AN EXISTENTIAL PHENOMENOLOGY OF LAW

PHAENOMENOLOGICA

COLLECTION FONDÉE PAR H.L. VAN BREDA ET PUBLIÉE
SOUS LE PATRONAGE DES CENTRES D'ARCHIVES-HUSSERL

104

WILLIAM S. HAMRICK

AN EXISTENTIAL PHENOMENOLOGY OF LAW: MAURICE MERLEAU-PONTY

AN EXISTENTIAL PHENOMENOLOGY OF LAW: MAURICE MERLEAU-PONTY

WILLIAM S. HAMRICK
(Southern Illinois University at Edwardsville, U.S.A.)

1987 **MARTINUS NIJHOFF PUBLISHERS**
a member of the KLUWER ACADEMIC PUBLISHERS GROUP
DORDRECHT / BOSTON / LANCASTER

Distributors

for the United States and Canada: Kluwer Academic Publishers, P.O. Box 358, Accord Station, Hingham, MA 02018-0358, USA
for the UK and Ireland: Kluwer Academic Publishers, MTP Press Limited, Falcon House, Queen Square, Lancaster LA1 1RN, UK
for all other countries: Kluwer Academic Publishers Group, Distribution Center, P.O. Box 322, 3300 AH Dordrecht, The Netherlands

Library of Congress Cataloging in Publication Data

Hamrick, William S.
An existential phenomenology of law.

(Phaenomenologica ; 104)
Bibliography: p.
Includes index.
1. Law--Philosophy. 2. Existential phenomenology.
3. Merleau-Ponty, Maurice, 1908-1961. I. Title.
II. Series.
K348.H36 1987 340'.1 87-7976

ISBN 90-247-3520-3

PRINTED IN THE NETHERLANDS

ACKNOWLEDGEMENTS

I am indebted to many people for their careful and patient criticisms of this essay at its various stages of development. Chief among these is Professor Simone Goyard-Fabre of the Université de Caen, France, who contributed much to the way that my initial reflections came to bear fruit. Professor Goyard was also of enormous personal help during a previous *séjour* in France which, among other things, permitted me the opportunity to discuss with her almost daily Merleau-Ponty's phenomenology and law.

I am also grateful for criticisms by the members of the British Society for Phenomenology, before whom were presented several earlier versions of parts of this essay. I owe a similar debt of gratitude to the members of the Society (and others) who have offered criticisms of revised versions of those papers that subsequently appeared in the *Journal of the British Society for Phenomenology,* and I am especially indebted to Professor Wolfe Mays, Editor of the *Journal,* for his helpful comments. Likewise, I would like to thank Mr. Neil Duxbury of the Faculty of Law, London School of Economics, for his many suggestions which improved the final copy of this book.

I would also like to thank Professors James Marsh, formerly of St. Louis University (and now of Fordham), and Herbert Spiegelberg of Washington University in St. Louis—neighbors and friends both—for their continued encouragement and beneficial criticisms. Both have been immensely helpful all along the route, although I do not venture to impute to them approval of the final result. Likewise, despite the considerable aid received from all those noted above, I am certain that I have not satisfied anyone completely, and responsibility for the eventual flaws in the essay is indisputably mine alone. Finally, but hardly least, I am grateful beyond words to M. Dominique Paret for providing me the means to produce the typescript for this essay. Without his kindness and generosity, it would have taken much longer to see the light of day.

Paris, May 1985

CONTENTS

PART TWO: THE PHENOMENON OF LAW

ABBREVIATIONS*

AD	*Les Aventures de la dialectique*
CAL	*La Conscience et l'acquisition du langage*
E	*Éloge de la philosophie*
HT	*Humanisme et terreur*
OE	*L'oeil et l'esprit*
PM	*La Prose du monde*
PhP	*Phénoménologie de la perception*
RC	*Résumés de Cours*
S	*Signes*
SNS	*Sens et non-sens*
VI	*Le visible et l'invisible*

*Quotations from these primary works of Merleau-Ponty will be included in the text without footnotes. The editions cited will be listed below under Works Consulted.

"[C]an one ask of a philosophy questions that it has not asked itself? . . . . My point of view: a philosophy, as a work of art, is an object which can generate more thoughts than are 'contained' in it (can one enumerate them? Can one count up a language?) which keeps a sense out of its historical context, which only *has* a sense out of this context."

—*Le visible et l'invisible,* pp. 252, 253

INTRODUCTION

The following pages attempt to develop the main outlines of an existential phenomenology of law within the context of Maurice Merleau-Ponty's phenomenology of the social world. In so doing, the essay addresses the rather narrow scholarly question, If Merleau-Ponty had written a phenomenology of law, what would it have looked like? But this scholarly enterprise, although impeccable in itself, is also transcended by a more complicated concern for a very different sort of question. Namely, if Merleau-Ponty's phenomenological descriptions of the social world are correct—as I believe they largely are—then what are the philosophical consequences for an adequate understanding of law?

Such a project may well occasion a certain surprise amongst observers of the contemporary philosophical landscape, at least in what concerns the terrain of continental thought, and for two different reasons. The first is that, although interest in Merleau-Ponty's work remains strong in the United States and Canada, his philosophical standing in his own country has been largely eclipsed[1] by that of, first, his friend/estranged acquaintance, Jean-Paul Sartre; by various Marxist philosophies and critical social theories; and finally by those doing hermeneutics of language. In my view, current neglect of Merleau-Ponty's thought in France is most regrettable. I intend to show that, among other things, once a phenomenology of law is pried out of his writings, it will be seen to have a most timely relevance to the contemporary state of society on both sides of the Atlantic, and particularly in France and the United States. I shall come back to this.

Surprise may also be generated, secondly, by the suspicion—or, indeed, conviction—that, considering the development of Merleau-Ponty's own philosophy, he might not have wanted any such project to be attempted in the first place. For, his last writings certainly signal a desire to go beneath phenomenology in certain important ways in order to express a more primordial relationship to Being than appeared possible in the relationship of consciousness—even a body consciousness—and its objects. Why, then, should we return to a method beyond which he had himself apparently grown? It is impossible to deal summarily with this objection, reaching as it does the very sense of Merleau-Ponty's *oeuvre*. Rather, I shall consider it on its own merits in a separate discussion below, at the end of this chapter.

Since Merleau-Ponty himself never wrote a phenomenology of law, this essay is necessarily interpretative as well as descriptive, and it is fair to acknowledge three sorts of dangers inherent in interpretation. The first is that of finding only what we want to find in a text, a temptation which Merleau-Ponty himself pointed out in the "Avant-Propos" of the *Phénoménologie de la perception*. Although it is not entirely clear to me whether the author considers this kind of danger merely a hazard or an inevitable pitfall, I have done my best to avoid it by citing carefully for the reader all the important texts from which my interpretation derives. I have confined myself to what is expressly in the texts themselves or what can be deductively derived from them—since if one is committed to the truth of a given proposition, one is also committed to all that is implied by that proposition.

A second sort of danger is that of historical bias caused by enhancing one's interpretation in the light of subsequent philosophical movements. Certainly, the temptation has been great to compare and contrast Merleau-Ponty's thoughts on language, history, art, and creative expression generally with current philosophical trends. But although contrast is an important philosophical tool which can greatly illuminate one's subject, I have not drawn these particular ones here because they would lead us too far afield. They are other stories, best left for other times and places.

The third sort of danger involved in interpretation is that of extrapolating from the texts to weave a design where none existed. Or, perhaps one could say it amounts to taking a button and sewing a vest on it. Why this is a danger for the present enterprise has to be understood in terms of the content and development of Merleau-Ponty's own works in what concerns the origin of culture—and hence law—from the world of perception. Because it was, after all, perception and the structures of the perceived world that both formed the source of his philosophizing and set its watermark. The "primacy" of perception means, in his view, among other things, that "The certainty of the idea does not found that of perception, but rather rests on it in that it is the experience of perception which teaches us the passage from one moment to another and brings about the unity of time. In this sense, all consciousness is perceptual consciousness, even the consciousness of ourselves. . . . The perceived world is the always presupposed foundation of all rationality, all value, and all existence."[2]

But at the same time, the "thesis" of the primacy of perception was not for its author a dogmatic doctrine. Rather, as James M. Edie has remarked,[3] the stress was much more on its thetic character, and the task imposed was to verify it in detailed and careful phenomenological descriptions of all kinds of meanings which emerge from the interactions of consciousness and its world. In other words, what the "thesis" mandated was a vast program of phenomenological studies of all regions of the *Lebenswelt,* including those that are historic, political, moral, legal, aesthetic, and so forth. Unfortunately, as one knows well, death tragically intervened before Merleau-Ponty began many of these analyses and before many others, once begun, were completed. Consequently, although Merleau-Ponty interested himself, even passionately at times, in the network of complex relationships making up the social world, not all of what he had to say received the attention—and still less the sympathetic development—it deserved. This is certainly the case with respect to his remarks about law.

For, rather than a full-fledged phenomenology of law, what one finds throughout Merleau-Ponty's writings—from one end of his career to the other—are illuminating remarks about law and right as such (*le droit*), particular positive laws, the administration of justice, the ideal of respect for law, the relationship of politics and principles, rights and authority, and so forth. In addition, most of these remarks are nested in his more intense interests in politics, history, economics, morality, and even art.

Furthermore, Merleau-Ponty tells us that, although the perceived world comprises the "foundation" of that which is cultural, it does not follow that the latter may be deductively derived from the former. As *The Prose of the World* indicates, its author proposes "on the contrary to recognize the order of culture as an original order of the advent of meaning" (112).[4] As a result, we may not simply or straightforwardly "read off" the structures of legal experience and the legal world from those that are perceptual (and which are more completely described in the texts). Many of the structures of the perceived world will be present in the legal world, but in novel forms. There will be, in other words, both similarity and difference.

In addition to this sensitivity to difference as well as similarity, the best defense against the danger of extrapolation is, once again, to confine oneself to the texts and what can be deductively derived from them. Also, as we shall see below, even on Merleau-Ponty's own view, texts have an expressive power which gives us a legitimate way to transcend them in the sense of making them say more than they have already said. This remains to be demonstrated, to be sure, but it is in any case a conclusion that is required by Merleau-Ponty's own phenomenology of expression as well as by statements such as that cited at the very beginning of this essay.

In pursuing the legal significance of Merleau-Ponty's writings, we shall see that there obtains a kind of reciprocal relationship in which what he tells us about law sheds more light on his view of the social world as a whole, whilst, inversely, his descriptions of other aspects of the social world will help us get clearer about his view of law. This fact, coupled with the way that his references to law are usually situated in a matrix of other social concerns, dictate the strategy to be followed in working out a phenomenology of law as Merleau-Ponty might have done it. Namely, we shall first follow out his descriptions of the various aspects of the social world as they appear to those who live them in order to recapture the concrete setting of law. This is not to be construed as a general or complete account of Merleau-Ponty's phenomenology of the social world, for that would be neither desirable nor necessary. It would not be desirable because it would sweep much too broadly for present purposes, and it would not be necessary because there already exist several texts dedicated to that task.[5] Rather, I shall attempt a fresh perspective emphasizing, however selectively, what is particularly relevant to an understanding of law. Therefore, in Part One below, we shall install ourselves in the social world as Merleau-Ponty describes it, in order to comprehend how he sees the phenomenon of law as part of this larger whole. This comprehension, in turn, will be the subject of Part Two. Part One will be largely expository, therefore, except for the interpretative stance of the perspective selected, certain critical remarks about other commentaries on Merleau-Ponty, and finally my own interpretations of the significance of certain primary texts.

In Part One, Chapter I will deal with Merleau-Ponty's concept of intersubjectivity, Chapter II with history and the origin of meaning, Chapter III with ethics, and Chapter IV with politics. Of these chapters, the last is arguably the most important from the perspective of Merleau-Ponty's own concerns for the social world. But it is also the most significant for the subsequent project of describing the phenomenon of law in Part Two. This is so because, as we shall see below in some detail, almost all of Merleau-Ponty's remarks about law are situated in a political context. Given the fact that this book is about a French philosopher, but addressed mainly to an English-speaking readership, it becomes crucial to understand the political-legal context in which Merleau-Ponty's thought is found. Chapter IV will provide this context in two ways. First, it will outline Merleau-Ponty's own political itinerary. This story is most commonly what is told about Merleau-Ponty's thought and politics, and it has been done elsewhere in much greater detail than here. But second, what is far more rarely attended to, Chapter IV will attempt to elucidate Merleau-Ponty's own view of the nature of politics itself as an intersubjective enterprise which is at once a historically weighted as well as limitedly free medium of creative expression. In Part Two, we shall see that law shares this same common characteristic, whether it be a question of codified systems of Continental law or those of common law derivation in Anglo-Saxon countries. This is not to say, however, that Part Two will attempt to relate what Merleau-Ponty says about law to all the salient features of both kinds of legal systems, and I shall return momentarily to this limitation.

To be sure, one can expect overlaps from chapter to chapter, and not only for the usual reasons involved in carrying along an argument across a large organizational pattern. The overlaps here will also flow from Merleau-Ponty's own work—given his beliefs in the unity of consciousness, the interpenetration of various kinds of social meanings, and the concentricity of all philosophical problems. His philosophical development is not linear, but rather web-like. Perhaps this is even inevitable in philosophies which seek to understand the concreteness of human experience; the process metaphysics of Alfred North Whitehead comes to mind as a similar example. In any case, on Merleau-Ponty's view, "Phenomenology is only accessible through the phenomenological method. Let us try then to deliberately tie together the celebrated phenomenological themes as they are tied together spontaneously in life" (PhP ii). And if we do so, it will follow that the themes of the various chapters below will not be insular, atomistic units, but rather interdependent parts of a social network. The differences between these chapters, therefore, will reduce largely to a choice between what shall lie at the focal-point and what will form the supporting background context.

In Part Two, Chapter V will take up the phenomenon of law in terms of both its origins and essential structure, and argue that, as in politics, Merleau-Ponty would also have thought law according to the model of language proposed by Ferdinand de Saussure. In addition, Chapter V will compare and contrast Merleau-Ponty's view of law with that of H.L.A. Hart in order to illustrate an important contemporary theory of law with which the former's linguistic model is in large part most congenial.

Chapter VI will consider the structure and functioning of law in society, and in this wider social context demonstrate certain criticisms which Merleau-Ponty's phenomenology would advance against Hart's concept of rules. Most of these criticisms revolve around the abstractness of the latter's view as well as the way it construes the relationship of legal rules to social institutions. Also in connection with the theme of law in society, Chapter VI will address the nature of judicial decision making and from within the consideration of a number of cases outline a position Merleau-Ponty would probably adopt on certain crucial issues in contemporary jurisprudence.

Chapter VII, finally, will address several interlocking themes contained within the relationship of law and morality. These include law and its relationship to nature and natural law theories, interests and justice, and the ideal of respect for law and fidelity to it. In so doing, Chapter VII will also continue certain criticisms of Hart concerning the social functions of law, and will attempt to show why Merleau-Ponty could have adopted (and adapted) a certain line of argument in that regard borrowed from John Finnis, J.R. Lucas, and Lon L. Fuller.

Across all three chapters, then, Part Two will show how the results obtained through working out the phenomenology of law can effectively relate Merleau-Ponty's philosophy to other sectors of legal philosophy—particularly, but not exclusively, to certain major thinkers in Anglo-American thought. In this way, phenomenology can be integrated anew into the on-going flux of the history of philosophy which surrounds, supports, and will eventually transcend it. There is no contention that Merleau-Ponty's thought can answer all questions which legal philosophers could put to it, but it is still true that it has much worthwhile work to do. This is to say that, while there is no desire to try to force Merleau-Ponty's phenomenology to speak to all the main questions in the philosophy of law, the texts will be exploited fully for all that they can say of relevance to legal philosophy. Similarly, there will be no attempt to force Merleau-Ponty's thought to interpret all the salient features of all legal systems, but we shall try to discern all that the texts can tell us about a number of features of the legal world as it is constituted in the consciousnesses of embodied legal subjects. The concern here will not be to understand this or that legal order or all of them, but rather law as such as far as Merleau-Ponty's phenomenology of the social world can shed light on it. In this respect, a number of illustrations have been selected from Continental legal systems and from the substantially different common law systems of England, Commonwealth countries, and the United States. Similarly, a number of legal theorists from both kinds of traditions have been cited where appropriate.

The distinction in each of the above contrasts between what this book will and will not do is important, and should not, therefore, be underestimated. Each negative half of these contrasts declines an invitation to do violence to Merleau-Ponty's texts by stretching and pulling them so as to make them speak (a) with voices different from that of the author and/or (b) with a voice in the first place where originally there had only been silence. I have sought a scrupulous balance between the sceptical doubts of those who thought the texts could yield too little and those who wanted too much. The former group, I believe, have been answered in full. In the latter group, however, are certain readers of earlier versions of this manuscript whose generosity in time and written comments will have to be repaid in a subsequent and different kind of volume in which in my own voice I will attempt a synthesis of an existential phenomenological approach to law, on the one hand, and the critical legal studies movement, on the other.

The final task of Part Two, which will be taken up in the Epilogue, will consist in the attempt mentioned above to demonstrate the timely relevance of Merleau-Ponty's views for the contemporary political landscape. In particular, I shall try to show that the problems of the ideal of fidelity to law, the tenability of democratic liberalism, the relationship of politics and principles—all specifically addressed or implied in *Les Aventures de la dialectique*—remain today just as valid and pressing for the reasons Merleau-Ponty gave as they were exactly thirty years ago.

Before proceeding on to future implications, however, we shall pause to look backwards to the texts themselves in order to take up the objection outlined above concerning the relationship between Merleau-Ponty's earlier and later writings. For it is plainly important to acknowledge, not least for the sake of intellectual honesty, why Merleau-Ponty probably would not have attempted to extend his phenomenology as I shall do, and then to state why I am doing it even so.

The best way to begin is by contrasting the relationship between phenomenology, metaphysics, and science in the earlier works with what one finds in the later writings—particularly *Le visible et l'invisible* and *L'oeil et l'esprit*.[6] This discussion will also have the double benefit of providing the necessary groundwork for understanding much of Merleau-Ponty's position on history, nature, and Marxism, on the one hand (see II.5), and law and nature, on the other (see VII.1).

The nub of the earlier position is that there is no inconsistency between phenomenology and metaphysics correctly understood because they are, in fact, identical. A metaphysics of this genre articulates human consciousness—which is before, prior to, founds, and transcends the evidence of the object, even while existing only in relation to it. This sort of metaphysics thus stands in opposition to the natural attitude, scientism, and positivism, as equally against abstract scenarios played out in inner mental theatres and the "high altitude thinking" of traditional speculative systems.

In this view, meta-physics thus becomes possible only when, "ceasing to live in the evidence of the object—whether it be a sensorial or scientific object—we perceive indissolubly the radical subjectivity of all our experience and its truth value" (SNS 163). This means, among other things, paying attention to the essential incompleteness of experience—both of the incarnate *cogito* as well as the phenomenal field of perceptual and cultural objects as they come into being before us with their focal-point and incomplete horizonal structures. As against the closed and finished world of scientific objects, the perceived world is, as Malebranche said—and which Merleau-Ponty was fond of repeating—"an unfinished task." But in the concrete intentionality of experience—through which property Husserl underlined the fact that all consciousness is consciousness *of* something—consciousness is itself incomplete, and so is the metaphysics which would try to understand it. In relearning to see the world, metaphysics has even the same goal which the "Preface" of the *Phenomenology of Perception* had told us is the purpose of the phenomenological reduction: "Metaphysical consciousness has no objects other than daily experience: this world, others, human history, truth, and culture. But, instead of taking them as completely finished, as consequences without premises and as if they were self-evident, metaphysics discovers their fundamental strangeness for me and the miracle of their appearance" (SNS 165).

It also follows that such a phenomenological metaphysics would be the very opposite of a system conceived as a closed network of concepts and propositions to express the nature of reality. Such classical attempts at philosophical construction are flawed because, first, *concepts* assume a false completeness of fully formed objects in the perceived world as in that which is cultural. The lived world, on the contrary, is first and foremost *pre-conceptual.* And second, *systems* of concepts assume the thoroughgoing rationality of the universe, and so cannot grasp what is truly meta-physical—our "thick," paradoxical, lived contact with the world. Even the very notions of truth and value "lose all meaning beyond human perspectives," and "Metaphysical consciousness . . . dies on contact with the absolute because it is itself . . . the living connection of myself with myself and of myself with the other" (SNS 167).

Turning now to the "physics" rather than the meta-physics, let us note that Merleau-Ponty's discussions of science proceed along two considerably different paths. The first of these leads to a view of science as the second-order expression of the life-world. As constructed on more primordial soil, it stands in relation to what we live in the way that a cartographer's map reflects the terrain over which he or she has walked. But science forgetfully generalizes from the human perspective of the scientist to the unjustified conclusions of the non-existence of the observer on the one hand, and of the completeness of the fully formed, complete universe on the other. Therefore, "scientific views according to which I am a moment of the world are always naive and hypocritical, because they presuppose, without mentioning it, this other view, that of consciousness, by means of which a world first prepares itself around me and begins to exist for me" (PhP iii).

The other vein of Merleau-Ponty's reflections on science is considerably different, and more conciliatory, than the first. In this perspective, science is not so much false as it is abstract. It is, or can be, a legitimate description of the facts, and its objectifications may therefore be true, although not an adequate expression of the totality of existence. This is the case not only for the social and natural sciences generally, but even, for instance, for the ways in which the latter would analyse the body.

But even if science is not totally wrong, it is not totally right either, and even in Merleau-Ponty's most conciliatory reflections on science, there is still a strong insistence on the rejection of causal thinking and—what goes along with causal thinking—considering human existence under the same categories appropriate for describing nature.[7] In existential phenomenologies, such as that of Merleau-Ponty, Husserl's protest against the "naturalization of consciousness" was transmuted into the distinction between (human) existence—which is an être-*au*-monde"—and the mode of being appropriate to things, which are "dans le monde." Another way to say it is that there is an irreducible difference between the meta-physical and the physical (world of nature, described by science): "man is the being who is not content to coincide with himself, as a thing does, but who represents himself to himself, sees himself, imagines himself, and gives himself exact or fantastic symbols" (S 285).[8]

From the rejection of causal thinking as appropriate for understanding human existence, and the claim that human existence is distinct from thing-like being, Merleau-Ponty draws four conclusions which are fundamental to his phenomenology of the social world, and which should be contrasted with his later writings. The first of these is that nature is not morally or, still less, religiously, normative for the development of human existence. This is so because, for the same reasons that we are distinct from things, there is no human nature at all: "It is impossible to superimpose on man a first layer of behavior which would call 'natural' and a fabricated cultural or spiritual world. Everything for man is fabricated and everything is natural, as one could say, in this sense that there is no word or behavior which does not owe something to simply biological being—and which at the same time does not escape from the simplicity of animal life" (PhP 221). For instance, "The Japanese smiles in anger while the Westerner goes red in the face and stamps his foot or else goes pale and speaks with a hissing voice" (PhP 220).

The manner of using one's body thus transcends one's biological equipment, such that what is 'natural' for us is as much cultural convention as it is biological. Since there are "*many ways for a body to be a body, many ways for consciousness to be consciousness*"(PhP 144), it follows that "The body is the bearer of an indefinite number of symbolic systems of which the intrinsic development surely exceeds the signification of 'natural' gestures, but which also collapses if the body ceases to punctuate their exercise and to install them in the world and in our life" (RC 18).

The second conclusion which is important in Merleau-Ponty's phenomenology of the social world is that nature is not normative for the direction and guidance of human culture as a whole any more than it is for a given person within it. It is true that Merleau-Ponty does say that "There is something to say in favor of the 'natural light'. Men secrete culture in some way without willing it. The human world, so different as it is from the natural or animal world, is in some fashion *natural for man*" (SNS 208-09). But one must not make too much of such remarks, especially in a moral or religious context. For he also held that the "natural light" "is an opening to being" which manifests itself "as well in the most cruel forms of sadism as in Italian painting" (S 304).

Rather, the main part of Merleau-Ponty's argument that nature cannot be normative for the development of any given culture turns on the fact that, in experience, culture and nature are always given together in a mélange. They are not separate and distinct, each self-contained and distinguishable from the other. Hence there is no immutable substratum of nature to which cultures should respond. Thus also, in his course at the Collège de France on "Le Concept de Nature," we find Merleau-Ponty criticizing Marx as follows: "The most famous of philosophies of history rests on a concept [of nature] which has never been elucidated and which is perhaps mythical. Pure object, being in itself, in which all is contained, and which however cannot be found in human experience because, from the first, the latter shapes and transforms it. Nature is for this experience everywhere and nowhere, like an obsessive fear" (RC 93).

Moreover, nature cannot provide the coordinates for making cross-cultural comparisons any more than it can be a normative guide for the development of a particular culture. This is the third important fact about Merleau-Ponty's phenomenology of the social world which will be contrasted with the later works below and in Part II (see VI.1). Over and over again, one sees him resisting cross-cultural comparisons and even declining the invitation to consider similarities between different cultures in different times and places. In Heidegger's suggestive phrase—to which I shall return below in Part II—it is not "identity" that is defended, but rather "difference." Just as there are several ways for a body to be a body and consciousness to be consciousness, so also there are various ways for cultures to constitute themselves—none more or less naturally than another. All are necessarily related to nature as a base, in some sense, but none is a determined mediation of it.

Thus in his well known essay, "From Mauss to Claude Lévi-Strauss," Merleau-Ponty considered that culture is "a transformation of nature, a series of mediations in which structure never emerges right away as a pure universal. How to call, if not history, this milieu in which a form weighted with contingency suddenly opens a cycle of the future and commands it with the authority of what is instituted" (S 154)?

The essential point to grasp here is that the relationships of culture and nature are such that, between cultures, similarities are downplayed for the sake of differences, closeness (in customs, mores, law, and socio-political institutions) is replaced by distance, and the identity or communality of belonging—to the same base of nature, "the good earth," and so forth—whilst not denied, lies rather in the background of the more prominent disjunctiveness of separate cultures creating truth and humanity within them. There is little room, if any, for any trans-cultural guidelines for the development of a particular cultural "interworld" which is "history, symbolism, [and] truth to make" (AD 269).

The fourth theme, finally, from Merleau-Ponty's phenomenology of the social world consists of the irreducible reality of history itself, on both individual and public levels, and of the corresponding layers of "sedimented meanings" which create a matrix of past conditioning influences of which our situated freedom must take account across all levels of meaning of our lifeworld. Both these themes will figure prominently in Chapter II below, but they are in any case well-enough known not to require a separate discussion here. Rather, they will be employed below to point up a crucial contrast with Merleau-Ponty's last writings which, among other things, espouse the possibility of interrogating a pure immediacy of experience unfiltered by any historically sedimented meanings from one's personal and social life.

Such are, in brief outline, the leading ideas involved in Merleau-Ponty's earlier discussions of phenomenology and metaphysics and some main implications of those discussions for the relationships of culture and nature which are important for his phenomenology of the social world. In the later works, by contrast, there obtains a considerably different conception of phenomenology and metaphysics with correspondingly different implications for the relationship of culture and nature. Metaphysics is no longer a synonym for phenomenology, and the metaphysical in humankind is no longer identical to the pre-objective phenomenal body and its motor-intentionality. Rather, the most basic referent of the metaphysical lies deeper than consciousness and its objects, and in fact makes them both possible within its totality—namely, "the flesh." Meta-physics thus becomes an infra-physics. It is not that the phenomenological descriptions of the earlier writings have been abandoned or repudiated. Rather, it is that their author evidently saw a need to go farther, a need created mostly by his changing views of the philosophical significance of language. As will be detailed in the following chapter (I.3), these changes constituted a major upheaval in his thought and led to his final notion of the flesh as something more fundamental and radical than the relation of (a body) consciousness and its objects, and which grounds them both.

Thus, Merleau-Ponty tells us that, for example, between the hand that explores and what is touched there must exist "on principle some relationship, some relatedness according to which they are. . . the initiation and the opening to a tactile world" (VI 176). The foundation of that relatedness consists of being part of the common flesh of the world. The flesh, in turn, is that by which "he who sees can only possess the visible if he is possessed by it, if he is *of it*. . . . The thickness of the body, far from rivaling that of the world, is on the contrary the only means that I have of going to the heart of things, in making me world and in making them flesh" (VI 177-78).

There can be no exact frontier between body and world since we are both perceiving as well as perceived—visible manifestations of the flesh of the world. The body as perceiving—what was before termed the "phenomenal body"—and as perceived, previously termed the "objective body" (VI 180), give it the structure of "Visibility" as well as make it part of flesh: "Visible and mobile, my body is of the number of things, it is one of them, it is held in the tissue of the world and its cohesion is that of a thing. But, because it sees and moves itself, it holds things in a circle around it. They are an annex or an extension of itself, they are incrusted in its flesh, they form part of its full definition and the world is made of the same stuff as the body" (OE 19).

What flesh itself is has no name in traditional philosophy (VI 183, 193). It "is not matter, spirit, or substance. To designate it, one would have to use the old term of 'element,' in the sense in which one would employ it to speak of water, air, earth and fire—that is to say, of a *general thing,* a middle path between the spatio-temporal individual and the idea, a sort of incarnate principle which imports a style of being everywhere in which a bit of it is found. Flesh is in this sense an 'element' of Being" (VI 184).

My visibility is also termed a reversibility in the sense that my perceiving body can be perceived, my touching hand can also be touched, and so on. This reversibility or "chiasm" of the flesh, which the last sentence of the main text of *The Visible and the Invisible* calls "ultimate truth" (VI 204), is essential to understanding my being part of nature. This Merleau-Ponty makes plain in his course, "Nature and Logos: The Human Body," at the Collège de France: "We had shown in preceding years that external nature and life cannot be thought without reference to perceived nature. It is now the human body (and not 'consciousness') which must appear as that which perceives nature of which it is also an inhabitant. . . . It envelops a philosophy of the flesh as visibility of the invisible. . . . It is a lexicon of corporeity in general, a system of equivalences between the inside and the outside which prescribes to one to accomplish itself in the other" (RC 176, 178).

If, then, the totality principle of Merleau-Ponty's later thought consists of an "element" of Being out of which both perceived things and we ourselves—and, therefore, consciousness—are made up, what becomes of the claims in the early and middle works about the social world? First, it would not follow that there was an immutable substratum of human nature, but it certainly would come about that consciousness and all its constituted social meanings have a much closer tie to nature than merely being based somehow on it. And in addition to the weaker claim that human beings have the task of creating their own meanings in relation to important natural "givens" in terms of the body and the external world, there would also follow the much stronger assertion that human beings cannot be adequately described in terms completely different from those judged appropriate for things.

Second, the same conclusion would apply, *mutatis mutandis,* for a whole society as well as for its individual members. The vast welter of, say, social living arrangements, institutions, and traditions, would have not merely twin reference points in nature and human will. It would also be the case that the operative model to follow in their explanation would be the synthesis and coherence of culture and nature rather than disjunction and difference.

Further, third, it would also follow that more attention would have to be paid to trans-cultural similarities in addition to their differences. Presumably all societies emerge from the same Being in whose emblematic flesh we live. Thus identities rather than differences, similarities rather than disconnexions, and belongingness rather than unrelatedness, would form important features of an empirically adequate social phenomenology, and would jointly serve as a balance wheel to the earlier accounts. Extending a statement from the *Phenomenology of Perception* cited earlier, since there are many ways for a consciousness to be a consciousness and many ways for a body to be a body, there could be also a multiplicity of different styles of being flesh. And in this variety of styles one would find the locus and ground of cultural diversity. But at the same time, it is the *same flesh,* and the same basic fact of belonging to it would lie at the base of all societies. And if this is so, it would seem to follow, then, that some important claims of Merleau-Ponty's earlier phenomenology of the social world would have to be at least seriously adjusted, but not entirely given up, in the sense that their descriptive value can remain intact whilst their ontological value is emptied.

Another way to say this is in terms of the philosophical necessity of thought. That is, it is one thing to point to our deeper, pre-conscious relationship with Being which we effect through the chiasm of flesh of the world and of ourselves. But it is also necessary for philosophers to be able to think it, as Merleau-Ponty himself insists: "One must think the flesh, starting not with substances, body and spirit, because then it would be the union of contradictories, but rather, as we said, as element, the concrete emblem of a manner of general being" (VI 193-94). But how, exactly, are we to think correctly our relationship with this "element," this unity of the visible, nature, and logos?

Jean-Paul Sartre proposed that we consider it essentially as "envelopment." He writes that "the understanding of existence and life, for Merleau, is conditioned entirely by this cardinal principle: envelopment. He makes us understand by that. . . . that Nature is right up in us and, so that to see but the moon or a neon advertisement, what is required is a natural appropriation of internal and external being. We are in being, it envelops us, it is in us, fundamental and contingent, and it transcends itself towards gesture and speech. In us it makes itself flesh—the word is Merleau's himself—and when we perceive the world through our body, we make it flesh and in turn, we make ourselves its flesh."[9]

But if we follow Sartre's suggestion of thinking flesh as envelopment, what could be the role of phenomenology in such thought? Certainly one finds in the later texts a continuity of phenomenological descriptions in what concerns the body, the other, language and art, but rather than having any ontological weight, they appear more like the charming, intriguing play of light on the surface of the water—supported by the deeper currents below, but telling us nothing about them. For if we think our relationship with Being through its emblematic flesh as an envelopment, and the center of this envelopment is the chiasm, it would follow that a phenomenology must be installed at this chiasm itself. Now, the last line of the text of the "Notes de travail" which follow the text of *Le visible et l'invisible* tells us that "*Matière-ouvrée-hommes = chiasme*" (p. 328). The project of doing a phenomenology of the flesh would therefore be installed at the "openedness," of describing the unity of the perceiving-perceived which makes consciousness possible, *and not the other way around.* This is so because flesh is the more primordial totality out of which consciousness and things emerge. And once the sovereignty of consciousness has been given up—even that of a body-consciousness—what would such a phenomenology look like?

Marc Richir recently has attempted to answer to this question as follows. He observes that "The flesh is the *Horizonhaftigkeit,* the 'system' of its interior and exterior horizons which open as well . . . to the non-phenomenal of the phenomenon and, through it, to other phenomena—as to the non-phenomenal of an incarnate perception . . . there is perception in the phenomenal (the visible, the perceptible) only because there is the non-phenomenal in the phenomenal and because there is the phenomenal in the constitutive non-phenomenal of perception (seeing, feeling) itself, and of all these terms that we only distinguish by reflection, there is . . . *chiasm*. . . . [The opening or chiasm is] really the key to every phenomenon, and through it, of all constitution."[10]

The openness of the chiasm is also the incompleteness of experience, and Richir argues accordingly that "The new departure which Merleau-Ponty announced . . . resides in *the principal unfinishedness* of the world of phenomena, and of ourselves, which constitutes in reality the *opening* itself of perceptual faith to the world, of perceptual faith to itself, of myself to the other, of the perceptible to the intelligible, of the mute world to expression. It is, for us, without doubt, the most profound and durable lesson of the work of the later Merleau-Ponty . . . that all being, of whatever sort it might be, is always and on principle *unfinished,* open in an unceasing way to horizons of finishedness which are themselves irreducibly traversed with unfinishedness."[11]

What, then, is the task of phenomenology? Richir concludes that "philosophy—and thus phenomenology—if at least it wishes to remain faithful to its demand to *show* by speech the world and ourselves in the silence of their origins, can only be 'perceptual faith *interrogating* itself about itself' (VI 139, emphasis added): not, thus, that it would be a question of reducing our astonishment before the world and converting it into a universe of reasons, of thoughts, or of concepts, but on the contrary, of *making it speak* from its very place."[12]

There are several points to notice about these passages from Richir's richly suggestive article. However, I will content myself with only two. First, I would suggest that the incompleteness "of the world, of phenomena, and of ourselves" is not at all a new point of departure in Merleau-Ponty's later works. It is, after all, as we have seen above in Part I, the basis on which he criticized science as naive and hypocritical, and it is further the basis for his fondness in quoting Malebranche to the effect that the world is "an unfinished task." What is new about the later works is that this claim of incompleteness is pushed beyond the perceived world to Being itself.

Second, and more importantly, we have no clues either in the passage cited above or in the rest of Richir's article about just how phenomenology could "show by speech the world and ourselves in the silence of their origins." Perhaps at bottom this is so because speech itself emerges from, and incarnates, flesh, just as consciousness does, and it cannot celebrate its own birth. But even if we waive this difficulty, speech would still have to give us words to enable the phenomenologist *think* this chiasmatic relationship.

Perhaps the difficulty of getting any words at all to do this is reflected in the fact that Merleau-Ponty's most extensive exploration of the chiasm is not in terms of language at all, but rather in the domain of painting. Indeed, *Eye and Mind* could well be seen in part as showing how the chiasm can be performed. Merleau-Ponty says, for example, that "It is in lending his body to the world that the painter changes the world into painting. To understand these transsubstantiations, one must recover the operative and present body, which is not a bit of space or a bundle of functions, but rather an intertwining of vision and movement. . . . The visible world and that of my motor projects are total parts of the same Being" (OE 16-17).

With regard to the chiasm of seeing and seen, touching and touched, he observes further that "once this strange system of exchanges is given, all the problems of painting are there. They illustrate the enigma of the body and it [painting] justifies them. Because things and my body are made of the same stuff, it is necessary that its vision operates in some way in them, or again that their manifest visibility doubles itself in it with a secret visibility: 'nature is on the inside,' says Cézanne. Quality, light, color, depth, which are there before us, are only there because they awaken an echo in our body, because it bids them welcome" (OE 21-22).[13]

And finally, Merleau-Ponty tells us that "Painting awakens and carries to its last power a delirium which is vision itself, because to see is to *have at a distance,* and painting extends this bizarre possession to all aspects of Being, which must make themselves visible in some way in order to enter into it. . . . the painter, whatever he might be, *while he paints,* practices a magical theory of vision. One must admit to him that things pass into him or that, according to the sarcastic dilemma of Malebranche, the mind goes out through the eyes to stroll among things" (OE 26-28).

But once again, where are the words to express this magic, to allow us to think this mysterious and silent origins of the world and of ourselves? I do not think it accidental that, the closer one draws to the deepest connections imaginable for Merleau-Ponty between ourselves and Being, gestures replace words, and performance—such as that of the artist—takes the place of philosophy. There is a hunger after immediacy here for which words are obstacles, and Sartre's remarks on Merleau-Ponty's concern for painting are very instructive. The former points out that the philosopher, being quit of *savants* who are engaged in high-altitude thinking, seeks Being among other men, among:

> those who think heavily and slowly, with their hands, with their eyes, with the whole body—rarely with words, and above all not at first. Brute life is there, raw and unrefined, immediate with no self-consciousness, as well as the body and spontaneity. Merleau very soon came to painting, loved it, and wrote about it because he held that a painter thinks: about the object, at the end of his brush, and by the very posture of his whole body. Ambiguity came to him from that: one half of himself absorbed himself in understanding gestures without words—it is to do them. (He spoke very well of a short fillm which shows Matisse painting.) The other half of himself was nowhere else or, if one prefers, it was the same as the first half. Very simply, it was empty: he *did not really do* the gestures that he redid, he *was not* a painter, it was a new exile.[14]

The upshot is that there is in Merleau-Ponty's later texts a drive toward immediacy in the relationship of the flesh to Being from which consciousness and probably language itself comprised an exile. For analogous reasons, there appears to be little room in his nascent ontology for the fourth important motif of his phenomenology of the social world described above, namely the irreducible reality of history and the sedimentation of meaning. For, in this immediate chiasmatic contact with Being, where is all that had been learned from Hegel and Marx, and Freud—illuminated not least through Merleau-Ponty's own pages—about history, the sedimentation of both personal and cultural meanings, and the necessity for hermeneutical interpretation? For a phenomenology that must use words and the historically conditioned understanding of concepts, the flesh would be far from immediately available. It would be, rather, as the painter Paul Klee described himself in what was to be his epitaph, "ungraspable in immanence" (OE 87).

In the light of the later texts, therefore, phenomenology must appear in a position somewhat analogous to that of science in the earlier works, namely, less false than abstract. Even so, there are three reasons why I want to follow out paths implicit in the phenomenology. First, the most important of the later works—*Le visible et l'invisible*—is such an incomplete book of uncertain direction. As James Edie points out, "It is not a book. Even in its more finished sections it is really only the incompletely corrected notes for a book. It has many stream-of-thought passages which go on without paragraphs for pages. Merleau-Ponty recognized its unfinished and uncorrected nature, its lack of rigor, its lack of consistency, its lack of elementary clarity."[15]

Second, as pointed out above, nothing in the later writings declares false what preceded them in terms of either method or content. Accordingly, I will even cite occasionally certain illuminating passages from the later works, particularly *L'oeil et l'esprit* and *Le visible et l'invisible,* which cohere particularly well with the earlier writings. And third, I am not at all convinced that the project of the later works is sound. Or at least if it is, it is still unhelpful for revealing much of the reality of the social world and of the *engagement* of human existence within it. Hence much, though not all, of the last writings—for the reasons given above in connection with history and the sedimentation of meanings—is unilluminative of the phenomenon of law. As a result, the reader will find considerably more of Hegel, Marx, de Saussure and Weber in what follows than of, say, Heraclitus or of the later Heidegger.

NOTES

1. One recent counter-example consists of the volume of essays about Merleau-Ponty's thought in the journal *Esprit,* Number 66, June 1982. Its more than fifteen essays are of unusual breadth and concern themselves with Merleau-Ponty's writings on socio-political matters, painting, language, ethics, and the relationship between his phenomenology and *Le Visible et l'invisible.* One of these essays (by Marc Richir) will be analysed below in some detail.
2. "Le Primat de la perception et ses conséquences philosophiques," *Bulletin de la Société Française de Philosophie,* XLI, 1947 (séance du 23 novembre 1946), p. 120. For Merleau-Ponty (pp. 142-43), it is perception which effects our most primordial relationships with things, other people, and the world around us. The "primacy" of perception also means that all levels of consciousness of our life-worlds remain perceptual to at least some degree and that one can discover in the "highest" strata of consciousness the fundamental structures of perception despite their qualitative changes.
3. James M. Edie, trans. and ed., *The Primacy of Perception and Other Essays* (Evanston: Northwestern University Press, 1964), p. xv.
4. This remark is repeated much later at S 85, and there Merleau-Ponty indicates that he is borrowing the word "advent" with its ascribed meaning from Paul Ricoeur.
5. Among others, the interested reader may wish to consult the following works: Barry Cooper, *Merleau-Ponty and Marxism: From Terror to Reform* (Toronto: University of Toronto Press, 1980); Sonia Kruks, *The Political Philosophy of Merleau-Ponty* (Sussex: The Harvester Press, 1981; published simultaneously by the Humanities Press, Inc., [Atlantic Highlands, N.J.]); Gary Brent Madison, *The Phenomenology of Merleau-Ponty* (Athens, Ohio: Ohio University Press, 1980)—in French, *La Phénoménologie de Merleau-Ponty, une recherche de la conscience (Paris: Editions Klincksieck, 1973); Albert Rabil, Jr., Merleau-Ponty: Existentialist of the Social World* (New York: Columbia University Press, 1967); and Laurie Spurling, *Phenomenology and the Social World: The Philosophy of Merleau-Ponty and its Relation to the Social Sciences* (London: Routledge and Kegan Paul, 1977).
6. An earlier version of this discussion was presented to the 1983 annual general meeting of the British Phenomenology Society meeting in St. Edmund Hall, Oxford.
7. For a fuller account of the role of nature in Merleau-Ponty's phenomenology of the social world, see below at III. 3,4 and VI.1, as well as William S. Hamrick, "Humanity, Nature, and Respect for Law," in A.-T. Tymieniecka, ed. *Analecta Husserliana* (Dordrecht: D. Reidel Publishing Company, 1983), pp. 245-56. The present essay goes beyond the earlier paper by coming to grips with what Merleau-Ponty wrote about nature and human existence after the formulation of his social phenomenology (in this Introduction) and by a much more extensive consideration of the main themes at issue (in Chapters III and VII below).

8. Cf. Martin Heidegger's parallel assertion and accompanying explanation that begin: "Das Seiende, das in der Weise der Existenz ist, ist der Mensch. Der Mensch allein existiert." *Was Ist Metaphysik?* (Frankfurt a.M.: Vittorio Klostermann, Neunte Auflage, 1965), pp. 15-16.
9. Jean-Paul Sartre, "Merleau-Ponty [I]," trans. William S. Hamrick, *Journal of the British Society for Phenomenology,* Vol. XV, No. 2, May 1984, p. 132. This was a previously unpublished manuscript, the initial version of the well known memorial article for Merleau-Ponty which appeared in the October 1961 issue of *Les Temps modernes* and was reprinted in Sartre's *Situations IV.*
10. Marc Richir, "Le Sens de la Phénoménologie dans *Le visible et l'invisible,*" in *Maurice Merleau-Ponty, Esprit* No. 66, juin 1982, pp. 138-39.
11. Richir, p. 132.
12. Richir, p. 132.
13. With regard to the last sentence, see also Malebranche's statement which Merleau-Ponty liked to quote in the early works, namely, that "sensations impinge respectfully." See also *L'oeil et l'esprit,* p.25: "our eyes of flesh are already much more than receptors for lights, colors, and lines: [they are] computers of the world which have the gift of the visible as one says that an inspired man has the gift of tongues."
14. Sartre, p. 136.
15. "Merleau-Ponty: The Triumph of Dialectics over Structuralism," *Man and World* 17: 299-312 (1984) at p. 310. Reprinted (and cited) in J.N. Mohanty, ed. *Phenomenology and the Human Sciences* (Dordrecht: Martinus Nijhoff, 1985), p. 70.

PART ONE: THE SOCIAL WORLD

We shall not cease from exploration
And the end of all our exploring
Will be to arrive where we started
And know the place for the first time.

—T.S. Eliot, *Little Gidding*

I: INTERSUBJECTIVITY

For Merleau-Ponty, the social or cultural world—for the most part, these expressions are used interchangeably—takes shape in and through the cooperative and competitive efforts of society's members as they both constitute the sense of their lives and take up the fabric of meanings laid down by others in the institution of laws, customs, traditions, mores, and the like. This being so, an adequate comprehension of the social world demands first that one understand the intersubjectivity that precedes it (logically, not temporally) and makes it possible. Accordingly, the present chapter will sketch the main structures of intersubjectivity, but largely abstracted from its temporal thickness. Since the latter will entail a reference to history and institution, that part of the discussion will be left for the following chapter.

§1. Intentionality and the Body-Subject

Since intersubjectivity consists of a complex mesh of relationships between different subjectivities—what becomes the *intermonde* of the later texts, one has to first inquire into the meaning of subjectivity. The subject—in fact, Merleau-Ponty does not usually write about a "self"—is variously described across his texts as a body-consciousness, an incarnate *cogito,* or lived-body (*le corps propre*). But the lived body is not the sort of subject which one finds in much of traditional philosophy or for certain of Merleau-Ponty's contemporaries—most notably, Jean-Paul Sartre.[1] Indeed, Merleau-Ponty went to considerable pains to distance himself from a variety of other views on the subject. For example, when writing on "Marxism and Philosophy," he included a long, compendious passage which expressly distinguished the position of his "existential philosophy" from a subject or self conceived as (1) a Sartrean *pour soi,* (2) a pure knower, independent of all reference to other selves—under which indictment, in other texts, he usually includes the Cartesian *cogito;* (3) a complex of rigidly determined biological and social functions of natural/environmental stimuli—a view fashionable in certain sectors of behavioral psychology in the 1930's and 1940's; and (4) a Kantian legislating consciousness. Instead, in the warp and woof of daily social life, "the human subject" is the one that, "through a continual dialectic, thinks according to its situation, forms its categories in contact with its experience, and modifies this situation and experience by the meaning that it finds for them. . . . Transcendental subjectivity, Husserl says, *is* intersubjectivity.[2] Man no longer appears as the product of a milieu or as an absolute legislator, but as a product-producer, as the place where necessity can turn into concrete liberty" (SNS 237).

As a dialectic of producer and product, the incarnate *cogito* does enact a concrete liberty among others, as we shall see below, but it would be misleading to conclude from the above passage that the foundation of Merleau-Ponty's view of the self lies in economic relationships, or indeed in the social world generally. For, in the case of economic phenomena, to be a producer means to use tools, and to use tools implies (sophisticated) bodily behavior. It is, therefore, at the level of perception and behavior that we have our fundamental contact with the world, other people, and even ourselves. Thus, as Alphonse de Waelhens indicated in his "Preface" to *The Structure of Behavior,* a picture of human existence as peculiarly oriented to tools—Heidegger's *Dasein* analytics being the case in point—misses what is more primordial: "Heidegger always places himself at a level of complexity which permits one to imagine the problem resolved which now occupies us. . . . But the projects which, according to *Sein und Zeit,* generate for us the intelligibility of the real, already presuppose that the subject of daily existence raises his arm because he drives a nail and forges iron, focuses his eyes because he consults his watch, and orients himself because he drives a car."[3]

As a result, although Merleau-Ponty sees one strength of the Marxist analysis of consciousness as its discovery of social existence at the most "interior" dimensions of our lives—a dimension in which "economic and cultural determinations endlessly overlap and signify each other" (SNS 143)—it is still the case that, given the "thesis" of the "primacy of perception," perception and behavior constitute a more primordial level of life."[4] Hence the account of subjectivity and thence intersubjectivity must begin with perception rather than the social world itself. At the same time, however, since our principal concern is with the social world, this account of perception will consist of the briefest sketch, tailored to provide only what is necessary as a foundation for understanding the phenomenon of law.

In its perceptual life, the incarnate *cogito* consists of a "third genus of being" (PhP 350) because it is neither a purely subjective consciousness nor a solely objective body. It is, rather, a concrete unity of interdependent psychical and physical aspects or, as the much later text of *Signes* expresses it, a mélange of body and soul which Montaigne did well to describe as living in "a world for which we do not have the key, of being unable either to remain within ourselves or to project ourselves into things, and of living at the intersection of both" (S 251).

Living in a perceptual circuit with things and other people means that the incarnate *cogito* is a Hegelian concrete universal, a "thought-in-act," because the body is a system of motor powers for exploring and making sense out of the world as it presents itself to us. As consciousness, the lived-body is intentional, but that intentionality is a motor-intentionality because *le corps propre* is an "I can" in addition to an "I think." It is "the place of a certain praxis, the point of departure from which there is something to do in the world. . . . one could say equally that we are conscious because we are mobile or that we are mobile because we are conscious. Consciousness, in the sense of awareness, and movement, in the sense of displacement in objective space, are two abstract aspects of one existence" (RC 16, 17).

Drawing on abundant evidence from Gestalt psychology, Merleau-Ponty was thus led very early on to an understanding of perception as an active process of spontaneously organizing a given field and which is, in consequence, neither completely passive nor sharply distinct from the "stimuli" which supposedly determine it. Or, as he would say much later in *L'oeil et l'esprit,* in perception "the whole affair is to understand that our eyes of flesh are already much more than receptors for lights, colors, and lines: they are computers of the world which have the gift of the visible as one says that the inspired man has the gift of tongues" (OE 25; see the Introduction, n. 13 above).

The spontaneous structuring of the perceptual field occurs pre-reflectively, requiring no intervening mental *acts* to accomplish it. It takes place "anonymously" in the sense that, non-personally, "one" (the French sense of *"on"*) rather than being consciously directed by an "I" (PhP 240). It is, to again use Husserlian language, a "passive synthesis" or constitution of the sense of things as they are presented to us in and through changing perspectives.

"Subject" and "object" in perceptual experience are, then, neither isolable, independent relata, nor are they fictions. Rather, they consist of interdependent aspects of new wholes called "structures." What is primary is the whole structure; its subjective and objective "parts" are subsequently distinguished features of it. Also, the spontaneous structuring of the perceptual field entails that the difference between sensation and thought is not that between chaos and order, since already in perception there is a fundamentally meaningful, sense-giving activity logically prior to the elaborations of a theoretical or reflective consciousness. As Cézanne showed us in trying to unite sensation and intelligence in painting, there is already an intelligible perceptual ordering which precedes that imposed by "the human order of ideas and sciences" (SNS 23).

But if this is so, both sides of a mind/body dualism collapse to a more fundamental unity. As a material object, the body could expectantly take into account the form of stimuli—as the Gestaltists say it can—only if "we introduce beside the objective body the phenomenal body, if we make of it a knowing-body and if, finally we substitute for a [Cartesian] consciousness as the subject of perception, existence, that is to say, being in the world through a body" (PhP 357). And thus also the failure of the mental side of such a dualism insofar as intelligence is already carnal. The psychical and the physical become interdependent features of a motor-intentional body as it explores and constitutes meanings in its world. "Body" and "soul" are therefore "only two aspects of . . . being in the world, in the same way that the word and thought that it designates must not be considered as two exterior terms [two independent entities] and the word bears its meaning as the body is the incarnation of a behavior" (SNS 96).

The philosophical significance of Gestalt psychology is, then, to show us that, as described above in the Introduction, not only the incarnate *cogito,* but also the perceived world as such, is a "third genus of being" uniting—and, at the same time, transcending—subjectivity and objectivity in a more primordial form or structure. Thus Gestalt psychology, "in revealing 'structure' or 'form' as an irreducible element of being . . . again places in question the classical alternative of 'existence as a thing' and 'existence as consciousness,' it establishes a communication between them as a mélange of the objective and the subjective" (SNS 150-51). And it is this conception of existence as a "third genus of being" that leads to the chiasm of the visible and the invisible in Merleau-Ponty's later works. As noted above in the Introduction, it is meant to oppose Sartre's dichotomy of being and nothingness with a "being of envelopment, what one could call the topology of being" which philosophy "tends to forget" (S 30).

But if philosophy was afflicted with this sort of amnesia, Merleau-Ponty found by contrast that the concept of structure was vigorously exploited in many other disciplines across his contemporary intellectual landscape—chiefly in linguistics, anthropology, sociology, economics, and history. The case of linguistics will be discussed below in some detail, and we shall in Part Two that linguistic structure will be central for understanding the phenomenon of law—particularly in regard to legal rules (V.3) and judicial creativity (VI.3). For Merleau-Ponty, in sum, both in the perceptual world and in the social world which takes up and modifies the former, "Whether it is a question of the individual fact of birth or of the birth of institutions and of societies, the original relationship between man and being is not that of the for-itself to the in-itself. . . . We have to recognize in some way primordial being which is not being-as-subject nor being-as-object, and which completely disconcerts reflection: from being to us there is no deviation and no gap" (RC 94, 95).

Such are, in brief outline, some main features of Merleau-Ponty's view of subjectivity, conceived as an incarnate *cogito,* and of its most primordial level of experience in perception and behavior. As we have seen above, the incarnation of form or structure effectively generates a philosophy dedicated to moving away from a number of parallel dualisms: mind and body, subject and object, perceiver and perceived, and the internal and the external. In each case, the *relata* comprise dual aspects of a more basic whole—effectively, a duality rather than a dualism. In the following pages, we shall find other dualisms to add to those rejected above—such as thought and expression, reason and passion, order and creativity and, immediately below, I and the other. For, as Merleau-Ponty wrote in *Sens et non-sens,* "A good part of phenomenological or existential philosophy consists in being astonished at this inherence of me in the world and of me in the other, of describing for us this paradox and this confusion" (p. 105).

§2. *Intersubjectivity*

The social world, for Merleau-Ponty, originates in intersubjectivity which is constituted as a mesh of complex relationships between different incarnate subjects. Thus his phenomenology is rooted in consciousness, even if it is a body-consciousness, and this unavoidable fact poses a serious, however well known, difficulty in accounting for intersubjectivity. This problem is essentially how to explain the fact that the other is present to me *as other.* That is, to be genuinely related to the other, there must be a commonality and sameness—the other is present to me as another *myself*—but, since the other is also *other,* there must be difference and distinction as well. Consciousness cannot be the author of this otherness for, as Merleau-Ponty said of Husserl's *Cartesian Meditations,* "The position of the other as another myself is in effect not possible if it is *consciousness* which must effect it: to have a consciousness is to constitute, and thus I cannot have a consciousness of the other because it would be to constitute him as constituting, and as constituting with regard to the very act by which I constitute him" (S 117).

This might look at first as though it were a peculiar rephrasing of the Cartesian legacy of the problem of "other minds." But this is, in fact, not the case. It is a very different question to ask, not how can I prove the existence of the other, or that this other (putative) person before me has a mind, but rather how can the other—whose existence is not in doubt—be present to me as other? The existence of the other is so much not in doubt that, even in introspectively trying to know myself apart from the other, I inevitably fail: "Each time I study my own feelings, I end up understanding them in terms of my behavior and as a modification of my relationships with the world" (SNS 93).[5] Or, as Merleau-Ponty wrote at the conclusion of *Éloge de la philosophie,* his inaugural lecture at the Collège de France, "At the end of a reflection which at first isolates him, but makes him better demonstrate the bonds of truth which attach him to the world and to history, the philosopher finds not the abyss of himself or absolute knowledge, but the renewed image of the world and himself situated within it among others" (p. 85).

How, then, can Merleau-Ponty's phenomenology satisfy both conditions of intersubjectivity, sameness and difference, without invoking the constituting powers of a reflective consciousness to do it? The solution to the first condition lies in the experience I have of my own body, in my anonymous, pre-reflective level of perception which is also presented to my consciousness. I am not a pure subject trying to account for a relationship with the other as object—the fundamental difficulty, Merleau-Ponty thinks, in both the Husserlian and Sartrian views of intersubjectivity. Rather, as a "third genus of being," the lived-body, in its most origin-ary, pre-reflective contact with the world and other people, is already both "subject" and "object" and transcends both. Consciousness does not constitute this relatedness to other people because the pre-reflective level of perception is already composed of one common texture of corporeal relationships. My bodily experience which is presented to my own consciousness already evidences the other at its very core. Thus, "If I experience this inherence of my consciousness in its body and world, the perception of other people and the plurality of consciousnesses no longer present any difficulty" (PhP 351).[6]

In *Sens et non-sens,* which appeared two years after the *Phénoménologie de la perception,* Merleau-Ponty described our relationship with the other as "no longer position of an object, but rather communication with a manner of being" (p. 163), and this language very strongly resembles that of his last writings in which he argues that the inter-world is founded on the fact that both I and the other are registers of being. A "philosophy of the flesh as visibility of the invisible" holds that "The schema of the lived-body, because I see myself, may be participated in by all other bodies that I see" (RC 176, 178). Then, as noted above in the Introduction, Merleau-Ponty proceeds to call this inter-corporeal reality "a lexicon of corporeity in general" (RC 178).

A much more detailed and concrete picture of how the other is presented to me must take into account several levels of experience in addition to our most primordial perceptual life. In the latter, as we have already seen, the very structure of perceptual objectivity implies the existence of the other, since perceived objects are presented to me as publically available, as qualitatively distinct from the privacy of imagination or ideas. But this is also true of cultural entities as well, beginning with the first of them by means of which all the rest exist, "the body of the other as a bearer of behavior" (PhP 401). For example, as André Malraux pointed out in *La Création esthétique,* "perception already stylizes. A woman passing by is not first for me a corporeal shape, a colored mannequin, a spectacle. She is an 'individual, sentimental, sexual expression,' a certain manner of being flesh given entirely in her step or even in the shock of her heel on the ground, as the tension of the bow is present in each fiber of the wood—a very noticeable variation on the norm of walking, looking, touching, and speaking which I possess in my presence because I am a body" (S 67-68).

Another, very different relationship in the social world consists of capital. Merleau-Ponty considers that Marx was correct to point out in *Das Kapital* that capital "is not a thing, but rather a social relationship between persons mediated by things" (AD 47). It is an example in the social world of what Gestalt psychologists abundantly illustrated in terms of perception, namely, that it is organized so as to achieve and maintain an equilibrium with one's environment. In the cultural world we attempt to establish and maintain an equilibrium with others in and through such social relationships as customs, habits, mores, conventions—as well as through social institutions such as law.

In the same way, Merleau-Ponty thinks that Marcel Mauss' researches pointed toward the conclusion—not formally drawn by him—that *mana* is "precisely evidence for the individual of certain relationships of equivalence between what he gives, receives, and returns, the experience of a certain distance between himself and his state of equlibrium with others, the first fact of a double reference of conduct to oneself and to the other, the demand of an invisible totality of which he himself and the other are in their eyes substitutable elements" (S 145-46).

Merleau-Ponty views Mauss' contributions to understanding intersubjectivity in the retrospective light of Claude Lévi-Strauss' cultural anthropology, to which he is substantially indebted in working out his phenomenology of the social world. For Lévi-Strauss, as for Merleau-Ponty, "structure" in intersubjective relationships constitutes the manner in which means of exchange such as *mana* are organized in society. They are cultural adumbrations of Gestalts in the perceptual world in which "subject" and "object" become indistinguishable features: "Social facts are neither things nor ideas, but rather structures" (S 146). And for Merleau-Ponty, as for Lévi-Strauss, society itself is a "structure of structures: how could there be no relationship between the linguistic system, the economic system, and the system of [blood] relationships which it practices" (S 147-48)?

It is true that the relationship of one structure to another can be "subtle and variable" in that they may be either "homologous" or "the counterpart and antagonist of the other"—which brings it about that "Society as structure remains a many-facetted reality, amenable to several views" (S 148). But it is still the case that structures are interdependent parts of a society as such, and each mirrors the whole in its own particular way. Both this concept of structure, as well as the "subtle and variable" fit of structures in a given society, will have the greatest importance for understanding the phenomenon of law (see VI.2, VI.3).

Merleau-Ponty has, in fact, many acknowledged, as well as unacknowledged, debts to thinkers such as Malraux, Lévi-Strauss, Marx, and Mauss, and we shall see more of these in the following chapters. But it turns out that it is language, rather than capital or *mana,* or even art which is, on his view, the social structure most illuminative of the commonality of intersubjective experience. As

Laurie Spurling has observed, "it is speech, above all, which develops, expands and puts flesh on the seed of intersubjectivity latent in all experience. In speaking, we participate in a cultural object, language, which is not of our own, individual making and into which we are immersed from birth."[7]

Language is as important as it is a complex topic in Merleau-Ponty's philosophy, and changes in his consideration of language did not so much follow the course of his own philosophical development as they did positively constitute it. Indeed, for a period of about ten years—from 1949-1959, as James Edie points out—Merleau-Ponty "frequently states his belief that the study of language is *the central* problem of philosophy, that even the phenomenology of perception must be understood in terms of the structures of language."[8] For this reason, and because only part of Merleau-Ponty's consideration of language deals with communication and the communality of intersubjective experience—our immediate concern here—I shall leave off a detailed examination of language (including the ways it manifests the communality of intersubjective experience) until the final section of this chapter and the one following. The latter will show how, among other things, Merleau-Ponty's appropriation of linguistic structuralism led to an outline of a philosophy of history.

Before going that far, however, we must first consider how Merleau-Ponty's phenomenology can satisfy the second condition of intersubjectivity, namely, how the other presents himself or herself to me as *other.* How can Merleau-Ponty account for the difference which is responsible for the fact that "I and the other are two *almost* concentric circles which are only distinguished by a light and mysterious slippage" (PM 186)?

In the first place, at the level of perception, otherness manifests itself, as described above vis-à-vis Malraux, in terms of particular, individuating styles of behavior. This is not a distinction in the common *what* that we do together day in and day out in our life-worlds, but in the *how* that we do it. This is plainly evident not only in Malraux's example of walking, but also in handwriting, laughing, speaking, bearing grief and sickness, and so forth.

A second distinguishing phenomenon is the essential privacy of experience, subjectivity that cannot be objectified, which brings it about that I shall never know completely how others experience, say, colors, love, or art. There is ineluctably a "lived solipsism that cannot be transcended" (PhP 411) but, at the same time, the balance wheel to solitude remains communication such that they are only "two moments of one sole phenomenon" (PhP 413). This is so because, in the perceptual circuit of the other, myself, and the world around us, the separation of consciousnesses "is only recognized after a failure of communication, and our first movement is to believe in a being undivided between us."[9]

For example, if a friend and I are looking at a certain landscape and I want to show him something that he does not yet see, I am not trying to describe an appearance in my private world for which I wish him to construct analogous images in his private world. Rather, "There is, and I well feel it if I get impatient, a kind of demand that what is seen by me is seen by him. But at the same time, this communication is demanded by the very thing that I see, by the reflections of sunlight on it, by its color, by its sensory evidence. The thing imposes itself . . . as real for any subject which takes up my situation."[10]

In the social world, as distinct from the perceptual, otherness manifests itself in ways much more immediately relevant for the phenomenon of law—particularly in the economic and political domains—in terms of conflicts of interests. Thus despite the intimacy and closeness of human relationships, there is, in the sort of world we inhabit, no pre-established harmony of needs and wants: the social world "is not a collective consciousness, but intersubjectivity, a living relationship and tension between individuals" (SNS 157). Intersubjectivity thus includes relationships as well as conflict, but the latter presupposes the former against which it stands out. Furthermore, since conflict differs both conceptually and existentially from alienation—a distinction consistently blurred by Sartre, at least in his early works—there really is an *inter*subjectivity with both subjective and objective aspects intact, rather than a Sartrian ensemble of negativizing and necessarily alienated subjects.

Practical consequences as well flow from this commitment to intersubjectivity, as we shall follow in detail throughout succeeding chapters. On the political plane, for example, a commitment to subjectivity underlies Merleau-Ponty's critique of Soviet totalitarianism in that the latter obliterates the subjective conscience and freedom of the individual in a total concern for the objective results of actions, rules, social policies, and history. And on the other hand, he will tell us that Western capitalistic democracies err by focussing exclusively on the subjective—settling on a morality of pure intentions, certain conceptions of individual rights, and the like—to the exclusion of the objective, dehumanizing consequences of social policies, laws, and positive moralities. Intersubjectivity is, then, both subjective as well as objective stubborn fact: "ultra-objective and ultra-subjective attitudes are only two aspects of one sole crisis of political thought and of the political world" (S 317).

Indeed, it would not be claiming too much to construe the *fil conducteur* of Merleau-Ponty's philosophy—from its earliest concerns with perception and behavior through its descriptions of the social world to his very last texts—as a determined attempt to chart a middle path between extreme subjectivism and extreme objectivism. This is as true of his theoretical research into the structures of perception and language, of his attempts to escape from an over-weaning idealism[11] without falling into a naive realism, as it is of his practical political involvement. The latter will be sketched below in detail (IV.1-3); for the present, let us consider the consequences for intersubjectivity in what concerns the nature of society itself.

It follows from Merleau-Ponty's striving for a living unity of objectivity and subjectivity in the relationships I have with others and the world around me that there is both room for privacy and individual rights, on the one hand, and a denial that society is composed of atomistic, individual consciousnesses, on the other. Thus society itself, which emerges from the mesh of intersubjective relationships, is neither a set of purely spatial, physical relationships as exist between things (see the Introduction above)—nor an ensemble of wholly subjective meanings founded on understanding the other. Rather, social relationships which form bases for interaction are themselves, as Lévi-Strass pointed out, structures simultaneously subjective and objective.

Thus, for example, the roles and status of members of society constitute such structures because roles are neither purely subjective conceptions nor are reducible to the objective profile of what the individuals whose roles they are usually do. (People habitually squint in bright sunlight, but it is no social role to do so.) Nor, for the same reason, is a role merely what a given individual may be objectively predicted to do by an external observer. Instead, roles are both objective and subjective in that they express rules that people are expected to obey according to some standard or norm. Society is consequently an ensemble of individuals whose concrete relationships are determined by rules that specify what is expected of people who fill roles, and which stamp their actions with a specifically meaningful character. So, for instance, much of what we permit a doctor to do to us even in a routine physical examination would be actionable under the criminal law if done in most other contexts.

But doctors are also individuals who may fill a variety of roles, and so a given society may be approached both individualistically in the sense of an ensemble of life stories of the particular members that make it up (the point of view of the biographer) or holistically in terms of the network of roles its members play (the perspective of the sociologist). Now within social theory, the debate between those favoring individualistic and those arguing for holistic accounts of society has generated a considerable literature ever since at least Hobbes (who strongly favored the former). But can one make any statements about society that do not finally reduce to those about the individuals that comprise it?

Merleau-Ponty's position on intersubjectivity entails the validity of both perspectives, but on balance inclines him to prefer holistic accounts which stress the kinds of "social facts" sketched above in terms of Mauss, Lévi-Strauss, and Marx. Such social facts, as well as institutions generally, express social interactions without being reducible to statements about any particular individual(s). Thus, on Merleau-Ponty's view, as in many other holistic accounts, society is not a whole in the way that a machine is the sum of its parts—say, as a clock is the sum of its wheels, levers, and gears. It is, rather, a Gestalt whole, the individual "parts" of which are—as described above—interdependent rather than independent. Such a Gestalt whole, therefore, cannot be understood by analysis in the way that a chemical compound can be broken down to its constituent parts or as a machine can be disassembled. Rather, it must be viewed as a developing organic whole which is why Merleau-Ponty very often links together in the same sentence descriptions of social structures and analogous relations between "parts" of the lived-body (see, for instance, PhP 202 and AD 162). It follows, therefore, that, as described above, individuals do not exist atomistically in *partes extra partes* relationships with each other, but rather as thoroughly mixed up in each other's lives.

This is not to say, of course, that individuality is not possible, or that the individualistic perspective pointed out above is after all false or misleading. But it was important for Merleau-Ponty, as we shall see below in terms of ethics (III.1), politics (IV.1), and law (VII.2), to distance himself from a naive and extreme individualism which underlay much of 19th-century liberalism in England and the United States as well as the liberalism of French politics for most of the first forty years of this century. Furthermore, it will be of some importance for those later discussions to pause for a moment here to consider another traditional aspect of the dispute between individualistic and holistic accounts of society, namely, the way the debate has been brought to bear on Ferdinand Tönnies' well known distinction between *Gesellschaft* (association) and *Gemeinschaft* (community). For, the individualistic perspective is certainly more appropriate for understanding the former than the latter, since there is usually little temptation to attribute any sort of group personality or character to, say, trade union groups or business organizations.[12] On the other hand, in families or tight-knit ethnic neighborhoods—two paradigm cases of *Gemeinschaft*—the opposite sort of attitude would tend to assert itself. Here, a given member of society is born into a certain family and community situation, and grows up with the consciousness of living a common history with a common set of symbols which links him or her—for better or worse—to the immediate companions[13] of his or her *Umwelt.* By this means, he or she effectively grows into a common culture and, in the same movement, society as a whole gains cohesion.

Merleau-Ponty has a vested interest in Tönnies' distinction for many reasons, the most important of which consists of his (Merleau-Ponty's) Marxist criticisms of Western, bourgeois capitalist societies. For, in stressing that intersubectivity differs substantially from a "collective consciousness," and in underlining the conflicts between justice and private interests in Western societies (see below at IV.3 and VII.2), he is evidently thinking much more of the individualistic perspective congenial to *Gesellschaft* than of the holistic approach to society appropriate to *Gemeinschaft.* Correlatively, his criticisms of law in capitalistic societies are also limited to the associative side of life. In actual fact, of course, law has a much wider importance in social life and is as crucial in what concerns *Gemeinschaft,* if not more so, than in the domain of

Gesellschaft. Why is it, then, that despite the pull of the holistic model of society, his vision became so narrowly focussed?

The answer is hardly clear-cut, but it seems to me that its most plausible reconstruction would run as follows. First, his phenomenology is committed to avoiding the abstractions of "high-altitude thinking" by always securing thought "in contact with the facts" (AD 255). Second, one of these facts is that, although all orders of meaning in the social world interpenetrate, one can come to dominate in a certain society in a particular historical epoch (PhP 202). Third, in Merleau-Ponty's own historical epoch, two particular orders of meaning dominated and effectively colored all the rest. One of these was the economic side of life—chiefly Western bourgeois capitalism with its political, moral, and legal reinforcement, on the one hand, together with its dishonest and hypocritical denials of violence, on the other. As we shall see below (IV.3), Merleau-Ponty was very much inclined to Marxist criticisms of such societies in stressing the difference between formal and real values, and one way of phrasing this criticism in the present context is to indict such societies for hypocritical appeals to the harmony and peace of a non-violent society—in the sense of community—whilst the economic side of society—in which are to be found paradigm examples of associations—rested on violence and exploitation. Certainly in this kind of environment, fourth, Merleau-Ponty would be led to stress much more the conflicts of individual interests than he would a (misleading and false) collective consciousness.

Fifth, another fact of social life that dominated Merleau-Ponty's historical epoch and decisively influenced his view of society and of law, consisted of the horrors and chaos of war, on the one hand, and the threats of totalitarianism—in Nazi Germany and Stalinist Russia, on the other. Such events and upheavals could not have failed to sensitize Merleau-Ponty, as they did Albert Camus, to the necessity of disentangling the interests of the individual from those of the State, of distinguishing society at large from the State, and of asserting the dignity of individual subjectivity in the face of totalitarian wishes to see in every aspect of private life a political dimension.[14] Perhaps in the end, therefore, Merleau-Ponty conceived of *Gemeinschaft* as a regulative ideal for a world caught up in a struggle for economic justice in the West and for individual liberty in the East.

§3. The Bonds of Language: Communication and Structure

Merleau-Ponty's consideration of language is also situated within the framework of discerning both the commonalities and differences in intersubjective experience, although in ways that eventually surprised even himself and led to a decisive turning point in his philosophizing. His earliest writings on language, in both *La Structure du comportement* and *Phénoménologie de la perception,* develop a theory of meaning in relation to bodily gestures. In speaking (*la parole*), I take up a given language system (*la langue*) shared with others and with whom I participate pre-reflectively in a common texture of inter-corporeal relationships. And this is an approach to language which remained in some form or other throughout Merleau-Ponty's writings—from its most complete early presentation in "The Body as Expression, and Speech" in the *Phénoménologie de la perception,* running through *La Prose du monde,* his early articles on language reprinted in *Signes,* through *L'oeil et l'esprit* and *Le visible et l'invisible.*

In each case, although Merleau-Ponty was certainly sensitive to individual differences expressed through distinctive styles of speaking and different empirical languages, he still stressed the communicative function of language, the living bonds of unity it forges. Since speech and the expressive body are immediately continuous with perception, "Language can vary and amplify inter-corporeal communication as much as one would like: it has the same elasticity, the same style" (S 27). The lived-body, mind-in-act, is an essential part of expression and speech. Since, as described above, bodily gestures are not the mere outer re-presentations of an inner reality, spoken words are not just the external "clothing" of thought (PhP 445). In both cases we are face to face with dual aspects of a concrete reality, and "perception, history, and expression" (S 94) are three interdependent parts of the social Gestalt. Indeed, in the bodily dialectic of speaking and listening, words and silence, my unity with the other is so close that "I *become* the one whom I hear" (PM 165). Just as I am installed in space and time by the living and thick presence of my body, speech and language install me in the life of the other: "Speaking and understanding, action and perception, are only completely different operations when I reflect" (PM 28). In speech, "I project myself into the other, I insert him into me, our conversation resembles the struggle of two athletes at two ends of the same rope. The 'I' who speaks is installed in his body and in his language not as in a prison, but rather as in an apparatus which transports him magically into the perspective of the other" (PM 28). Indeed, "in the exercise of speech, I become the one to whom I am listening" (PM 165).

After having finished the *Phenomenology of Perception,* Merleau-Ponty began to read seriously the works of structuralism and scientific linguistics. His first course in the philosophy of language was presented (in the University of Lyon) in 1947 and 1948, and he expanded and developed this course to be given at the Sorbonne in 1949. It is this latter course we have in the form of *Consciousness and the Acquisition of Language* and, as noted above, this research merely constituted the first step in a decade-long obsession with structuralism, chiefly with the work of the pioneering Swiss linguist, Ferdinand de Saussure.[15] Merleau-Ponty was particularly interested in two interlocking Saussurian distinctions—that between "*la langue*" and "*la parole,*" which together comprise "*le langage*"—and, secondly, that which concerns the "synchronic" and "diachronic" functions of language. We shall consider the former distinction here, but leave the latter for the following chapter (at II.5), since it is particularly concerned with the temporal depth of historicity in experience and with the sense of history itself.

La langue denotes a language as in speaking of, or in, the French or English language; it consists, therefore, of a fixed structure or syntax of words (*les mots*) and rules for usage. It is the linguistic equipment which one takes up in concrete speech acts which in turn comprise *la parole,* some (infelicitous) translations of which consist of "power of speech" or "human speech." *La langue* is, for de Saussure, "a system of signs expressing ideas, and by this means comparable to writing, to the alphabet of deaf-mutes, to symbolic rites, to forms of politeness, to military signals, etc., etc. It is only the most important of these systems. One can thus conceive of *a science which studies the life of signs at the heart of social life;* it would form a part of social psychology; and consequently of general psychology; we shall call it 'semiology.'"[16]

As a grammatical system, *la langue* is a form of social order, an integral part of the social structure by means of which intersubjectivity becomes a living reality. Thus, as we shall see below (II.2), it also has a historical depth because it forms part of the context of sedimented meanings we take up and appropriate in our everyday lives. As a result, de Saussure could underscore the fact that, as Merleau-Ponty repeated in virtually the same words, *la langue* is "a treasure deposited by the practice of *la parole* in subjects belonging to the same community, a grammatical system . . . [which] is not complete in any [particular individual] but only perfectly exists in the group."[17]

Merleau-Ponty was most particularly interested in this dialectical relationship between *la langue* and *la parole,* in which the former funds the latter with structure whilst the latter sediments new meanings which accumulate in the former. They are two aspects of the same concrete whole, and neither ultimately can be understood without the other. From the point of view of intersubjectivity, they give us different perspectives in that *la langue* is a form of social order providing a kind of cohesion for at least the majority of a particular society, whilst *la parole* shows us more individually and more dynamically how incarnate *cogitos* constitute what is perhaps the most important dimension of the life-world.

For, although *la parole* does have a copying function in what concerns the transmission of received thought, doctrines, and social meanings generally, this function constitutes neither the entire role of human speech nor what is most essential to it. The latter, rather, consists of creative expression which leads to the sedimentation of new meanings. "That is why," the *Phenomenology of Perception* tells us, "we have been led to distinguish a secondary speech which translates acquired thought and an original speech which first makes this thought exist for ourselves as well as for the other" (p. 446). In creative expression we take up, but also transcend, available significations and rules for usage, and new sedimentation occurs. We can coin new words, develop new genres of literature, and exploit new styles of expression in poetry (and in non-verbal artistic media as well). In each case, new use has been made of the linguistic equipment available to all; new life has been breathed into it such that, as Merleau-Ponty puts it, "we feel that *something has been said*. . . . It is precisely this 'coherent deformation' (A. Malraux) of available meanings which orders them in a new sense and makes listeners, *but also the speaking subject,* take a decisive *step*" (S 114-15).

Correlatively, it is by means of an *illusion* that speech manifests itself to us as already contained in language: "Speech, insofar as it is distinct from language, is that moment when the significative intention still silent and wholly in act proves itself capable of incorporating itself into my culture and that of the other, of forming me and of forming him in transforming the sense of cultural instruments [*la langue*]. It becomes 'available' in turn because it gives us after the fact the illusion that it was contained in the already available meanings, when in fact, by a sort of *ruse,* it only evoked them to infuse them with a new life" (S 115).

In the dialectical movement between *la parole* and *la langue,* on Merleau-Ponty's view, words thus have less a fixed signification than a use-value. They have a value "in the sense in which one speaks of the value of a piece of change which one can use to pay for an infinite number of objects" (CAL 257). Thus, if life can be breathed into words and expressions and styles of speaking—if, in short, use values can be created—they can also be withdrawn. Use-values can atrophy and enter "into decadence by the sole fact that they have been used and have lost their 'expressivity'"; language is, consequently, "a moving equilibrium" (S 108).

Language has at least one other crucial intersubjective role, reflection on which occupied Merleau-Ponty very early on and led eventually to the crisis in which he abandoned structuralism altogether in favor of the dialectics of *The Visible and the Invisible.* This function of language concerns the search for truth and the founding of universality. As James M. Edie observed, "In his 1952 paper addressed to the Collège de France (in support of his candidacy for the chair of philosophy) he . . . says that in a series of further studies which he has undertaken since 1945, and which will definitely fix the philosophical significance of the earlier works, he is turning to language. . . . to 'the field of knowledge properly so-called.' There are then two tasks before him: (1) a theory of truth, and (2) a theory of intersubjectivity. These tasks will be achieved in two books on the theory of truth, namely, *The Prose of the World* and *The Origin of Truth.* He states clearly, even in this very preliminary study, what will turn out to be the major problem and ultimate stumbling-block of his whole investigation of language: 'Language leads us to a thought which is no longer ours alone, to a thought which is presumptively universal, though this is never the universality of a pure concept which would be identical for every mind. It is rather the call which a situated thought addresses to other thoughts, equally situated, and each one responds to the call with its own resources.'"[18] Well, *The Origin of Truth* was never written, and *The Prose of the World* was abandoned in mid-stream. What, then, went wrong?

Effectively, Merleau-Ponty was trying to hold together two incompatible positions, and *The Prose of the World* was shelved when the futility of such a project finally became inescapable. One of these positions was, as described above, a phenomenology of language as expression and communication in the life-world, and the other consisted of a structuralism which focussed on language as a tool of knowledge, as a set of logical a prioris imbedded in a depth grammar, to use Noam Chomsky's well known phrase, which binds all empirical languages. Merleau-Ponty recognized early on the affinities of structuralism with Husserl's *Fourth Investigation* in which the latter defended what the former could never accept, namely, "a complete theory of pure grammar as the first level of formal logic, a depth grammar coercive on all natural languages."[19] But, for the reasons given above in the Introduction vis-à-vis nature, consciousness, and truth, Merleau-Ponty could not see in language any deeper structure than the powers of communication which lay on the surface. Or, rather, the interactions of the structures of *la langue* and the power of speech (*la parole*) are always bent to a communicative purpose: "Phenomenology studies the act of speaking; Structuralism studies the presupposed rules. The two, he claims, can be related dialectically."[20] Thus, in the last analysis, Merleau-Ponty sought "to turn structuralism into a branch of dialectical phenomenology and to show its existential and experiential roots."[21]

But this attempt was doomed to failure as he came later to completely appreciate the full import of structuralist claims, as he had apparently not done earlier. Phrased in terms of universality, the only sense of it that he would accept in his earlier writings consists of "the ability of speakers of natural languages to make themselves intelligible, little by little, to one another. This is an 'existential' or 'affective' universality, not the logical sub-structure demanded by Husserl. The logical aprioris of pure grammar are ruled out in favor of the 'oblique' or 'lateral' universality of the incomplete but sufficient comprehensibility which we effect in actually speaking to others."[22] In installing myself culturally in the lives of other people, "I confront them, I show one to another, I make them compossible in an order of truth, I make myself responsible for all of them, I create a universal life" (S 93-94). Further, as Merleau-Ponty writes à propos of Lévi-Strauss, the experience studied in anthopology shows that "we live in the unity of one sole life all the systems of which our culture is make up. There is some knowledge to draw from this synthesis which is us. . . . a lateral universal which we acquire by ethnological experience, incessantly tested by myself towards the other and by the other towards me" (S 150).

But the universality in language and truth demanded by structuralism is *radically* (at the root) different. It springs not from the play of language on the surface of intersubjective relationships, but rather from the presupposed rules of depth grammar that make the former possible. It constitutes, then, an original level of meaning somehow beyond all human beings and binding on them. Thus, as James Edie summarizes the *dénouement* of Merleau-Ponty's dawning recognition of this fact:

> It is as if . . . Merleau-Ponty never fully recognized or appreciated the fact that phonology, and hence all of contemporary linguistics relies on a binary logic (the only kind of logic a computer, for instance, can use). The whole system of phonological oppositions in all natural languages is based on the possibility of speakers of those languages being able to recognize sounds emitted as noises from the vocal apparatus of native speakers as opposable, according to rule, in binary fashion, to all the other sounds recognized as standing for phonemes in those languages. This, he could hardly have missed, but it took a good deal of time for it to sink in. When, later on, he was faced with the prospect of the necessity of choosing between structuralism and a dialectical description of lived experience, it was structuralism which he rejected.[23]

The whole of this reaction to structuralism will be central to understanding Merleau-Ponty's perception of natural law theories (see below at VII.1), just as the dialectical relationships between *la langue* and *la parole* will comprise an essential part of the structures of law itself (V.2,3). Taking into account, therefore, Merleau-Ponty's ultimate rejection of structuralism as well as the fact that he never disavowed the dialectical relationships between *la langue* and *la parole,* once disentangled from the additional baggage of claims about a depth grammar and an ideal language, all subsequent references to de Saussure's work in the following pages will be restricted to what Merleau-Ponty found acceptable in it. Structure therefore may be kept and preserved as essential to the phenomena which define the social world, even if structural*ism* is not. Further, I shall use Merleau-Ponty's descriptions of the dialectic of speech and language to illuminate other, tightly related aspects of his phenomenology of the social world, beginning in the following chapter with history and the appearance of meaning.

NOTES

1. For reasons given below in the text, I think Merleau-Ponty's view of the body-subject does in fact differ substantially from the *pour-soi* of Sartre's early writings. In the long run, how much a distinction is possible from Sartre's later writings is debatable and turns on how consistent texts such as *La Critique de la raison dialectique* and the posthumously published *Cahiers pour une morle* and *Les carnets de la drôle de guerre: Novembre 1939-Mars 1940* can be with, say, *L'Être et le néant*. And it will be even more interesting to make comparisons and contrasts with all of Sartre's unpublished writings once they finally appear.
2. The ascription of this statement to Husserl also appears in the *Phénoménologie de la perception* and in *Les sciences de l'homme et la phénoménologie,* cited in *Bulletin de Psychologie,* n° 236 (novembre 1964), p. 143. But as Herbert Spiegelberg has pointed out, such a quotation has never been found. See *The Phenomenological Movement: A Historical Introduction,* 3rd Edition (Dordrecht: Martinus Nijhoff, 1982), pp. 580-81, n.2.
3. Alphonse de Waelhens, "Une Philosophie de l'ambiguïté," the Preface to Merleau-Ponty's *La Structure du comportement* (Paris: Presses Universitaires de France, 1942), p. v.
4. It is a bit misleading, therefore, to say, as Albert Rabil, Jr., does, that *"the social world is also primordial.* It is already there, given, prior to my attempts to account for reciprocity. The human world, like the natural world, leads us back to the lived or existential world." *Merleau-Ponty: Existentialist of the Social World* (New York: Columbia University Press, 1967), pp. 36-37. This sense of "primordial," that is, being given in experience, is different from, but related to, the one under discussion here and which is invoked by de Waelhens above (note 3).
5. This claim about the inevitable futility of introspection should be considered together with Sartre's contentions that, for years, Merleau-Ponty engaged in serious and disciplined introspection, plumbing the depths of his own experiences and memories in an (unsuccessful) attempt to recapture the immediacy of his own childhood. See his "Merleau-Ponty [I]", trans. William S. Hamrick, *Journal of the British Society for Phenomenology,* Vol. XV, No. 2, May 1984, p. 130.
6. For a more detailed and extremely lucid account of the way Merleau-Ponty attempts to account for intersubjectivity, see Gary Brent Madison, *The Phenomenology of Merleau-Ponty* (Athens, Ohio: Ohio University Press, 1981), pp. 37-45.
7. Laurie Spurling, *Phenomenology and the Social World* (London: Routledge and Kegan Paul, 1977), p. 52.
8. James M. Edie, "Merleau-Ponty: The Triumph of Dialectics over Structuralism," *Man and World* 17: 299-312 (1984) at p. 304. Reprinted (and cited) in J.N. Mohanty, ed. *Phenomenology and the Human Sciences* (Dordrecht: Martinus Nijhoff, 1985), p. 64.
9. "Le Primat de la perception et ses conséquences philosophiques," *Bulletin de la Société Française de Philosophie,* XLI, 1947 (séance du 23 novembre 1946), p. 125.
10. "Le Primat de la perception et ses conséquences philosophiques," pp. 124-25.
11. Sartre also complained with some bitterness, and considerable sarcasm, of the idealistic basis of their common philosophical training— with particular reference to the idealism of their teacher, Léon Brunschvicg. For Sartre's critique of the latter's "sinister and cozy idealism," see "Merleau-Ponty [I]," pp. 128-29.
12. This claim is culture-bound to the degree that it is largely true in Western capitalistic societies. For instance, one of the gloomiest statements in the English language is "I only work here." (One would not say of one's family home, "I only live here" unless that particular family had already lost a good share of its community.) But on the other hand, this claim is not nearly as true of cultures such as that of Japan. Perhaps in some way its truth or falsity depends on

whether it is a question of guilt cultures, like those of the West, or of shame cultures, like those of the East—and also of the original Americans. See William S. Hamrick, "Redeeming the Earth: Tragic Wisdom and the Plains Indians," *Journal of the British Society for Phenomenology,* Vol. XVI, Number 1, January 1985, pp. 36-54.

13. The Latin word "socius," from which we derive "society" and "la société," originally meant "companion."
14. There is perhaps no better example of this danger, and of the moral dilemmas it poses, than the play, *Pack of Lies.* This particular piece of theatre should be required viewing for all members of intelligence-gathering communities (not in Tönnies' sense!) of freedom-loving, democratic societies.
15. See de Saussure's *Cours de linguistique générale,* édition critique, préparé par Tullio de Mauro (Paris: Payot, 1976), especially pp. 23-38.
16. De Saussure, p. 33.
17. De Saussure, p. 30.
18. Edie, p. 63, citing the English translation, "An Unpublished Text," in *The Primacy of Perception and Other Essays,* ed. James M. Edie (Evanston: Northwestern University Press, 1964), p. 8.
19. Edie, p. 62.
20. Edie, p. 67.
21. Edie, p. 69.
22. Edie, p. 65. He also notes that, "since Merleau-Ponty will never fully agree to the structuralist requirement that the laws of language are foundational and universally valid for *any* and *every* natural language, he states that his method is only a 'methodological' rationalism which must not be confused with a 'dogmatic rationalism.'" (pp. 64-65, citing "An Unpublished Text" at p. 10.)
23. Edie, p. 66.

II: HISTORY AND THE ORIGIN OF MEANING

Philosophy, in Merleau-Ponty's view, always comprises a return "to an intersubjectivity which, ever more closely, binds us to the whole of history" (S 141). Accordingly, history is a subject with which Merleau-Ponty is concerned again and again throughout his works, from the earliest up to the very last writings. Across these texts, he is concerned to argue that history provides intersubjectivity with temporal depth by (i) furnishing a dimension of historicity to an individual consciousness, by (ii) anchoring our incarnate freedom in an established order of sedimented meanings, and finally by (iii) elaborating our relationships with others in the creation of truth, meaning, and rationality.

Furthermore, Merleau-Ponty's analyses of (ii) and (iii) and even occasionally (i) as well, are taken up in two distinct, but related, epistemological inquiries which are constantly interwoven in his writings. The first asks about the sense of history or, in other words, about questions usually associated with the philosophy of history. The second investigation, however, concerns the appearance of meaning *in* history or, to turn it around, the role of history in the appearance ofsense. Additionally, Merleau-Ponty distinguishes "personal" from "public" history (RC 59). For the former, he confines his attention largely to Freudian inquiries into sexuality. In the context of public history, on the other hand, he examines a different ensemble of causal theories represented by Marx and subsequent Marxists who propounded political theories based on an economic determinism. As we shall see below, Merleau-Ponty finds much more inspiration in the younger, rather than the elder, Marx because the *1844 Manuscripts* does not fall prey to what he (Merleau-Ponty) sees as a chief vice in *Capital,* namely, the view that history embodies a mechanical dialectic, like a clock ticking off the advance of world events, independent of human will.

In what follows, I shall be concerned with Freud only marginally because what Merleau-Ponty says about it will have only a minor relevance to law (see VI.3). What will prove to be more legally important, however, will be the philosophy of history and its connection with language, as well as the role of history in the appearance of meaning.

§1. The Historicity of Consciousness

History, whether we refer to our own personal histories or to the accumulated record of cultural events in the social world, is not an external addition to a body-consciousness.[1] Rather, it is on the "primordial institution of the body that all symbolic elaboration is founded" (PM 63, n.). The structure of time-consciousness, the analysis of which Merleau-Ponty borrows largely from Husserl's *Vorlesungen zur Phänomenologie des inneren Zeitbewussteins*—but with several additions or misrepresentations, depending on one's point of view—makes the lived-body inescapably and essentially historical before any elaborations of the social world. "Historicity," that is, a lived history, is ineluctably a dimension of consciousness because it is not left for a (logically) subsequent, mental reconstruction or series of re-presentations. This is so because no specific mental act(s) is (are) required to relate us to our past experiences or to verify their presence to us. Correlatively, history does not appear in Merleau-Ponty's phenomenology as it does in philosophies such as classical British empiricism—as a problem to be solved and as a threat to the integrity of consciousness. Thus he does not end up with the sceptical quandaries of Hume's *Treatise* which in effect could not explain what its author lived, whilst the latter could not live what he had explained.

Merleau-Ponty avoids this incoherence because the time-structure of consciousness inserts us into history as a thick temporal presence. Phenomenologists have always been obsessed with the unity of consciousness or, more fundamentally, showing that there can be *a* unitary consciousness. Particularly set against the sceptical arguments of Hume, Merleau-Ponty saw clearly, as Husserl had, that the former's difficulties in accounting for memory, personal identity, and the persistence of a world not dependent on our mental acts all stemmed from his instantial, or atomistic, concept of time—the quanta of which had no instrinsic connection with each other. Thus memory became a problem—how to be sure one instant had correctly grasped another, but only in re-presentation—and personal identity turned into an enigma.

In the absence of any persisting mental substance à la Descartes, and faced with the Humian challenge, Merleau-Ponty, like Husserl, espoused the age-old philosophical task of "saving the phenomena." He attempted this not merely by offering descriptions of a continuity of lived time or of its evident presence in memory, or of our feelings of personal continuity, or of our belief in a world continuing without the help of our mental acts to keep it going. Hume, certainly, was willing to accept all these descriptions, and he pointly observed that, out of his study, the philosopher could not in fact do otherwise. Rather, Merleau-Ponty uses Husserl's reflections on time-consciousness—as well as Heidegger's *Being and Time* which is, of course, greatly indebted to the former—to meet Hume on his own level with a new analysis of time-consciousness. Or, what is the same, he proposes a different structure of consciousness.

This is to say that time, rather than being a series of disconnected instants or present "nows," is such that each present is constituted as a Gestalt in the sense of being a focal-point with horizons of pastness and futurity already built into it. The present appears in the context of the past which, as background, influences or conditions its appearing. In a similar way, the present already has as part of its structure or sense as present an anticipation of the future a-borning—exceptions being made for aberrant mental states such as catatonic trances or drugged conditions of a similar nature. The flux of time-consciousness, as Husserl showed, consists therefore of the advent of a future which passes through the present and finally "shades off" (*Abschattungen*) into the past. The life of a body-consciousness is thus a temporal unity of past, present, and future—what Heidegger called an "ek-stase"—which gives our lives a fundamental cohesion (PhP 481). And this cohesion emerges not with reflective, positing acts of higher levels of consciousness—what Merleau-Ponty termed, following Husserl, an "intentionality of act"—but rather at the level of the "one," the anonymous, non-personal, pre-reflective level of perception and behavior at which we find "operative" intentionality— in Husserl's idiom, *fungierende Intentionalität* (PhP xiii).

Moreover, it is at this same, more origin-ary level of intentionality that the historicity of consciousness is first deepened by gaining an established purchase on the world, namely through the medium of bodily habits. For it is the habitual body in Merleau-Ponty's early works that plays the role of institution in his later ones. It does this by rescuing the freedom of consciousness from the necessity of being, à la Sartre, a continual, instantaneous meaning-giver. That is, freedom is already present in the most basic level of perceptual life as a spontaneous, non-determined structuring of a perceptual field. It is continually elaborated, sometimes deepened and not infrequently frustrated, across many kinds of experiences in the social world—from freedom of styles of bodily expression in manifesting one's individuality, through the liberty of creative linguistic expression, to freedom of thought and conscience in higher-order intellectual projects. Liberty, at whatever level, neither emerges from, nor operates in, a vacuum apart from the circumambient world and other people. Freedom is situated and conditioned, both spatially and temporally, and the anchor for this conditioning is the habitual body through which the "I can" of the corporeal schema becomes the "I can continue to." Habit can therefore furnish our liberty with a certain stability and permanence of being established in the world among others because the temporal continuity and durational thickness of a certain pattern of behavior serves as a framework for subsequent creativity and autonomy.

In short, therefore, the habitual body grounds a more meaningful, because lasting, equilibrium with one's milieu. As the last chapter pointed out, this is a behavioral goal not only in the perceived world, but also throughout the social as well, so that various kinds of habits there too serve the same function. To paraphrase Kant, habits without creativity are blind, whilst creativity without habit is empty (of effective force).

§2. Constitution and Institution

In the social world, it is institutions more nearly than behavioral habits that solidify this goal of equilibrium and cement the historical unity and identity of a society. This is so not only of the institution of language, as we saw in the last chapter, but also of durable political structures, judicial institutions, and the like.

Merleau-Ponty defines an institution as that which is created out of the "events of an experience which can endow it with durable dimensions, by relation to which a whole series of other experiences will have meaning, will form a thinkable continuation or a history—or again, the events which depose in me a meaning, not as a relic and residue, but as an appeal to a continuation, the demand of a future" (RC 61). Institutions are thus not pure objects, devoid of any reference to the consciousness(es) that create and sustain them. They are, rather, like perceptual objects, structures of a concrete intentional bond of objectivity and subjectivity. As Alfred Schutz puts it, the "texture of meaning" of the life-world "originates in and has been instituted by human actions, our own and our fellow-men's, contemporaries and predecessors. All cultural objects—tools, symbols, language systems, works of art, social institutions, etc.—point back by their very origin and meaning to the activities of human subjects. For this reason we are always conscious of the historicity of culture which we encounter in traditions and customs. This historicity is capable of being examined in reference to human activities of which it is the sediment."[2]

For Merleau-Ponty, institutions serve two basic sorts of purposes, the first of which is, as noted in the previous section, to serve as the kind of balance wheel for consciousness. Institution of meaning, as in the case of bodily habits, rides in tandem with constitution to give it stability and temporal duration. As a body-consciousness takes up its situations and attempts to make sense of them, its liberty is always based on the "sedimented" layers of past meanings (S 115) to which Schutz refers above, and to which it must react in some way or other. In turn, consciousness has not only the power to constitute new meanings but also to institute them—to sediment new layers of meaning both perceptually, linguistically—as described in the previous chapter—and across other orders of meaning in the social world as well. Thus to live is "to continue a vortex of experience which is formed, with our birth, at the point of contact of the 'beyond' and he who is called to live it" (RC 66).

On the one hand, then, Sartre was not wrong to consider as self-deception the belief that all our meanings and commitments are imperviously secure in being: meanings are established—for a while—and what we like to view as permanent and ineradicable is in reality considerably more fragile. As with the essential incompleteness of the perceptual object, which is continually being "filled in" in the passive synthesis of new temporal perspectives, so also with meaning-structures in the social world. Constitution still goes on because, among other reasons, what we live is still nuanced, ambiguous, indeterminate and thus, to use the language of Merleau-Ponty's later works, open to interrogation. This is not only true of personal experiences between specifiable individuals in developing patterns of relationships in love, friendship, and so forth. It is also the case much more generally throughout the social world—in language, economics, politics, religion, law, and philosophy itself. It is even true of the so-called exact sciences, such as mathematics, and Merleau-Ponty inherited Husserl's sensitivity to the crisis in its foundations at the end of the 19th-century and in the beginning of our own. I shall come back to this vis-à-vis the nature of truth and its relation to nature.

But on the other hand, even if all our meanings are non-permanent and subject to change, it is equally true that we do not have to re-create or re-validate them in every choice. Were this Sartrian picture the case, human beings would be "condemned to an incredible tension" (AD 269). The lived-body is not, for Merleau-Ponty, "a pure power of signifying, centrifugal movement without opacity, without merit, which rejects on the outside, in the signified, history and the social, reduces them to a series of instantaneous views" (AD 267). For, since through institutions consciousness is open, rather than closed, to history and the social world, the institution of meanings and institutions created can serve a second purpose for consciousness, namely to be effective media for the varied and complex ways I belong to the same world as the other. Thus Merleau-Ponty tells us that, because of the instituting capabilities of consciousness, the other is not merely "the negative of myself," co-existence is possible because an institution "is not the immediate reflection" of the other's actions, and finally that institution is, "between others and myself, between me and myself, as a hinge, the consequence and guarantee of our belonging to the same world" (RC 60).

This close connection between the viability of institutions and the perception of belonging to the same world is perhaps most acutely evident in cases in which fundamental changes are wrought in familiar institutions such as those of language, positive morality, religion, and law, or in socially pathological cases, that is, in the presence of a breakdown of social order. For when institutions that have bound our life-world are wrenched out of their familiar shapes, we are apt to feel cast adrift and alienated (unless we are already so alienated that we are more than ready to issue in a new order of things). At the level of personal history, such reactions can give rise to schizophrenia and other similar forms of mental difficulties.[3] At the level of public history, a multiplicity of reactions are possible, ranging from desperation and despair on the one hand, to civil disobedience and revolution on the other.

In his lectures on "'Institution' in Personal and Public History," Merleau-Ponty sheds further light on the dialectical relationship of constitution and institution across a number of different kinds of examples of the latter. First, he observes that there is a "rhythm of conservation, recovery, and transcendence of past events . . . which is characteristic of institution" (RC 61) which one finds in puberty. Consequently, "there is something like an institution even in animality . . . and even in human functions which were thought purely 'biologically'" (RC 61). Institutions are not closed off, however, unavailable to further interrogation even, or especially, in human sexuality. Rather, just as puberty is related to adult life, what was instituted in the past "can give way to an indefinite *research* in Kafka's sense, or to an indefinite elaboration" (RC 61).

In illustrating a very different sort of example, Merleau-Ponty remarks that the same "rhythm of conservation, recovery, and transcendence of past events" is present in "the institution of a work of a painter, of a style in the history of painting" (RC 63). When painters confronted the problem of perspective, for example, Merleau-Ponty considers that they did not approach the problem directly, but only obliquely through a diversionary problem. By this "subterranean logic,"[4] they were thus able to take up an ensemble of past history in art—rather than rejecting it outright—recover from it the necessary tools to express themselves perspectivally, and finally transcend given traditions by instituting a new one. Such a mode of approach created, "much more than a *problem,* an interrogation of painting which suffices to give a common meaning to all its endeavors and to create a history" (RC 63). (Elsewhere, Merleau-Ponty extends this "subterranean logic" far beyond the domain of painting to effectively the whole of human life: "Personal life, expression, knowledge, and history advance obliquely, and not straight towards ends or towards concepts. What one searches for too deliberately, one does not find" [S 104].)

Two other examples of institutions, which will both turn out to be important for understanding Merleau-Ponty's view of law, and will be discussed more fully below in separate sections of the present chapter, consist of language and the development of knowledge. In terms of the first of these, we have already followed his reliance on de Saussure's distinction between *la langue, la parole,* and *le langage;* the remainder of the structure of language is given in the latter's discussion of the synchronic and the diachronic which, as we shall see below, plays a significant part in Merleau-Ponty's consideration of the philosophy of history. The second example, however, concerns the role of history in the development of knowledge in the sense that, as detailed more fully below, there is no truth for Merleau-Ponty in an a-historical, pre-existent systems of truths—a "heaven of ideas" (RC 46)—which gradually reveals (part of) itself in history, with its historical adventures being conceptually distinct from it. Rather, the adventures of experience are essential for understanding both the development and the nature of knowledge: "The historicity of knowledge is not an 'apparent' characteristic which would leave us free to analytically define truth 'in itself.' Even in the order of exact knowledge, it is to a 'structural' conception of truth (Wertheimer) that one must turn. There is truth in the sense of a common field of diverse enterprises of knowing" (RC 64).

There is, perhaps, no better set of illustrations of this "field of diverse enterprises of knowing" than that provided in Thomas Kuhn's *The Structure of Scientific Revolutions.*[5] In Kuhn's view, the history of science is constituted by a dialectic between two sorts of periods of inquiry. The first, which is a period of "normal science," takes place under the influence of a certain established paradigm. In the wake of this institution, scientific activity becomes mostly elaborative research. But the second period is quite different. It is "crisis science" which is carried on when a existing paradigm—say, Galilean-Cartesian physics—is challenged and overthrown in the upheaval of a "paradigm shift" to a successor—in this case, Newtonian physics. In the constitution of the Newtonian model, as well as in its institution as the reigning paradigm, there was both a conservation of the previous paradigm, in that it was not abandoned as totally false, and a recovery in the sense that the data and reasoning operative in the previous paradigm were integrated in a more adequate interpretation. And finally, there was transcendence in that the new paradigm provided not only more adequate explanations than its predecessor, but also had the power to account for certain phenomena which remained inexplicable under the old paradigm—in the present case, causation at a distance[6]—or else to account for the same phenomena in a better way.

Merleau-Ponty's own way of phrasing Kuhn's insights is in terms of a certain doctrine's becoming a "classic" and a "second truth" which has been taken up into another, more adequate point of view (S 16-17). Thus, for instance, "The theses of Marx can remain true as the Pythagorean theorem is true, no longer in the sense that it was for him who invented it—as an identical truth and as a property of space itself—but as a property of a certain model of space among other possible spaces" (S 16). Whilst some truths, to be sure, end up being transformed into "messages" and others into abandoned museum pieces—metaphysical systems, particularly—others somehow never lose their ability to speak to us even if, like the thought of Pythagoras, Descartes, or Marx, they are no longer accepted as Absolute Truth. One is forced to consider them if one wants to go further, and these are the classics: "One recognizes them in that no one takes them literally, but on the other hand new facts are never absolutely beyond their competence, they draw from them new echos, and they reveal in them new reliefs. . . . We say that Marx is in the process of passing to the level of this second truth" (S 16-17).[7]

When we dig further into the dialectical relationship of constitution and institution, we find two other facts which will be important for an understanding of law (see VI.2). The first is that many of the sedimented meanings of the social world have been established not by assignable individuals in the presently existing life-world, but rather by anonymous others in the distant past, the results of whose efforts are still visible. This is more so to the degree that a society endures and maintains its traditions, but in all developed cultures, present generations form their own world-views and arrange their societies on the basis of anonymously generated concepts such as those embedded in literature and philosophy, political and religious institutions, legal codes, uncodified common law traditions, and so forth.

Societies can thus live their inheritances pre-reflectively, even in ignorance of the original meanings of the concepts involved in their formation. For instance, it is possible, and perhaps even probable, that the majority of the population of the United States have no clear idea of the original meanings of the concepts of natural rights and property which are embedded in their Declaration of Independence and Constitution to which they give lip-service and allegiance. This claim is different from, but related to, another that suggests that many Americans are probably not familiar with the texts themselves. But perhaps both assertions, if true, help to explain the (appalling) results of a poll a few years ago in which, when presented with the Bill of Rights in somewhat altered verbal form, many of the populace denounced it as communist propaganda.

The second feature of the dialectical relationship between constitution and institution which will be central to the phenomenon of law (see VI.2) concerns the fact that, whilst passive acceptance of tradition, inheritance, and so forth, is always possible and even necessary for the reasons that consciousness needs institution in the first place, our incarnate freedom must still adjust its heritage to meet the needs of changing times. New meaning must be constituted; there must be transcendence in addition to conservation and recovery because, just as in the perceptual world certain visual or tactile "data" can lose their suggestive abilities to speak to our bodies, so too, in the cultural world, particular meaning structures can lose their affective power and become decadent—the "dead wood" of the past. This is as true of law, social and political policies, artistic genres, and the like, as it is for language, as we saw in the previous chapter's discussion of meaning as use-value. In this way, social policy or styles of art or constitutional interpretation in the courts can change just as can the mores of a whole culture or sub-cultural group.

Stated in terms of the freedom evidenced in the constituting and instituting activities of consciousness, this means that, although the present is situated in the context of its past actual world—and thus must necessarily take it into account in some way or other—the past does not shackle the present into conformity with it. The present cannot be undertood adequately as a function of the past, but it is necessarily influenced by it—if only negatively—so that the past has a certain incontestable weight. Causal deterministic thinking is thus rejected for whole societies as much as for individuals: "The spirit of a society realizes itself, transmits itself, and perceives itself by the cultural objects that it gives itself and in the milieu of which it lives. Its practical categories sediment themselves there, and in return they suggest to men a manner of being and of thinking" (SNS 232). Law is, as we shall see below (VI.1), a way of responding to this suggestion to enforce upon the social world a form of order according to a welter of competing and collective value-judgments.

At the level of personal history, Merleau-Ponty's debate with determinism is carried on largely with a number of psychologists writing in the 1930's and early 1940's as well as with Freud. Although, as noted above, Merleau-Ponty's consideration of Freud is only tangential to an understanding of law, there are certain approaches the former takes to the latter which are certainly pertinent to the claim that there can be truth "in the sense of a common field of diverse enterprises of knowing" (RC 64). And these more general questions about knowledge and truth clearly will be relevant to the nature of law.

In Merleau-Ponty's earlier writings, his treatment of Freud merely tended towards Sartre's denial of the unconscious and opposed to Freudianism a philosophy of form (Gestalt) in which no one order of meaning—say, the sexual or the economic—is such that all others can be reduced to it. As with the sense of structure which the last chapter elaborated, the life-world is rather an atmosphere in which all layers of meaning are total 'parts' of the same Gestalt and each can assume the role of focal-point against the background of the others.

But although this part of Merleau-Ponty's view never changed, he came to see his early treatment of Freud as too simplistic. Thus in his course at the Collège de France on "The Problem of Passivity: Sleep, the Unconscious, and Memory," he held that interpretations of Freud as a determinist makes us lose sight of the latter's most essential contribution as well as that aspect of it which is most relevant to Merleau-Ponty's own conception of truth. Namely, there is the incontestable fact that "the analysis of behavior always finds several layers of meaning which all have their truth, that the plurality of possible interpretations is the discursive expression of a mixed life in which each choice always has many senses without one being able to say that one of them is alone true" (RC 71).

The unconscious, indeed, is rehabilitated to such an extent that he says "The unconsciousness of feeling would thus be a secondary formation, contemporary with a perception-consciousness system, and the primordial unconsciousness would be the allowing-to-be, the initial yes, the indivision of feeling" (RC 179). Thus, from this perspective, it is not surprising to read in Merleau-Ponty's last written essay on Freud[8] that the unconscious stands for a certain "latency" of experience, a certain involuntary layer of meanings for us to take up, interpret, and to use for orienting our lives with others in the interworld.

The upshot is, then, that in the dialectic of "conservation, recovery, and transcendence," Merleau-Ponty wants to reformulate "certain Freudian concepts in a better philosophy."[9] But the transcendence eluded Merleau-Ponty inasmuch as his philosophy had not provided him with "the means to better express this *timeless,* this *indestructible* in us which is, says Freud, the unconscious itself, [therefore] it will be better to call it the unconscious—on the sole condition of knowing that the word is the index to an enigma—because it keeps as algae or a pebble which one picks up, something of the sea from which it was taken. . . . Phenomenology and psychoanalysis are not parallel; it is much better to say that they both direct themselves toward the same *latency.*"[10]

In the last analysis, therefore, Merleau-Ponty's "solution" to the problems posed by Freud was couched in terms of the incarnate freedom of *le corps humain,* a liberty bearing the sedimented weight of past personal and interpersonal experiences. As Albert Rabil, Jr. remarks, "his solution was similar to that of Jacques Lacan, namely, to recognize the unconscious as possessing an intentionality of its own, different from the intentionalities of the subject, but in a *dynamic relationship* to those intentionalities. Thus the conscious and the unconscious are two structures which belong in different ways to the same phenomenon *le corps humain,* and do not, as in Freud's view belong to different phenomena altogether."[11]

If nothing else, for Merleau-Ponty, Freud's work establishes the influence of the unconscious as one ingredient in the sedimented meanings of an individual's life. And it is this fact which will emerge in Part II as relevant to law, in terms of an analysis of judicial decision making and the interlacing of principles and politics. For, as we shall see, it has been a key issue for certain legal philosophers that a judge's sub-or unconscious motivations and values play a not inconsiderable role in deciding what will count as law in the interpretation of, say, a particular rule. What the present discussion points to is the conclusion that all human beings—including, therefore, judges—are subject to such influences which may play instrumental roles in their motivations, value-systems, and conduct.

§3. *The Appearance of Sense in Public History*

These brief comments about Freud devolved from a consideration of Merleau-Ponty's remarks about liberty and truth, and these latter subjects themselves emerged from a view of the historicity of constitution and institution. We have been concerned with institution and the sedimentation of meaning within the general framework of describing how meaning appears to us and the role of history in that appearing. However, as yet we have seen very little of the actual workings of constitution. Thus the task of the present section is to recapture Merleau-Ponty's variable descriptions of the ways in which individuals as well as whole societies take up their past actual worlds and reinterpret them.

One finds throughout his writings at least four distinct descriptions of constitution which are never very carefully separated or systematically interrelated. Moreover, he uses these four descriptions when speaking, at times almost interchangeably, of meaning, rationality, and truth. Most unhappily, not only are no definitions of these basic terms ever to be met with in his texts, but also the precise relationships between them are never carefully spelled out. In the face of these ambiguities (surely, bad ones), then, let us first consider the case of meaning because of its more general character, and then go on to the more specialized ones of rationality and truth.

The first axis of Merleau-Ponty's thought on what it means for meaning to be constituted in consciousness is the already detailed morphological analysis of Gestalt structures. Here the essential ingredient in the manifestation of a meaning is the crystallization of a focal-point of clarity against background horizons of indeterminacy. There is the primary perceptual case, of course, in which visual, auditory, and tactile sense organize themselves spontaneously before us in these Gestalt forms. And, on Merleau-Ponty's view, it is the artist who is the most faithful and reliable witness to this primordial experience, as in the case of Cézanne whose main purpose Merleau-Ponty construed as reproducing on the canvas the spontaneous perceptual "impression of an order-aborning, of an object in the process of appearing and of congealing before our eyes" (SNS 25). But this type of experience of something "making sense," of our "getting clear" about something as it stands out from a background of non-sense also persists throughout the spectrum of experiences possible in the social world. "This experience of an event," Merleau-Ponty tells us, "which suddenly hollows itself out, loses its opacity, reveals a transparence and itself makes sense forever, this experience is constant in culture and speech, and if one wanted to contest it, one would no longer even know for what one is searching" (PM 170).

The first picture of what it means for sense to be constituted in consciousness is sometimes tightly bound up with the second image, namely, a convergence of perspectives. Social phenomena, as well as perceptual objects as described above, present themselves incompletely in a succession of perspectives which shade off into one another first in a "passive synthesis" and second, with regard to very complex social phenomena such as, say, the Vietnam War, free enterprise, or nuclear armaments, with the aid of a great many reflective acts to try to get clear about the meanings of these phenomena. Here, as in perception, there is a "filling in" of the perspectival content such that a sense emerges through a convergence of perspectives. (Conversely, the lack of sense emerging is tantamount to divergence of perspectives. Thus, for instance, in construing causal explanations in science, certain propositions may converge on the truth of a particular hypothesis, but sometimes the evidence presented may diverge from the explanation under consideration.)

The process of convergence (and divergence as well) may take a short time in the case of perception—establishing the nature of an indeterminate visual appearance ahead of me as I walk down the beach—or a very long time in the social world as successive historical perspectives build up a sense of something like, say, capitalism, free enterprise, feminism, or revolutions in popular morality. As we shall see below, Merleau-Ponty usually employs this second image of making sense while discussing the nature of rationality.

The third image of something's making sense is more complex than the first two because its constitutive activities both include as well as transcend what occurs in the formation of Gestalt structures and in the convergence of perspectives. According to this third image, "There is simultaneously decentering and recentering of the elements of our own life, our movement toward the past and the movement of the past toward us, and this work of the past against the present does not lead to a universal closed history, to a complete system of all possible human combinations with respect to an institution as relationships, for example, but to a tableau of diverse complex possibilities" (RC 64-65).

In the basic perceptual case, we exist in a circuit with the world which presents itself to us as "already there" before our perceptual contact, which the latter refinds rather than poses. The refinding consists of constituting a world already constituted before us because in this *redoublement,* (i) the world offers itself to us as anterior to our perceptions and (ii) at the same time, we do not limit ourselves to registering it. We engender it as "an open horizon of relations to construct" (PM 175). We structure and restructure the "given"—which is only the objective side of these subjective activities, the objective contribution to the subject-object mélange—by decentering and recentering it with new sense.

Certainly this third image of making sense expresses certain constitutive activities of consciousness which are possible at the level of perception, but it is perhaps especially appropriate to invoke in the discussion of intellectual change and the development of knowledge as discussed above vis-à-vis Kuhn and Merleau-Ponty's conception of a classic and its "second truth." This is so because the progress of thought in any given discipline is rarely, if ever, an unbroken, linear unfolding of the consequences of previous doctrines. Rather, as Merleau-Ponty points out, when certain achievements are transcended, their claim to exclusive truth is decentered and they are recentered in a larger context in which their contributions have proportionately less weight. They become not completely false, but rather "especially simple particular cases in which certain possibilities of variations were not employed and which would only be misleading if one made of them the measure of being itself" (PM 141).

Thus within fundamental reinterpretations in the world of science, as Kuhn describes them in terms of paradigm shifts, or within others which occur in the course of assessing the significance of particular friendships, marriages, artistic genres, schools of criticism, and so forth, "a structure decenters itself, opens itself to an interrogation, and reorganizes itself according to a new sense which is, however, the meaning of this various structure" (PM 178). In Part Two below, at several junctures, we shall see that the same image of making sense is equally applicable to law.

The fourth way that Merleau-Ponty describes the constitution of meaning is in terms of the phrase borrowed from André Malraux, namely, a "coherent deformation" of existing traditions and other institutions. In *Signs,* this image is used as a synonym for decentering and recentering in the case of linguistic expression. To repair to part of a passage already cited in the previous chapter, Merleau-Ponty considers thus that, to create a French literature out of "the elements of the expressive apparatus" of the French language, it "was necessary to decenter and recenter them" and "It is precisely this 'coherent deformation' (A. Malraux) of available meanings which orders them into a new sense and makes listeners *but also the speaking subject,* take a decisive *step*" (S 114-15).

From all that appears, the notion of making sense as "coherent deformation" may well also serve as a synonym for the third image as well, and in any case seems to be equally serviceable for describing phenomena of, say, intellectual change. But whatever Merleau-Ponty might have thought of this putative synonymity and explanatory power, it is certain that he was in no case concerned to distinguish clearly the precisely relationships between the four images of making sense, and especially the last two. Nor does he indicate exactly how the "rhythm of conservation, recovery, and transcendence" which is characteristic of an institution fits together with the third and fourth ways, although it is surely fair to think that there must be a tight link between them. Perhaps after all, it is more a question of emphasis, with talk about decentering and recentering emphasizing discontinuity in intellectual advances, and phrases such as "coherent deformation" suggesting more a continuity with received traditions.

In any case, for Merleau-Ponty, we live an "immense history in which nothing is finished and nothing begins absolutely" (PM 56). We inhabit a "field of existence already instituted, which is always behind us and the weight of which . . . intervenes even in the actions by which we transform it" (RC 67). All consciousness, on Merleau-Ponty's view, is historical, and therefore all meaning and truth as well. The eternal dimension of humankind is rejected,[12] and presumably this rejection applies as well to the unconscious, despite its puzzling description as "timeless." There is no "heaven of ideas" because all meanings and truths are of historical, temporal origin and condition. Philosophy cannot be, therefore, a "tête-à-tête of the philosopher with the true, a judgment borne from on high upon life, upon the world, and upon history as if the philosopher *were not part of it*"(E 44). Merleau-Ponty also considers that it was to the credit of the younger Hegel that he was fully cognizant of this "historical inherence" of consciousness but, on the other hand, a failure of the later Hegel that he forgot this fact (SNS 111). And for Merleau-Ponty, as for Hegel, such a view has considerable implications for understanding rationality and truth.

§4. *Rationality and Truth*

There does not appear in Merleau-Ponty's writings a clear-cut, unambiguous definition of rationality; rather, he discusses it in different ways in different contexts. Basically, his approach to it is of a piece with the way he treats the now thread-bare 17th-and 18th-century debates about how one might prove the existence of the external world. Rationality is no more a problem, on his view, than is the world itself, and this is so because of the collapse of false subject-object dichotomies. Consequently, Merleau-Ponty can write that "Rationality is not a *problem,* there is not behind it an unknown which we would have to deductively determine or to prove inductively starting with it: at each instant we assist in this wonder of the connection of experiences, and no one knows better than we how it happens because we are this knot of relations" (PhP xv-xvi).

This does not mean that the author believed that people are spontaneously disposed to act rationally, or that a human being is naturally a "rational animal." On the contrary, writing as he did at a time and place when Europe as a whole was convulsed with destruction, terror, and fear, he was under no such illusions. What is meant, rather, by the assertion that rationality is no problem is that, just as in the primary *analogon* of perception, our thoughts are already in a fundamental intentional relation with the world such that the classic problems of correspondence theories of truth and of representational thinking is dissolved. This is why Merleau-Ponty said that, as noted above in the Introduction, "The perceived world is the always presupposed foundation of all rationality, all value, and all existence."[13]

This is also why, on his view, that "The most important achievement of phenomenology is without doubt to have joined together extreme subjectivism and extreme objectivism in its notion of the world or of rationality" (PhP xv). And it is only in the light of such an accomplishment that rationality can become visible: "There is rationality, that is to say: perspectives blend, perceptions confirm each other, a meaning appears. But it must not be posed apart, transformed into absolute Spirit or into a world in the realist sense. The phenomenological world is not pure being but the meaning which shows through at the intersection of my experiences and those of the other, by the gearing in of the one to the other. It is thus inseparable from subjectivity and intersubjectivity which become unified by the recovery of my past experiences in my present ones, and by the recovery of the experience of the other in mine" (PhP xv).

Rationality thus gets worked out in a merging and engaging of intersubjective perspectives, and this happens not only in perception to distinguish veridical from illusory experiences, but also across all levels of experience in the cultural world. In addition, as noted above, the experience of falsification is shaped by dissonance, disconfirming and conflicting perspectives. It is impossible to assign a certain weight *a priori* to conflicting perspectives, in testimony to which difficulty there is a well known debate in the philosophy of science about the theoretical possibility of defining in advance how much evidence is needed to disconfirm a hypothesis or theory. And with particular reference to Marxism, as we shall see below in Chapter IV, Merleau-Ponty struggled persistently to hold on to that interpretation of history in the face of ever increasing conflicting perspectives.

But despite the theoretical difficulties of defining *a priori* the amount or kind of evidence presented in divergent perspectives required to falsify a particular hypothesis, such experiences of falsification do occur just as surely as do those of convergence and the appearance of rationality. Perhaps in both cases, as Aristotle remarked in a different context, the decision lies with perception rather than definition, such that in politics as well as in other social decisions, "the rational course to follow" appears at the intersection of harmoniously converging perspectives—although, as with the essential indeterminacy of the perceptual object—always with an ambiguity which prevents any absolute assurance. History is in this fashion doubly perspectival—actions are performed from a certain perspective on the past, and the actor's own concrete situation aims toward an uncertain future from his or her own particular point of view. "The highest point of truth is still thus only perspective" (PM 184), and because of this fact, the interrogation of historical events must take account of their essential ambiguity—their *Vielseitigkeit,* as Max Weber termed it, "the plurality of their aspects" (AD 28).

Objectivity does not exist in spite of these consequences of perspectives; on the contrary, it exists in and through them. As Merleau-Ponty approvingly summarized Weber's view, "Historical comprehension does not thus introduce a system of categories arbitrarily chosen, it only presumes the possibility for us of having a past which would be ours, to recover in our liberty the work of so many other liberties, of illuminating their choices by ours and our choices by theirs, of rectifying one by the other, and of finally being in truth. There is no greater respect, more profound objectivity, than this claim to draw from the same source from which all history comes" (AD 32).

Thinking in historical perspective is perhaps not a sufficient condition of rationality and objectivity, but Merleau-Ponty quite clearly insists time and again that he considers it a necessary condition. In a manner reminiscent of Kant's criticism of traditional metaphysics for having transcended the bounds of sensory experience, Merleau-Ponty criticizes interpretations of history—and, above all, political programs for the present and future—which succumb to the temptation of high-altitude thinking beyond the history to which they would apply. He usually refers to such views which take refuge in a "heaven of ideas" as "ideologies," that is, doctrines propped up by ideas out of contact with stubborn, contradictory facts and supported primarily by the wish that they be true. The fact that one cannot successfully engage the field of the practical by mere deductions from a set of *a priori* principles— a notion central to his political critique of certain forms of liberalism, as we shall see below (IV.2)—means in part that the perceived world "destroys neither rationality nor the absolute. [Rather,] It seeks to make them come down to earth."[14] And, as we shall also see in Chapter IV, such a claim was also to be prophetic inasmuch as it was to express the eventual outcome of his continuing interrogation of Marxism.[15]

When we move from a consideration of rationality to that of truth, we first find that, although the latter is not identical to meaning or rationality, Merleau-Ponty nevertheless does not sharply distinguish them. For this reason, the various descriptions of constitution are often applied to truth as well. Moreover, truth and rationality are particularly blended together in the analysis of the sense of history, and the majority of Merleau-Ponty's remarks about truth occur in that framework. Thus, what is most appropriate here is to draw some general conclusions about truth from the philosopher's meaning as such, and then to apply these remarks to the philosophy of history.

First, since all meaning is of historical origin and condition, and since what is true is meaningful, truth is also historical. Since there are no eternal truths, and since history is not complete or finished, the philosopher, on Merleau-Ponty's view, "feels himself as all other men caught up in it and in the face of a future *to be made*" (SNS 236). Further, in stressing the notion of truth to be made, as well as that of the historicity of truth itself, there appears to be a considerable similarity between Merleau-Ponty's views and William James' contention that "The truth of an idea is not a stagnant property inherent in it. Truth *happens* to an idea. It *becomes* true, is *made* true by events. Its verity *is* in fact an event, a process: the process namely of its verifying itself, its *veri-fication*. Its validity is the process of its valid-*ation*."[16]

James also held, as Merleau-Ponty would later, that there is a tight relation between the origin of meaning and intersubjectivity. Sense appears at the intersection of my and the other's perspectives on our life-world. In at least his published writings (see note 12 above), Merleau-Ponty joins James in rejecting a classical rationalist model of knowing in which, within the private introspection of one's own consciousness—an introspection which is privileged because both private and incorrigible—truth is discovered (intuited). Nothing new would then be learned in communication, there would never occur the reversals of thought, the challenges, the problems which make up the discourse that, for example, Montaigne loved so well and about which he wrote so poignantly. Since the development of meaning is tied to the *adventures* of experience, as we have seen above, Merleau-Ponty, like James, rejects "the great assumption of the intellectualists," namely, "that truth means essentially an inert static relation. When you've got your true idea of anything, there's an end of the matter. You're in possession; you *know;* you have fulfilled your thinking destiny. . . . nothing more need follow on that climax of your rational destiny. Epistemologically you are in stable equilibrium."[17] Truth and meaning generally are not firm or permanent acquisitions, and we cannot expect them to manifest the apodicticity of an everlasting, secure possession. Theories, even (or especially) in fields such as economics and politics, such as Marxism, *"become instruments, not answers to enigmas, in which we can rest."*[18]

Necessity is thus set, for Merleau-Ponty, in the context of a more pervasive contingency, reason amidst unreason, sense against a background of non-sense, and meaning is situated betwen crucial experiences and absurdity. Commitments become tenuous in the face of such ambiguity, even in what we take to be the most assured of meanings. The same change and reformation which occur in our perceptual life take place across all experiences of the life-world; differences between them are largely of degree and speed of change. In science, certainly, but also in mathematics and geometry, as mentioned above in passing, the last hundred years have seen profound changes and crises in their foundations which would have been unthinkable earlier. Thus, for instance, Euclid's geometry appeared for centuries to be self-evidently true (at least in its axioms) and a secure and permanent possession, but it did not turn out to be that way for Riemann. Correlatively, Euclidean geometry became a "classic" with its typical "second truth."

Still less, of course, do we have any certainty in personal or political commitments. Their truth is not given to us like a package; they are to be achieved, if possible—sometimes veri-fied and sometimes not. The contingency of experience robs us inexorably of the assurance of success which we are inclined to project on the world. Thus, despite the subjective certainties of the parties involved, respected teachers can turn out to be charlatons, friendships can prove illusory, marriages can and do frequently turn out to be mistakes, political commitments can be rendered obsolete by the changing shape of national and international situations, and so on and on.

Nevertheless, the other side of the coin of contingency is that we must act anyway and that there is some meaning which anchors as well as mandates an *engagement* without guarantees. Thus the two quotations from Montaigne which preface Merleau-Ponty's appreciative reading of his predecessor, four centuries removed: "I commit myself with difficulty" and "One must live among the living" (S 250).

§5. *The Sense of History*

Merleau-Ponty's considerations of the role of history in the appearance of truth, meaning, and rationality, are also closely bound up with an interrogation of the meaning of history itself, and his reflections on this subject devolve from essentially two distinct sources. The first is the structuralist linguistics of de Saussure—as noted above (I.3), before the truth claims of structuralism finally sank in—and the second source consists of a complex of arguments and counter-arguments extracted from Marx, certain Marxist writers such as Georg Lukács, and Max Weber. But even despite Merleau-Ponty's eventual abandonment of structuralism, and Marxism as well, it is worth looking at what he derived from both sources of inspiration because of the relevance of his remarks to the phenomenon of law (see VII.1).

In his inaugural address to the Collège de France, Merleau-Ponty briefly summarizes his sense of the promise offered by de Saussure's work for a philosophy of history. Using almost the same words as appear in the relevant passages of *Consciousness and the Acquisition of Language,* he writes that "The presence of the individual to the institution and of the institution to the individual is clear in the case of linguistic change" (E 64). For here "The contingent fact, recovered by the will to expression, becomes a new means of expression which takes its place and has a meaning in the history of that language. There is here a rationality in contingence, a lived logic . . . and Saussure could have well outlined a new philosophy of history" (E 75).

The lived logic develops from the relationship of the synchronic and diachronic aspects of language. As de Saussure sees it, the evolution of a given language (*la langue*) is such that a constituted language such as French, English, or German may be studied in its historical developments and as related to other language systems. This perspective on a system of word meanings and rules for usage comprises the "diachronic" aspect of language which contrasts with the "synchronic" aspect, namely, a static cross-slice of the development of a language at a certain time. The synchronic is the point of view of "speaking subjects" for whom their language makes up a solidary system.[19] But in the diachronic point of view, no such system need appear, for in the development of a given linguistic system, or in tracing the connections of one linguistic system with another, what may very well appear from this perspective is a disordered collection of linguistic facts.

As a result, the synchronic refers to its evolutions from one state to another—the history of language being only a succession of synchronies. The "lived logic" of the historical development comes, therefore, not from the objective record of changes across a certain temporal duration, but rather from the "inside," as it were, from understanding the coherent, systematic order which a culture imposes on its linguistic heritage to maintain it as a useful, meaningful, and adequate tool of expression.

It is true that Merleau-Ponty sometimes misinterpreted de Saussure in falsely identifying *la parole* with the synchronic and *la langue* with the diachronic (see, for instance, S 107). And there seems little doubt either that, as Laurie Spurling phrases it, "Merleau-Ponty tailors de Saussure's structural linguistics very much to his own purposes, and, indeed, as has been pointed out, manages to misrepresent structuralism in the process."[20] Spurling's references to this misrepresentation consist, first, of a remark by Paul Ricoeur that, for the science of structural linguistics, language is an object to be studied, while for phenomenology, "language is not an object but a mediation, that is to say, it is that by which and through which we move towards reality (whatever that may be)."[21] And second, Spurling considers James M. Edie's statement in his preface to the English translation of *La conscience et l'acquisition du langage* that "The fact of the matter is that, for Saussure, both synchrony and diachrony are aspects of *la langue,* whereas the study of what Merleau-Ponty calls *la parole,* the speech act as such, falls wholly outside the scientific approach to language defined in Saussure's structural linguistics."[22]

Although there is clear textual evidence that Merleau-Ponty is occasionally guilty of the first confusion, or deliberate misinterpretation, described above—that is, falsely identifying speech with the synchronic and language with the diachronic—I am inclined to think that he can better defend himself on the matters with which Edie and Ricoeur are concerned. First, as regards Ricoeur, Merleau-Ponty can certainly reply that it is true that science is concerned with objectivity and that his emphasis does, in fact, fall on the speaking (and writing) subject. But he can also point out that, as we saw above in Chapter I, what is essential here is the single, unitary structure of *la parole* as it takes up, interprets, and sometimes creatively modifies the linguistic tools given in *la langue.* Neither *la parole* nor *la langue* ultimately can be understood apart from one another, any more than—and for the same reasons that—the perceptual object can be understood apart from the percipient. The primary structure, *la parole-la langue,* is "*the life of signs* at the *heart of social life*"—or at least the most important example of such life—which forms the object of the science of semiology.[23]

Accordingly, de Saussure contended that, and Merleau-Ponty certainly agreed, "*la langue* is necessary so that *la parole* would be intelligible and produce all its effects; but the latter is necessary so that *la langue* establishes itself; historically, the fact of *la parole* always comes first . . . it is *la parole* which makes *la langue* evolve. . . . There is thus interdependence of *la langue* and *la parole;* the former is at the same time the instrument and the product of the latter."[24] What this means, then, is that the primary focus of structural linguistics is *la langue*—this constitutes its objectivity—but at the same time, *la parole* is not the same as subjectivity. Rather, it is the living use of an objective, constituted linguistic system, in the study of which we are always referred back to the former. As we have seen above in the Introduction, it was precisely for Merleau-Ponty the naīveté and dishonesty of science to constitute its objects out of the living texture of perceptual relationships and then consider them as a purely objective, self-enclosed universe (PhP ii-iii). Rather, as Schutz indicated above, "All cultural objects—tools, symbols, language systems, works of art, social institutions, etc.—point back by their very origin and meaning to the activities of human subjects."[25]

By the same token, it is difficult to see how it could be true that, as Edie claimed, "the study of what Merleau-Ponty calls *la parole,* the speech act as such, falls wholly outside the scientific approach to language defined in Saussure's linguistics." If it fell *wholly* outside the compass of semiology, the latter could refer to no structure, no "life of signs," and, since in that case *la langue* would amount to a self-enclosed system, finally no synchrony. For the same reason, it also cannot be true that, for de Saussure, "synchrony and diachrony are aspects of *la langue,*" where this is meant to exclude all reference to *la parole.* For, as we saw above, the synchronic consists of the perspective of "speaking subjects" for whom their *langue* forms a solidary system.[26]

Turning from these objections to Merleau-Ponty's appropriation of Saussurian linguistics, let us look at the ways in which he considered de Saussure's thought useful as at least part of a model for a philosophy of history. He begins by perceiving an analogy between the "reciprocal relations" of "productive forces and forms of production, and more generally historical forces and institutions," on the one hand, with *la parole* and *la langue* in any given state of synchrony, on the other (E 75). Just as the meaning of language, its internal logic which constitutes it as a "system of signs," is generated and nourished by the creative expression of speech, each institution from one historical epoch to another is a "symbolic system" that those who live it appropriate as a certain "style of functioning"—that is, they give it its "use value" (E 75). Following the course of history from a diachronic perspective would reveal ruptures, fissures, incongruities, and enigmas as to how they mesh in a single, coherent fabric. But once looked at from the synchronic point of view, we can see that the symbolic system of a culture—represented by its institutions of say, property, classes, positive morality, judicial institutions, and so forth—"affects molecular changes which produce a meaning which is neither thing nor idea, in spite of the famous dichotomy, because it is a modulation of our co-existence. It is in this fashion that . . . there exist historical forms and processes, classes, epochs of which we ask ourselves where they were" (E 76).

In the wake of Merleau-Ponty's abandonment of structuralism, it is fair to ask, as he never did, whether any value remains in de Saussure's linguistics for understanding history. That is, Merleau-Ponty's rejection of the ultimate truth-claims of structuralism did not entail the abolition of language and speech themselves and the dialectical, communicative relationship between them. And, as we saw at the end of the last chapter, Merleau-Ponty had every good phenomenological reason to retain them. In a parallel way, whatever the eventual fate of structuralism, can we still adhere to synchronic and diachronic *descriptions* of history?

From all that appears, there seems to be no good reason why we may not do so. For one thing, the fate of the phenomena is surely independent of that of theories used to explain them. Second, history may be in fact much more complex than what can appear at the intersection of synchronic and diachronic axes of thought. But even if so, one could well argue that the descriptive value of structuralism is such that it ought to be reintegrated into the history of thought with the "second truth" of a "classic." Structures can and do persist without structural*ism*. And third, as I shall show in Chapter VI below, the synchronic and the diachronic are particularly illuminative of judicial decision making. (The same Saussurian concepts will also be employed in Chapter IV in connection with politics and in Chapter V vis-à-vis legal rules.) Consequently, it appears reasonable to conclude that history may still be viewed synchronically and diachronically, and that in a number of different contexts these concepts can be useful for understanding a lived logic of necessity amidst contingency, the emergence of sense against a background of non-sense.

The access to Merleau-Ponty's other source of inspiration about the philosophy of history—seen through the writings of Marx, Lukács, and Weber—consists of the tight connection between history and nature (RC 92-93), on the one hand, and the second and third images of making sense—the convergence and divergence of perspectives as well as the decentering and recentering of existing meanings—on the other. If anything, Marxism is clearly a certain perspective on the relationship of history and nature, but in Merleau-Ponty's view, although history does teach us something about the cultural organization of nature, exactly what it teaches us is the reverse of what he takes Marxism or, at any rate, various Marxists, to claim. In terms of the logic of history, the truth disclosed in it consists of mostly what remains after something else has been falsified. This is to say that the process of verification is really much more one of falsification, and Merleau-Ponty's descriptions of it approximate more nearly what one finds in the historical Darwin than the Darwin which the former criticizes.

More precisely, history somehow works to eliminate the irrational, what will not cohere with the perspectives of the time: "Of the course of things itself we know only that it will eliminate sooner or later irrational historical forms. . . . This elimination of the irrational can end up in chaos if the forces which destroy these forms do not turn out to be capable of constructing new ones. There is no universal history. . . . The historical meaning is immanent in the interhuman event and is as fragile as the latter. But precisely for this reason, the event can take on the value of a genesis of reason" (E 59-60). However, to say that there is "historical meaning in the interhuman event" must not mislead one to think that there is one sole meaning waiting to be disclosed. Rather, as Max Weber held, "history has, not a direction[27] like a river, but sense that it teaches us; not a truth, but errors to avoid" (AD 41).

The sense of history is not really what is worked out for us because "There is less a sense of history than an elimination of non-sense" (AD 55), and the character of this elimination is expressed as follows: history "eliminates men and institutions that do not respond to existing problems—not that everything that happens deserves to be, but that everything that disappears merits disappearing" (SNS 184-85).[28] It follows from this negative working of history, for Merleau-Ponty, that the experience of truth in a historical matrix is never conclusive because the sense of history only takes shape from a certain point of view and never excludes absolutely other ways of looking at things. For this reason, "Each of our perceptions is faith" (SNS 317) and because of this perceptual faith, "The philosopher recognizes himself as one who has inseparably a taste for evidence and the sense of ambiguity" (E 10-11).

Since, on Merleau-Ponty's view, there is no destiny in things any more than there is a logic solely in the diachronic unfolding of a language, history is essentially a structure of the subjective and the objective. Historical epochs are marked much more by "an interrogation on the possibility of man" than by "an immanent solution" (AD 36). And the results of these interrogations consist of what Max Weber called "intelligible nuclei" which comprise "typical ways of treating natural being, of responding to others, and to death" (AD 25). No intelligible nucleus of values establishes any immutable *natural* way of relating to other people, nature, and to death because, as detailed above in the Introduction, there is no fixed substratum of human nature (any more than there is an ideal language of which all empirical languages are imperfect approximations). Humankind, like truth, "is to be made" (AD 146), and hence Merleau-Ponty's appreciation of the Marxist—and effectively Jamesian—emphasis on *homo faber:* "Truth is thus itself conceived as a process of indefinite verification. . . . The *Stimmung* of Lukàcs and, we believe, of Marxism, is thus the conviction of being not in the truth, but at the threshold of truth, which is simultaneously very close—indicated by the whole past and present—and at the infinite distance of a future which is to be made" (AD 73-74).[29] The legal significance of this and kindred statements will emerge in Part Two in terms of natural law theories and certain presuppositions of Anglo-Saxon common law (see VII.1,2); the ethical and political dimensions of Merleau-Ponty's view of history and the creation of meaning, on the other hand, will comprise the remaining two chapters of Part One.

NOTES

1. Thus Alfred Schutz, elaborating on the *Phenomenology of Perception:* "Man finds himself at any moment of his daily life in a biographically determined situation, that is, in a physical and socio-cultural environment as defined by him, within which he has his position, not merely his position in terms of physical space and outer time or of his status and role within the social system but also his moral and ideological position. To say that this definition of the situation is biographically determined is to say that it has its history; it is the sedimentation of all man's previous experiences, organized in the habitual possessions of his stock of knowledge at hand, and as such his unique possession, given to him and to him alone." *Collected Papers,* ed. Maurice Natanson (The Hague: Martinus Nijhoff, 1962), I, p. 9. (Footnotes from the above passage have been omitted.)
2. Schutz, p. 10.
3. For further particulars on this subject, see William S. Hamrick, "Language and Abnormal Behavior: Merleau-Ponty, Hart, and Laing," *Review of Existential Psychology and Psychiatry,* Volume XVIII, Nos. 1, 2, & 3, 1982-83 (but actually published in 1985), pp. 181-203.
4. It does not appear in either *La Prose du monde,* the *Résumés de Cours,* or in *Signes,* but it finally does come out in *L'oeil et l'esprit* (at p. 90), that Merleau-Ponty derives this concept of indirect problem solving from Erwin Panofsky. See also below in Chapter III where this model of problem solving is discussed in terms of the process of making moral decisions.
5. Chicago: University of Chicago Press, 1962. See especially Chapters IX, "The Nature and Necessity of Scientific Revolutions," and X, "Revolutions as Changes of World View."
6. There is really a double transcendence here in that the paradigm shift allowed one to see as causation what had not been thought to be such. As Kuhn points out, in the early stages of the shift to the Newtonian paradigm, one refused even to label as causation what Newton was describing.
7. It is fair to observe that today the same very probably may be true of Merleau-Ponty's philosophy itself.
8. "Préface" to *L'oeuvre de Freud et son importance pour le monde moderne,* Dr. A. Hesnard (Paris: Payot, 1960), pp. 5-10.
9. Merleau-Ponty in Hesnard, p. 7.
10. Merleau-Ponty in Hesnard, p. 9.
11. *Merleau-Ponty: Existentialist of the Social World* (New York: Columbia University Press, 1967), p. 290, n. 20 (emphasis mine). See also the article to which Rabil refers in the same place, "Note sur le problème de l'inconscient chez Merleau-Ponty," J.-B. Pontalis, *Les Temps Modernes* XVII (1961), pp. 287-303.
12. For a fresh perspective on this subject, see Jean-Paul Sartre, "Merleau-Ponty [I]," trans. William S. Hamrick, *Journal of the British Society for Phenomenology,* Volume XV, Number Two, May 1984, pp. 134-35.
13. "Le Primat de la perception et ses conséquences philosophiques," *Bulletin de la Société Francaise de Philosophie,* XLI, 1947 (séance du 23 novembre 1946), p. 120.
14. "Le Primat de la perception et ses conséquences philosophiques," p. 120.
15. Relative to the preceding note as well as to the sentence referenced by the present one, consider the following statements from a lecture which Merleau-Ponty gave at the Collège de France just a little over two weeks (on 17 April 1961) before he died: "How does philosophy develop a bad ambiguity? Like 'overview' thinking," exhaustive, possessing the thing 'in thought,' philosophy wanting to be all, is nothing; it does not inhabit the things it discusses. . . . It lacks everything, both the particular and the universal. By contrast, it must

have both. This thought will not have the character of an overview, the pretense of living at a distance, of seeing, haunting, contemplating. . . . By contrast, what is needed is a manner of thinking which is at the same time concrete and universal." "Philosophie et non-philosophie depuis Hegel," notes de cours, texte établi et présenté par Claude Lefort, *Textures,* Nos. 10-11 (1975), pp. 145-173. Cited in the English translation, "Philosophy and Non-Philosophy Since Hegel," trans. Hugh J. Silverman, *Telos,* No. 29, Fall 1976, pp. 43-105, at p. 97. See also here James L. Marsh, "Phenomenology as Ideology Critique," *Philosophy Today,* Fall 1980, pp. 272-84.

16. "Pragmatism's Conception of Truth," in *Pragmatism: A New Name for Some Old Ways of Thinking* (New York: Longmans, Green, and Co., 1910), p. 201.
17. James, p. 200.
18. William James, "What Pragmatism Means," cited in *Pragmatism: A New Name for Some Old Ways of Thinking,* p. 53. Cf. John Dewey, *The Quest for Certainty* (New York: Capricorn Books, 1960). See especially Chapter II, "Philosophy's Search for the Immutable," and below at Chapter III, n. 20.
19. Ferdinand de Saussure, *Cours de linguistique générale,* édition critique, préparée par Tullio de Mauro (Paris: Payot, 1976), p. 128.
20. Laurie Spurling, *Phenomenology and the Social World* (London: Routledge and Kegan Paul, 1977), p. 59.
21. Paul Ricoeur, "New Developments in Phenomenology in France: the Phenomenology of Language," *Social Research,* Vol. 34 (1967), p. 16, cited in Spurling, p. 187.
22. James M. Edie, foreward to *Consciousness and the Acquisition of Language,* trans. Hugh J. Silverman (Evanston: Northwestern University Press, 1973), pp. xxx-xxxi.
23. de Saussure, p. 33.
24. de Saussure, pp. 37-38.
25. See note 2 above.
26. de Saussure, p. 128.
27. Merleau-Ponty employs here the word "sens" which enjoys the double meaning of "sense" (or "meaning") and "direction." It is a word which he also profitably exploits when concerned with the connection of motor-intentionality and the constitution of meaning.
28. One should note at least in passing the affinities of Merleau-Ponty's view with that of Karl Popper in his *The Logic of Scientific Discovery* (London: Hutchinson, 1959), Chapters VI and VII.

    In the same vein, Merleau-Ponty borrows appreciatively from Max Weber the notion that we are constantly faced with "a tableau of diverse, complex possibilities, always bound to local circumstances, engraved with a co-efficient of facticity, and of which we cannot say that one would be *more true* than the other, although we could say that one is more false, more artificial, and has less of an opening on a less rich future" (RC 65). For this reason, "truth is not adequation, but anticipation" (PM 180-81).
29. See Gary Brent Madison, *The Phenomenology of Merleau-Ponty* (Athens, Ohio: University of Ohio Press, 1981), p. 264. Speaking to Merleau-Ponty's view of history in later works such as *Signs,* he writes: "Thus for Merleau-Ponty there is a logic in history since history is the 'inscription of Being,' but this logic does not override man and does not do away with contingency and human freedom. It is man in his freedom and creativity who makes history and is responsible for it by letting Being be. . . . Thus if Merleau-Ponty's philosophy is not a quietism before an overpowering force or transcendence, neither is it a form of Promethean humanism."

III: ETHICS

One would search in vain throughout Merleau-Ponty's writings for anything like a systematically developed ethics. Instead, what one finds is a variety of remarks about ethics, morals, and morality which are usually, but not always, situated in the context of his more comprehensive concern for politics, which is the subject of the following chapter. Furthermore, just as he is not ordinarily inclined to disentangle clearly his moral from his political concerns, he equally makes no sharp distinctions between morality, usually thought of as referring to human behavior; morals, interpreted as the rules, norms, or codes employed in acting morally; and (normative) ethics, the principles of goodness that are reflected in morals. But it is also clear that Merleau-Ponty usually employs these terms in the senses specified, and those are, consequently, the ways that they will be used here.

To be more precise about the context of Merleau-Ponty's moral concerns, his remarks about ethics, morals, and morality are woven into his constant attention to not only daily politics, but also the economic dimension of social life, the experience of war, and Marxist reflections on these diverse phenomena. As he explained in 1947, "In the coexistence of men to which these years have awakened us, moralities, doctrines, thoughts, and customs, laws, works, and words express themselves in each other, and everything signifies everything" (SNS 269). And again, "economic phenomena being at the heart of society, economic decomposition does not leave intact the cultural heritage. It is a fact that, in our present situation, there is not one of the terms of the moral vocabulary which has not become equivocal, not one of the traditional values which has not been contaminated" (SNS 207).

Furthermore, some things that Merleau-Ponty did not explicitly say about ethics or morals can be made to appear as straightforward logical implications of his descriptions of human existence as we have followed them throughout this essay. As a result, the following picture of Merleau-Ponty's conceptions of ethics, morals, and morality will consist both of references to the relevant texts as well as deductions from them. The main lines of force in this picture organize themselves along four principal, overlapping themes: moral agency, autonomy as a source of value, teleology and responsibility, and an analysis of moral decision making. The reader will find in the second and third sections particularly certain anticipative overlaps with the following chapter in order to show the concrete circumstances Merleau-Ponty had in mind in framing his view of ethics and morals. Such overlap is indeed inevitable, given the usual political context for much of Merleau-Ponty's consideration of moral values. But in general, the present chapter will attempt to pry out the latter from environing political (and other) contexts so that it may be more clearly visible for itself.

§*1. Moral Agency*

By whom is the (morally) "good life," whatever it will turn out to be, lived? Taking into account the various senses of subjectivity rejected in the beginning of Chapter I, we can reliably conclude that the moral agent, for Merleau-Ponty, cannot be anything like a Kantian transcendental ego, or noumenal self, and still less anything resembling a Cartesian *cogito*. Nor can it be, at the opposite extreme, an organism whose behavior can be understood exhaustively as a set of conditioned responses to environmental stimuli—whether in the older, cruder versions, or in newer, more subtle ones. Performing a moral act or choosing to follow a moral rule, for Merleau-Ponty, would be, like doing any act or making any choice, conceptually different than an effect of past causes, and it takes root in the daily social life of the incarnate *cogito* which, in its economic dimensions, is a dialect of product *and* producer. Thus to say that the moral agent is the incarnate *cogito* is to see in another sector of existence "the spiritual function of the body and the incarnation of the spirit" (S 291). It is also to stress the moral importance of the fact that "Our century has erased the line dividing 'body' and 'mind' and sees human life as through and through spiritual and bodily—always based on the body and always interested, even in its more carnal modes, in personal relationships" (S 287).

When Merleau-Ponty reflects on what it means for the body-subject to act morally, the contrasting theory which he takes most seriously is that of Kant.[1] As a result, the salient features of the latter's ethics of practical reason will serve as a convenient touchstone at many places throughout this chapter to illustrate Merleau-Ponty's alternative programme. Beginning with the notion of moral agency, Merleau-Ponty certainly agreed with Kant that the moral life must be carried on by a self-directing reason. But, as we have seen throughout the preceding chapters, this reason cannot exist in the way Kant construes either *Verstand* or *Vernunft*. Since there is no clear division between "body" and "mind," there can be no "pure" reason apart from sensibility, no distinction between the internal and the external sufficient to constitute a noumenal self, and hence no frontier separating reason and feeling in the way Kant would have wished.

Such a view also entails abandoning two distinct, but related, pillars of Kant's ethics, the first of which is a conceptually clear and practically serviceable distinction between autonomy and heteronomy. As Paul Ricoeur would document later, the will is a complex, many-layered dialectic of the voluntary and the involuntary.[2] Because of this shift, and also because Merleau-Ponty, unlike Kant, is not committed to a Newtonian concept of nature, he can also avoid a certain tension in Kant's theory as regards being both free—from the point of view of the noumenal self—and determined—as concerns the body considered as part of the material continuum of nature—in one and the same action.

The abandonment of the second Kantian doctrine plays a much larger role in Merleau-Ponty's thought—especially about politics—than does his rejection of the first doctrine, and it also follows directly from it. This is the conception of the moral agent as a lawgiver who follows purely rational rules which have, in turn, an *a priori* truth value. For Merleau-Ponty, neither ethics itself nor the morals one would adopt as a result of being committed to a certain ethics consists of a system of pure ideas. There can be no purely formal rules in a Kantian sense, on Merleau-Ponty's view, because there is no available source from which they could be generated. Blurring the distinction between the body and mind, and consequently between autonomy and heteronomy, reason and feeling, leaves no pure Kantian *Verstand* or *Vernunft,* where "pure" means precisely uncontaminated by the data of sensory intuition. Furthermore, although of course Kant would not himself argue for any of these alternatives, there is no *a priori* truth to be found (i) in nature—for the reasons given above in the Introduction and in the last section of the previous chapter. Nor can it be derived (ii) from a "metaphysical heaven" of ideas (SNS 141); as also noted in Chapter II, for Merleau-Ponty, such does not exist. All truth is both empirically based and the outcome of human projects. Nor can purely formal moral rules be derived (iii) from human nature because, as described above in the Introduction, on Merleau-Ponty's view there is none. A moral universality must entail cross-cultural similarities and comparisons, but these could only be founded on the fact of having similar bodies. And this will not do, for Merleau-Ponty, "because exactly what is proper about the human body is not to behave according to nature" (PM 113).[3]

Nor, finally, (iv) can history provide any moral absolutes for, as we have seen (II.5), its logic is rooted in contingency. Values, as truths, are given to us in a Weberian fashion, as "resisting nuclei in a diffuse milieu; like perceptual objects, they are defined and circumscribed only via the complicity of a background and thus suppose as much darkness as light" (PM 159).

It is relevant to such a statement to observe that, as William Frankena has pointed out, "no deontologist has presented us with a conflict-and-exception-free system of concrete rules about what we are actually to do."[4] For Merleau-Ponty, such a system could exist only at the level of ideas, if at all, and not in practice in the kind of world we inhabit. And since "The perceived world is the always presupposed basis of all rationality, all value, and all existence,"[5] the truth of moral rules can only be empirical and contingent. This contingency is such that, as Albert Rabil, Jr., has remarked, moral principles "exist bound up with the facts. Thus in order to deal with an ethical problem, principles and facts must be derived together from the total situation. As the situation changes, the principles, like the facts, cease to be relevant, and a new configuration must be grasped in its totality."[6]

Another, exceedingly important way that Merleau-Ponty's approach to ethics differs from that of Kant concerns the nature of society. For the reasons given in Chapter I, the interworld cannot be a network of separate and self-contained moral legislators in the way in which Kant conceived a kingdom of ends. As James L. Marsh has said, "Human consciousness, rather than being isolated and atomistic, is flooded with otherness,"[7] an incontestable reality which gives the lie to the exaggerated sense of individual discreteness which, in the wake of a Kantian inspiration, characterized the political and moral philosophies of the pre-war generation in France (see IV.2) as well as in England and the United States during much of the 19th and early 20th-centuries. Such mistaken views denied the exterior for the sake of the interior as part of an "optimistic philosophy which reduced human society to a sum of consciousnesses always ready for peace and happiness" (SNS 246).

By contrast, as in the political realm, since reality is fundamentally adversity, "In a period of sharpened class struggle, a proletarian party cannot be sincere with everyone. Either it is sincere toward the proletariat, and thus it is necessary that it deceive capitalism, or else it conforms to prior commitments, to formal and universal rules of morality, and then it betrays the proletariat as a class. . . . the postulate of a truth and a morality common to everyone is an improbity for a man of Marxist politics because Marxism is a theory of revolution, it opposes two worlds, the one capitalist and the other proletarian; and it forces us to choose between them" (SNS 280). Although Merleau-Ponty was eventually to give up Marxism as an interpretation of history, he never abandoned the moral ideals of proletarian humanism, as we shall see later in this chapter and in the one following, and consequently, he still adhered to the fundamental tenets of the reasoning expressed in this passage from his essay "For Truth."

It is not only at the level of global political struggles that Merleau-Ponty considers that Kant's picture of society as a kingdom of ends is false. It also fails, in his view, to describe adequately the moral dimensions of personal relationships. To show that this is the case, he provides a long, detailed analysis of Simone de Beauvoir's novel, *L'Invitée*. He also finds in the latter's intriguing story grounds for (i) asserting that acting morally does not amount to following purely rational, *a priori* rules and (ii) blurring the distinction between autonomy and heteronomy.

In this tale, as Merleau-Ponty considers it in *Sens et non-sens,* Françoise and Pierre are lovers creating a false morality in an artificial world. It is false because their position rests on a mistaken belief in pure sincerity—they *are* their pure intentions and love for the other, or at least this is the case for Françoise—and it is artificial because it is lived out solely at the level of ideas.

The game is up when a third party—*l'invitée,* Xavière—comes between them. Françoise could pretend to surpass jealousy and to treat others, including Xavière, as Kantian ends in themselves, only by supporting the myth of being an interior consciousness rather than a lived-body. But her world collapses when this phantasy is seen through: "She has sacrificed everything to this myth, she has become incapable of drawing out of herself an act which was hers, to live in the intimacy of her desires, and that is why she has ceased being precious to Pierre as Xavière knows so well how to be. This purity, this disinterestness, this morality which one admired, she has come to hate them because they were all part of the same fiction" (SNS 58). Her awakening occurred as she finally recognized the existence of the other. When she finally "accepted the objective shape of her life which she sees in the look of others, how could Françoise hold as indubitable the feeling which she has of herself" (SNS 58-59)?

It would not be wrong to say that Françoise is jealous, that Pierre represents desire, and that Xavière is coy. But the truth runs deeper than this psychological explanation. It is a metaphysical, rather than a psychological, drama in the way that Xavière throws into question all the psychological devices by means of which Pierre and Françoise thought their love invulnerable. This is so because "Françoise believed that she could bind herself to Pierre in leaving him free, not distinguishing between herself and him, willing herself in willing him as each wills the other in the Kantian kingdom of ends. The appearance of Xavière reveals to them not only a being from whom their values are excluded, but also that they are excluded one from the other and each in itself. Between Kantian consciences, agreement is always self-evident. They [Pierre and Françoise] discover inherence, the Hegelian self which seeks the death of the other" (SNS 56-57).

Beneath their putative generosity, Pierre and Françoise really carry out a "very calculated enterprise" toward others because the latter are merely frustrated "annexes" in their world. This is so because, within the Sartrian perspective from which de Beauvoir is writing,[8] the other is the source of all of consciousness' problems: the meaning of our acts (for us) resides in our intentions, but the menace of the other is to try to make us be what he or she perceives and judges us to be. This is "because we recognize in them the exhorbitant power to *see us.* Françoise will be what Xavière thinks of her, with no recourse, as long as Xavière exists. From this stems the crime that ends the book, and which is no solution because Xavière dead will eternalize the image of Françoise that she bore within her at the moment of dying" (SNS 64).

Since, then, the other essentially constitutes the threat of the meaning of our actions changing outside us and without our assent, this fact yields for de Beauvoir the Sartrian conclusion that we are in no case responsible for what others think of us: "Any behavior will be always absurd in an absurd world and we shall always be able to decline responsibility for it" (SNS 67). In the framework of the dichotomy of the for-itself and the in-itself, two other conclusions follow here, one of which Merleau-Ponty accepts and the second he does not. The former is that the characters of *L'Invitée* "do not find good and evil in things, they do not think that human life has, by itself, definite demands and carries within itself its rule like that of trees or bees. They take the world (including society and their own bodies) as an 'unfinished task,' according to the profound phrase of Malebranche, they interrogate it with curiosity" (SNS 68).

But if nature is not morally normative, as we have seen above in the Introduction, neither can norms be found solely in consciousness, or the Sartrian for-itself. In other words, the conclusion which Merleau-Ponty does not accept here is that of a morality of pure intentions—whether it be framed in a Kantian or Sartrian context. Moral responsibility does not stop at the frontier of one's intentions; rather, it also extends to the consequences of one's actions (S 90). The proponent of a morality of pure intentions is the "moral man" of whom Merleau-Ponty wrote in *Sens et non-sens:* "We have unlearned 'pure morality' and have learned instead a sort of popular immoralism which is sane. The moral man does not want to dirty his hands. . . . The people do not have that liberty. The mechanic in the garage, if he wanted to live, was indeed obliged to repair German cars. . . . We are in the world, mixed up with it, compromised with it. . . . This division between the interior and he exterior is abstract, as is the division between intentions and their results" (SNS 259-60).

By contrast, what one cannot bear with Pierre and Françoise is the artificial life-style of attempting to live within a self-enclosed framework of pure intentions and of thereby being their own norms, "it is, in a word, that they think as they act and act as they think" (SNS 68). But, on the other hand, does it follow that an absolute immoralism is the final conclusion of an "existential" philosophy? Merleau-Ponty thinks not, and he ends his analysis of de Beauvoir's story by observing that our actions may be nuanced and ambiguous, but they are still meaningful. It is not true that they lack sense just because one can make them appear that way by taking a distant-enough viewpoint, as Voltaire did in *Micromégas.* Rather, our liberty gives us the continuing task of making sense out of the world and instituting those meanings where possible. The moral significance of this fact, for Merleau-Ponty, is that, first, "true morality" does not amount to respecting objective values somehow inscribed in the stonework of the universe. "Exterior rules" and "objective values" in that sense are eschewed because "there are no ways *to be* just and *to be* saved" (SNS 71).

But second, the task of constituting and instituting meaning is still represented in the characters of Pierre and Françoise in terms of their "good faith," "fidelity to promises," "respect for the other," "generosity," and "seriousness" (SNS 71). Value "is there. It consists of being actively what we are by chance, of establishing this communication with the other and with ourselves for which our temporal structure offers us the possibility and of which our liberty is only the outline" (SNS 71). In so saying, Merleau-Ponty touches on a theme to which he returns again and again in the context of politics and law, namely, that of recreating values by working to change the social world so that such values may be really instantiated. I shall come back to this in section 3 below, in connection with the teleological character of Merleau-Ponty's ethics, as well as throughout Chapter IV.

§2. *Autonomy and the Problem of Violence*

To say that morality rests upon an autonomous choice of one's situations rather than following exterior rules or norms establishes a tight link between the contingency of values and a contextualist ethics. That is, the very ethical nature of a given problem does not appear unless and until it is clear that its solution rests upon a free, autonomous decision by a given moral agent. The agent cannot decide if the solution appears already given, *a priori,* via "objective values"; there is no decision to be made other than assent or refusal. Thus, as Rabil indicates, "far from ethics depending upon immutable principles, the case is that to make ethics depend on such principles is to divorce oneself from existence, to cut oneself off from other men and to survey the world with a truth brought to it from another region."[9]

I shall say more about this connection between the contingency of values and a contextualist ethics below in terms of moral decision making. I introduce the subject here in the framework of Merleau-Ponty's defense of autonomy. For, a contextualist ethic, far from detracting from personal autonomy and our possible respect for human beings as ends in themselves—an ideal which Merleau-Ponty defends, once it is disentangled from the particular Kantian variant of a legislating consciousness—actually increases the likelihood of that respect by enhancing the notion of the self as free decision maker. It is true, for Merleau-Ponty, that the Kantian distinction between autonomy and heteronomy must be blurred, but to say that there is no exact frontier between the two does not mean—and Merleau-Ponty did not believe—that there is no difference either. In the context of politics, for instance, it is worth recalling that, even though he eventually abandoned Marxism, at a time when his political and moral thought leaned farthest to the left, he wrote that "To be a Marxist . . . is not to renounce being an individual so as to be blended into the world proletariat. It is to rejoin the universal, but without leaving off being what we are" (SNS

264-65). Furthermore, in an interview "On Madagascar," which appeared in *L'Express* on 21 August 1958 (and was later reprinted in *Signes*), Merleau-Ponty gives an ostensive definition of the "moral attitude" itself precisely in terms of autonomy and the right of self-determination of third-world countries as against European colonization (S 409).

The best way to see what view of autonomy Merleau-Ponty does defend, beyond the minimum level of having some responsibility in creating meanings, is to examine the twin problems of respect and violence. For, of course, respect for persons—which blocked treating them as mere means to an end, or violently—was one of Kant's main reasons for insisting on the importance of autonomy. In Merleau-Ponty's view of the matter, on the other hand, things become much more complex and ambiguous, and his views changed dramatically in the historical development of his work from *Sens et non-sens* through *Humanisme et terreur* to *Les Aventures de la dialectique*.

In the first place, and this is common to all his writings on the subject, human beings are neither pure subjects nor solely things or objects—in a social context, the *manipulanda* of governments or despots. Rather, they are incarnate selves, and any ethics plays the life-world false which forgets or ignores either the subjective or objective dimensions of humankind. Following Marx, and again this is true of all his writings, Merleau-Ponty considers capitalism an immoral system because it reduces workers to mere means of generating wealth for others. And as we shall see in the following chapter, this violence was for him equally institutionalized in contemporary communism. Thus his political dilemma was simultaneously a moral one: the social world is not peopled by a network of noumenal selves, but it is equally not composed of—nor should it be—classes of pawns and controllers. Hence the dilemma amounted to the inability to choose without furthering some kind of moral degradation in the shadow of both the open institutionalization of violence in the U.S.S.R., on the one hand, which wrongly held itself to be the faithful bearer of Marxism, and, on the other hand, Western democracies which paid lip service to grand slogans invoking respect for all human beings, but which in fact rested on the violent exploitation of capitalism, colonialism, and the subjugation of racial minorities. He might well have added the subjugation of women as well, had the women's movement occurred in the 1950's, and he certainly was philosophically alive to the continual possibility of social movements such as feminism awakening us to the presence of institutionalized, sedimented meanings—here, an institutionalized violence carefully concealed in both capitalist and non-capitalist societies. I shall return to this subject below in the context of law (at VI.2).

Further, Merleau-Ponty's analysis of *L'Invitée,* taken together with his rejection of both an immutable human nature as well as the conception of the incarnate *cogito* as a legislating consciousness, imply that his view of respect for human beings cannot be anchored in the concept of a person as a rational being or a moral lawgiver. As far back as the *Phénoménologie de la perception* he wrote that "Human society is *not* a community of reasonable minds, and one has been able to understand it thus only in favored countries in which a biological and economic equilibrium had been obtained locally and for a while. The experience of chaos, on the speculative as well as other levels, invites us to locate rationalism in a historic perspective from which it pretended to escape on principle, to look for a philosophy which makes us understand the bursting-forth of reason in a world which it has not made and to prepare the living infrastructure without which reason and liberty empty themselves and decompose" (PhP 69).

Rather than follow these unfruitful modes of thought, Merleau-Ponty sought for a long time to tie together the notion of respect with that of the proletariat as the bearer of universal humanity. Thus, respecting human beings was bound up with overcoming conflicts of private interests, and this would come about when the latter were identified with the general, impersonal interest of all, and vice-versa. In short, respect became a goal, or limiting idea, which was possible to achieve by degrees here and now, but which was neither guaranteed in advance nor impossible on principle. When we take into account the consequences of our actions, it can, and frequently does, happen that, either at the level of personal relationships, classes, or at that of nation-states, legitimate interests clash irreconcilably. Thus, as Merleau-Ponty put it toward the end of his address to the Société Française de Philosophie, "Nothing guarantees us that morality is possible, as Kant said with a profundity which has not yet been exhausted. But no fate assures us either that morality is impossible. We perceive it in an experience which is the perception of the other and, for having evoked the threat that the plurality of consciousnesses places on it, we are more aware of what it has of the unhoped for, the difficult, and the precious."[10]

However, when in *The Adventures of the Dialectic* Merleau-Ponty finally came to repudiate Marxism, for reasons given in the following chapter, this political change also entailed a corresponding transformation of his view of respect for persons, especially in what concerns violence. There is no evidence that he ever gave up the view that humankind have moral rights to basic requirements of life and, if this is not part of the former, to work. And there is plenty of evidence to show that he never thought better of capitalism as a system for increasing human respect. He remained a "man of the left," and his "new liberalism" seemed precisely a more effective means to make regimes as well as movements truer to basic human rights, if not to a revolutionary spirit. But still in all, there was a profound shift in the way he looked at violence as an acceptable tool for promoting social justice.[11]

Merleau-Ponty's position on violence in his earlier texts, such as *Humanisme et terreur,* can be reconstructed briefly in four basic propositions. (1) As noted above, all present societies are violent; the only difference between those that are Marxist and those that are not is that the former, unlike the latter, honestly recognize this fact. This awareness, Merleau-Ponty believes, makes it more likely that violence can be transcended in the future. Also as pointed out earlier, (2) violence is unavoidable as long as there are social classes, this structure being itself violent, whatever the grand slogans or constitutional principles of liberal societies. (3) Violence cannot be avoided by a return to pre-war conceptions of persons as Kantian-like ends in themselves. This would ignore their real, existential relationships for the sake of a system of pure ideas, and this system gets shipwrecked both theoretically—in conflicts of irreconciable, valid claims to some good(s)—and practically, in the destructive hypocrisy of its blindness to its own violent consequences. Therefore, Merleau-Ponty quotes Hegel approvingly: "Terror is Kant put into practice" (HT 160).

An illuminating example of this contrast is the difference between ideals of human rights espoused by Jimmy Carter when he was a political candidate and, on the other hand, his perceptions of those ideals from within the framework of the Presidency. If anything, the latter is not an affair of relating to others in a system of purely rational principles or pure ideas, as President Carter was soon to discover across the experiences his Office thrust upon him. In politics, as also in what concerns morals, the emphasis in Merleau-Ponty's thought is not primarily values, principles, or rules, but rather being able to instantiate them in the field of the practical—in other words, to concretize morality. Or, as John Leonard advised in another context, "Demonstrate how complicated policy-making really is. *That* would be an education. The teacher would pay his dues as a citizen; the student would learn that truth is not some instantaneous revelation, immutably obvious in the fires of an existential moment, but only the grubby approximation of a shared ideal."[12]

And finally, (4) not all violence is sanctioned. The test is whether it helps the proletariat to gain political power,[13] and doubtless it was this part of Merleau-Ponty's view which was responsible for the scathing criticisms which the author received when the essays that make up *Humanisme et terreur* first appeared in various journals and newspapers. And Merleau-Ponty responded very bitterly in the "Préface" of the latter work (pp. 23ff.) denying that all violence is permissible. But despite the emotional intensity of his reaction, widespread misunderstanding was almost guaranteed in the absence of several necessary qualifications. For example, are all sorts of violent acts sanctioned, or only some? If the latter, which ones and why? Also, how is one to *know* which acts of terror will help the proletariat gain power? For Merleau-Ponty, this ought to have been an especially acute problem given the fact that, as noted above, moral responsibility embraces the consequences of one's actions in addition to one's intentions.

However Merleau-Ponty might have clarified his position within the framework of his earlier writings on politics and morality, the change in political philosophy represented by *Les Aventures de la dialectique* brought with it a fresh set of problems for understanding his views on the moral permissibility of violence. For, as we shall see below in the present section, as well as in the following chapter (IV.3), Merleau-Ponty's new programme of a non-communist left was centered on a "new liberalism" of a (non-violent) parliamentary democracy. Correlatively, therefore, giving up for good the notion of the proletariat as the true bearer of universality went hand in hand with forgoing revolution in the streets in favor of legislative solutions to problems of social justice.

Since *Les Aventures de la dialectique* ends with only a hopeful sketch of a new politics—and since his later interviews and articles in *L'Express, Le Monde,* and elsewhere, do not greatly elaborate the fundamental tenets of that politics—it is not well enough developed to answer certain questions about violence which have long been debated and sharpened in Anglo-American philosophy. One of these concerns the justification of civil disobedience and the use of violence as a legitimate tool for fighting oppression when the latter originates in the very functioning of the democratic system itself. What, for instance, ought the "new liberal" to do in the face of legislation or judicial decisions that disenfranchise a certain minority group to the profit of the majority? Another problem, which cuts across conceptual and tactical concerns, consists of whether in the new liberalism violence is disavowed for good or only as long as parliamentary democracy is (from its viewpoint) successful.

What is common to both these problems about violence is the complex relationship between values, formal rules, and social, political, and economic interests. This relationship will be explored in detail below in the context of law and justice (VII.2,3). Here, by contrast, a very brief overview will suffice to illuminate its connection with the two problems of violence just mentioned. That is, in *Humanisme et terreur,* as regards Western bourgeois capitalistic societies, the operative contrast had been between justice on the one hand, represented by the goals of proletarian humanism and, on the other hand, private, conflicting interests which expressed simultaneously an economic, political, and legal exploitation. As noted above, this was a conflict that could only be resolved morally by the eclipse of capitalism because in a capitalist society, following the categorical imperative by treating each person as an end in him-or herself would betray the proletariat. Sincerity towards *everyone* would be ineffective in principle for eliminating conflicts of legitimate interests and thus for remedying social injustice.[14]

But in *Les Aventures de la dialectique,* such conflicting interests are all to be accomodated somehow within the formal institution of parliamentary democracy. How formal rules of parliamentary democracy could be followed here by both citizen and legislator alike in the presence of what is perceived to be substantially unjust legislation or judicial decisions—which, although Merleau-Ponty does not expressly say so, he would almost certainly have construed as systemic violence—is the essential problem which underlies the two questions of violence posed above in the context of the new liberalism.

However Merleau-Ponty might have answered those questions, and hence also sharpened the relationship of moral values, formal rules, and interests, it is certain that, in the new liberalism of his last political writings, the goal of respecting others is not lost. Like the moral ideals of proletarian humanism and the notion of a universalizability principle which transcends personal interests,[15] the ideal of respecting others remained an end or regulative ideal to pursue in the task of sedimenting values. The hope that sustained the programme of the non-communist left was certainly that parliamentary democracy comprised, at least in the present historical epoch, the most probable means to achieve a society whose members could concretize their respect for each other. "As long as we live with others," Merleau-Ponty wrote, "none of our judgments on them is possible which excepts us and puts them at a distance" (E 49). And again, in writing of "the juncture of the individual and the universal," he concludes that "The central fact to which Hegel's dialectic returns in a hundred ways is that we do not have to choose between the *for-itself* and the *for-the-other*. . . . Others . . . are worth exactly what I am worth" (PM 120-21).

Intersubjectivity means that, as Sartre had announced in *L'Être et le néant,* choosing for oneself means choosing for everyone else as well. But this claim on us is certainly more problematic for the early Sartre[16] than for Merleau-Ponty, and the latter's preference for the Hegelian dialectic was also intended as a criticism of his friend/estranged acquaintance. For in the latter's view, social solidarity always has the formidable obstacle of a multiplicity of purely negative, unavoidably alienated consciousnesses. Regardless of what position one defends vis-à-vis the tenability of a Sartrian ethic, as we saw in Chapter I, Merleau-Ponty does not have to contend with the latter's problem of the other always haunting the for-itself and being the source of all its troubles. In the language of *The Visible and the Invisible,* the problem of the other is "not that of access to another nihilization, but like that of initiation to a symbolism and a typology of others in which *being for oneself* and *being for the other* are reflexive variants, and not essential forms" (p. 114n.). Hence "we are moments of the same syntax, we count in the same world, we reveal the same Being" (p. 115).

§3. *Teleology and Responsibility*

The main threads of our discussion so far all lead to the conclusion that, had Merleau-Ponty written an ethics, it would have been much more in a teleological rather than deontological vein. Overall, its concern—the good to be sought—is conceived largely in terms of the economic welfare of the proletariat, whether from a Marxist viewpoint or, as later, without appeal to the latter's doctrinal support. But it is also clear that, as in the conclusion of Merleau-Ponty's analysis of de Beauvoir's *L'Invitée,* social justice is not in his estimation the only moral problem. For he also praises qualities such as "fidelity to promises," "generosity," and so forth (SNS 71) which are, as noted above, central to personal relationships which do not have any necessary connection with social justice. Thus one may conclude that the good which forms the goal of his "theory" would consist of an imprecise mixture of general economic welfare together with a personal respect of a much wider sweep than the economic dimension of life. In addition, one would have to add to the list power—both personal and political—knowledge, plus whatever other necessary conditions of concretizing those values there might be.

The teleological character of Merleau-Ponty's ethics is also underscored by his insistence that moral responsibility extend to the consequences of our acts as well as to our intentions. And this view finds its fulfillment in *Les Aventures de la dialectique* (and in other later writings) in which the author praises Max Weber's "heroic liberalism" (AD 38). The latter's *Politik als Beruf* is approvingly quoted in relevant part as follows: "The morality of the heart [pure intentions alone] and the morality of responsibility [for the results of one's actions] are not absolute opposites, but complementaries of which the unity alone makes a man of political vocation" (AD 41). Precisely what Merleau-Ponty finds of value in Weber's work in this context is that the latter was able to transcend his earlier dualism of "the universe of knowledge and that of practice and . . . the opposed options of the ethics of responsibility and of the ethics of conscience" (RC 48). For Merleau-Ponty, Weber was himself led to see through his own research how these antitheses collapse: "The opposed options of the ethics of responsibility and the ethics of conscience are not exclusive: even pure consciences choose the moment to have their sincerity burst forth, and the estimation of the consequences is often a judgment of masked value" (RC 48-49).

Another main feature of the teleological character of his thinking about ethics consists of his concern, already illustrated above, to concretize values. So consistent is he on this score that what he wrote in June 1945 could have been repeated anywhere along the route of his political itinerary, even at the conclusion of *The Aventures of the Dialectic:* "We were not wrong, in 1939, to want liberty, truth, happiness, transparent relations between men, and we do not renounce humanism. The war and the occupation have only taught us that values remain nominal, and do not even count, without an economic and political infrastructure which makes them begin to exist" (SNS 268). It is not the renunciation of those values that is called for, but rather their actualization.

Merleau-Ponty's teleological concern for concretizing values in history is closely related to the notion of heroism that comes out strongly in *Sense and Non-Sense* and then seems to vanish. I think, however, that it is still very much present in *The Adventures of the Dialectic,* and by looking at the fate of the hero across Merleau-Ponty's works, we will gain additional purchase on the teleological character of his ethics.

In the concluding essay of *Sense and Non-Sense,* "Man, The Hero," the author describes his subject as the individual committed to the task of bringing values into being. He or she knows that reality is "adversity," that the enterprise is always haunted by contingency rather than being guaranteed success, but that the solace of despair is also unavailable because everything has meaning. Conscious of the fragility of meaning created, and that what sense there is always stands out as nuanced and ambiguous against a background of non-sense, "The contemporary hero is not a sceptic, a dilettante, nor a decadent. It is simply that he has the experience of chance, of disorder, of failure, of [19]36, of the War in Spain, of June [19]40. He is in a time in which duties and tasks are obscure. He demonstrates better than one has ever done the contingency of the future and the liberty of man" (SNS 330).

The contemporary hero knows, therefore, that, as Hubert and Patricia Dreyfus phrased it, "individual and social commitments can result in a moment of meaning which is its only reward. . . . Although we have no guaranty against disillusionment, we must trust such a moment and live by it as long as it seems significant to us. Injustice and non-sense are not eliminated, but the hero is all the more heroic for not being a saint but only a man."[17] As a result, *Sens et non-sens* ends by saying that, unlike Christian saints or "the heroes of past revolutions," the contemporary hero does not have the support of believing that his or her struggle "is already won in heaven or in History. . . . The contemporary hero is not Lucifer, he is not even Prometheus, he is man" (SNS 331).

What *is* humanity's only resource, and what is most important, is to keep its awareness of the contingency of maeaning, but also of the significance of what value is brought into existence morally, legally, aesthetically, politically, economically, and so on throughout all regions of the life-world. As noted above, Merleau-Ponty is fond of citing Malebranche's dictum that the world is an "unfinished task." This is a task which is essentially personal but also intersubjective: in the course of analyzing Hemingway's *For Whom the Bell Tolls,* he adds that "One dies alone, but one lives with others; we are the image that they make of us, there where they are, we are also" (SNS 329). (In *Consciousness and the Acquisition of Language,* he includes the *obiter dictum* that "Malraux, saying that 'One dies alone, therefore one lives alone', makes a false deduction. Life, in fact, radically transcends individualism and it is impossible to judge it in terms of death which is its individual failure" [p. 241].)

Consequently, the contemporary hero is radically different from (i) the Nietzschean *Übermensch* who is, in Merleau-Ponty's estimation, too isolated and not essentially *être-au-monde,* as well as from (ii) the Hegelian hero who is too bent on ferreting out the rational course of history (SNS 331). The contemporary hero also knows that "the value of man is neither in an explosive and maniacal sincerity, nor in a faith without discussion" (SNS 318-19). He or she is, in short, the ordinary mortal who, unsupported by an external justification, acts anyway such that humanity becomes, through his or her acts and those of others, in the haunting and challenging symbol of Giraudoux, "*la caryatide du vide.*"

Such are, in brief outline, Merleau-Ponty's earlier descriptions of what the contemporary hero is and is not. What becomes of the hero in his later works? This is necessarily a speculative sort of question, given the lack of any specific pronouncements on the subject, but I believe that a substantial part of the answer consists in his praise of Weber's "heroic liberalism" and in his own programme of legislative reform in the "new liberalism." From all that appears, Merleau-Ponty had it in mind that the "new liberal" legislator faced all the same possibilities, obstacles, hopes for reward, and contingency of success in instantiating humanizing values through the political process as did "the contemporary hero" of *Sens et non-sens.* And it seems that the same kinds of presuppositions carry over in the author's assessment of Weber's liberalism. The latter is heroic, first, because it does not oppose the internal to the external, the subjective to the objective, intentions to consequences of one's acts, and values to practicality. It is also heroic because "it recognizes the right of its adversaries, does not consent to hate them, does not elude confrontation with them, and, in order to defeat them, does not count on their own contradictions and on the discussion that reveals them" (AD 38).

It is not otherwise with the "new liberal" legislator. Parliamentary democracy intrinsically provides a forum for the presentation and confrontation of competing views, and its procedures for resolving conflict do not depend on finding internal contradictions in any given political program. But at the same time, parliament does not guarantee the non-communist left or any other party success in making real what is interpreted to be correct moral values. In short, the most likely interpretation of "the contemporary hero" of Merleau-Ponty's later writings—at least in what concerns politics—is the new liberal who chooses the legislative process to make the world a little less of "an unfinished task." The new liberal is the true humanist who eschews a sterile humanism, namely, a "philosophy of the inner man who finds no theoretical difficulty in his relations with others, no opacity in social functionings, and replaces political culture with moral exhortation" (S 282). Rather, the new liberal is a humanist in the sense of Machiavelli, that is, someone who espouses a philosophy which affronts as a problem the relation of man with man and the constitution between them of a situation and a history which would be theirs in common" (S 282-83). I shall have more to say about Machiavelli below (at IV.5). For now, let us conclude the present chapter by examining the last main theme in Merleau-Ponty's reflections on ethics, morals, and morality.

§4. *Moral Decision Making*

This last main theme consists of the process of making moral decisions, and although it is true that he provides us with no single, detailed description of this activity, it is still possible to construct a fairly clear picture of it from many scattered references throughout his writings and from certain conclusions drawn from the preceding sections of this chapter. Again, the most convenient way to present his views is to contrast them with their relevant Kantian counterparts.

For Kant, making a moral decision is essentially a matter of the properly motivated deduction of the requirements of practical reason—and hence of the immutable, objective, *a priori* moral law—as applied to a certain set of facts. One has a certain inclination to do something, expressed as a "maxim," and this usually—and debatable whether necessarily—is motivated by self-interest. One is aware of a present state of affairs, and one makes empirical judgments about the likely consequences of acting on one's own maxim. The moral agent discovers whether willing the maxim is the moral thing to do solely by reasoning whether it is consistent with the universalizability requirement of the categorical imperative. If and only if the maxim can be willed universally without contradiction can it correspond to the objective moral law. And last, but hardly least, willing morally can occur if and only if doing so stems from the one moral-making motive of willing out of reverence for the moral law. And Kant is quite specific in distinguishing this motive from (merely) willing in accordance with the moral law. He fully well admits that in any given decision-making context we can, and usually do, have a variety of motives at work. But he is equally clear in restricting the possibility of willing morally to doing so for the sake of the moral law. And this requirement implies in turn our introspective ability to unerringly discern which motive it is that finally directs our volitions.

Merleau-Ponty's picture of making moral decisions could hardly be further removed from the Kantian model, although it is true that, when he is concerned to distinguish political from moral decision making, the model for the latter he always has in mind is that of Kant or of neo-Kantians. But the task of concretizing morality demands another model, namely, that of the *artist,* and this is a view that tends to fly in the face of common sense. As Henry F. Nardone puts it, "The ordinary view of the situation is this: the moral man is the unimaginative but responsible individual who follows the customs of the group in which he lives; the artist is the imaginative but irresponsible individual in constant revolt against the establishment. . . . the true artist and the authentically moral person are, in reality, much more akin than the stereotyping would lead us to believe."[18]

Moral experience is much closer to artistic experience in Merleau-Ponty's view because, first, it is also an attempt at expression and institution of values in the face of adversity: the moral person, like the artist, is circumscribed and challenged by the limitations of his or her situation. Second, and even more important, there is an intimacy of all kinds of expression because they belong "in one sole order which the first act of expression instituted" (PM 120). Thus, for Merleau-Ponty, differences in artistic and moral expression are more nearly those of degree than of kind. (Furthermore, as we shall see below in Part II (V.1,2), this claim is also central for understanding the phenomenon of law.)

Merleau-Ponty in fact takes great pains throughout many of his writings to use the example of the artist to illuminate social phenomena, chiefly morality and politics, in what concerns their origins, organization, and functioning. For example, whilst describing Max Weber's analysis of the interpenetration of religious, economic, and legal meanings in a social system, he tells us that "The sense of the system in its beginnings is like the pictorial sense of the tableau which directs the gestures of the painter less than it results from them and progresses with them" (AD 26). And in turn, the link between aesthetic and perceptual experience is located in the "expressive operation of the body, begun in the least perception, which is amplified in painting and in art" (PM 117).

The picture of reason operative in moral decision making originates in and amplifies aesthetic feelings. It is not that making moral decisions is exactly like what the painter does at his or her canvas or the composer at the keyboard, but rather that there are, in Wittgenstein's idiom, strong "family resemblances." As against Kant, the structures of the situations are analogous in at least three respects. First, in terms of what is created, the moral agent, like the artist, tries to create the best "picture" possible in a given situation (RC 64-65). In moral experience, the "best picture" would be defined as that instantiating the richest set of humane possibilities, as described above, with the least possible harm to those involved.

The second close "family resemblance" between aesthetic and moral experience concerns the method of problem solving employed in both. As noted above in Chapter II, this method is characterized by the indirection of Panofsky's "subterranean logic" such that, when progress in creating sense or concretizing value occurs, it often comes about obliquely rather than straightforwardly. Thus moral values figure prominently in Merleau-Ponty's observation that "What one looks for too deliberately, one does not obtain, and ideas and values, on the contrary, are not lacking to him who has known how, in his meditating life, to set free their spontaneous source" (S 104; the same passage appears, in somewhat different form, at PM 159).

Moral and aesthetic experience are also analogous in that knowing what values to strive for in a given context is not something that can be deduced from *a priori* rules. Such decisions must be made from within the situation and, in the case of morality, if not art as well, demand a consciousness of the relevant past and likely future of the particular context. Progress is also oblique in knowing what values to attempt to bring into play because values themselves have an ineradicable ambiguity about them. In Weber's idiom, values "offer themselves first to our signifying and speaking life only like resisting nuclei in a diffuse milieu. They, like perceived things, get defined and circumscribed only through the complicity of a background and suppose as much shadow as light. . . . Even the purest truths suppose marginal views, are not entirely at the center of clear vision, and owe their sense to the horizon which sedimentation [of meaning] and language arrange around them" (PM 159-60).

This lack of absolute certainty about what values to strive for in a particular context does not mean that there can be no such thing as moral rules, as I shall show momentarily. What it does indicate is that a moral decision, just as one in art, is often an expressive step in a fog and "In morality, as in art, there is no solution for him who first wants to make sure of his step, to remain at each instant just and absolute master of himself. We would have no other recourse than the spontaneous movement which binds us to others in unhappiness and happiness, in egoism and in generosity" (SNS 9).[19] Moreover, it is in this "spontaneous movement," in morality as in art, that fogs lift, that through the convergence and divergence of evidential perspectives, we get clear about which decision to make. As the artist is guided by the emerging painting on his or her canvas and adjusts choices of intensities or hues of colors, compositional balance, or the prominence of line and form, so, too, the moral agent must remain sensitive to the effects of his or her acts in given situations and, in the light of the emergent Gestalt, assess their effects on the whole.

In addition to this "outer ambiguity," there is also an inner one that serves to further distance Merleau-Ponty's non-formal, contextual approach to ethics from that of Kant. Namely, as noted above in Chapter I, Merleau-Ponty's writings eschew introspection as a means of gaining a private and incorrigible access to oneself. Further, as Kant freely admitted, behind any given act of will there could be and usually is a variety of motives, of which any one or combination thereof might be its source. But Kant's claim, which Merleau-Ponty's texts abandon along with introspection as a means to self-knowledge, is that we are able in principle to unerringly select the one moral-making motive of willing out of all reverence for the moral law and then let that motive determine our will. In Merleau-Ponty's view, on the contrary, "There is no final moment of total, incorrigible clarity of oneself and of others, even at the moment of death, and we must act upon the judgments we make of ourselves (and others) as if they were indisputable, though they always are" (SNS 65). "The truth is that," he concludes, "our actions do not admit of a single motive and one sole explanation, and that they are, as Freud said profoundly, 'overdetermined'" (SNS 63-64). And as we saw above in Chapter II, for Merleau-Ponty the truth of Freudianism is, in part, that "each choice always has several meanings without our being able to say that one of them is the only true one" (RC 71).

The final aspect of moral decision making to examine before turning our attention to the context of politics, consists of the status of rules—a topic equally important in analysing legal experience (see V.2,3). Earlier on, rules came into view as "exterior rules" or "objective values" which Merleau-Ponty considers inconsistent with the assumption of human responsibility, or moral artistry in concrete situations. But giving moral rules such short shrift will not do, as neither will the too facile conclusion that Merleau-Ponty was a rule sceptic. For one thing, he refers to and accepts the existence of rules in other contexts, such as language. For another thing, and more significantly, if moral experience parallels that of the artist in certain crucial ways, it is also important to observe that artistic creation is not free from rules either. The latter, embodied in *technique,* consist of instituted, accepted (within a given tradition) procedures to follow, according to certain norms, for accomplishing some task with one's materials in a particular, specified manner. Similarly, in moral experience, rules would consist of empirical generalizations of ways to best concretize value in certain types of situations. They would refer to the likely effects of employing certain principles at particular times in situations resembling those of our past experience. As such, the same ambiguities which attach to principles derived from history would also attach to the rules referent to them. They would have, as in John Dewey's ethics, an "instrumental" value. As the latter insisted, and Merleau-Ponty certainly would have agreed, "A moral law, like a law in physics, is not something to swear by and stick to at all hazards; it is a formula of the way to respond when specified conditions present themselves. Its soundness and pertinence are tested by what happens when it is acted upon."[20]

Now Rabil has pointed out that "There is a certain advantage to this 'contextualist' view of ethics. For ethics ceases to be reflection on the 'ought' and becomes instead reflection on the given and on what of the 'ought' is possible within the given. That is, ethics, like politics, deals only with concrete problems. Indeed, it resembles politics above all in its concern with specific problems and with the most desirable possible solutions to those problems."[21] But Rabil also correctly notes a crucial, unresolved problem in Merleau-Ponty's thinking about ethics which is important not only to the topic of moral rules, but also to that of law (see VII.1,2). Essentially the problem which Rabil disengages from Merleau-Ponty's texts is whether it is history that teaches us the truth of moral principles to which we give expression in rules, or whether, on the contrary, we use those principles to interpret and morally judge history—or, without being viciously circular, somehow both?[22]

Suppose, for example, one were to ask Merleau-Ponty whether a certain moral principle could be true even if no society ever succeeded in bringing it into existence (or perhaps had never even thought of it). Could the truth of such a moral principle be independent of its lack of historical instantiation? (Analogously, was the Pythagorean theorem true before Pythagoras discovered it?

Would it have been true if no one had?) Now taking one aspect of Merleau-Ponty's phenomenology, that which deals with discovering principles in empirical facts—rejecting, as we saw above in Chapter II, non-historical truths—the answer would seem to be 'no.' But it is hard to square such a response with all that he wrote about the desirability of instantiating moral values themselves and especially with his view that a human being is *worth* treating as an end in him- or herself. *That* truth, as well as the moral ideals of proletarian humanism generally, tend to function in Merleau-Ponty's texts as non-historically derived and even as self-evidently true.[23]

Rabil does not himself attempt to resolve this problem of interpretation of Merleau-Ponty's reflections on ethics, and it is just as well because it is not clear that the texts themselves give us any possible resolution. Indeed, it is not certain that Merleau-Ponty even fully reognized the problems involved, let alone provided detailed, unambiguous responses to them. But the texts do suggest part of an answer that might be sketched out along two different, though related lines. The first of these is that history certainly has taught us the unacceptable—not to say, frightening and sordid—consequences of adopting any other moral view about the worth of humanity. That is, contrary views appear through the negative historical lens as lost illusions not to pursue (II.5). And the second line of argument might begin with the observation that history is only one source of evidence in such matters, to which must be conjoined not only present observation but also the anticipation of an uncertain future. And he could certainly argue that the instrumental conception of rules is enhanced by its ability to make rules flexibly respond to changing present and future configurations of events. Moreover, the same approach to rules and making moral decisions in settling conflicts amongst a multiplicity of perspectives obtains in politics and law as well. In those sectors also, as we shall now see, there is equally an interpenetration of the moral and the legal, the aesthetic and the political—all guided, when ideally so, by the aim of making the world a little more acceptable through the achievement of human respect.

NOTES

1. I am grateful to Professor Edward Ballard (then) of Tulane University for having long ago pointed me toward this most fruitful perspective on what Merleau-Ponty wrote about ethics.
2. Paul Ricoeur, *Le Volontaire et l'involontaire* (Paris: Aubier, 1951.
3. In the margin of his unfinished manuscript at this point, the author wrote: "The real problem is not that of resemblances, but of the possibility of *metamorphosis,* of taking up again. Resemblances are the exception." But see VII.1 under "permanent necessities" (HT 163-64).
4. *Ethics* (Englewood Cliffs: Prentice-Hall, Inc., 1973), second edition, p. 26.
5. "Le Primat de la perception et ses conséquences philosophiques," *Bulletin de la Société Française de Philosophie,* XLI, 1947 (séance du 23 novembre 1946), p. 120.

6. *Merleau-Ponty: Existentialist of the Social World* (New York: Columbia University Press, 1967), p. 248. The last sentence seems to me much too strong, since there can be many degrees of change from one situation to another, with corresponding changes in the applicability of moral norms. Taken literally, the last sentence of the passage cited would condemn us to a moral equivalent of Santayana's "solipsism of the present moment," against which Merleau-Ponty protested in his writings on time-consciousness in *Phénoménologie de la perception* and elsewhere.
7. "Phenomenology as Ideology Critique," *Philosophy Today,* Fall 1980, p. 276.
8. "Whether this was borrowed from Sartre is questionable. Certainly in a general sense it was very much in the framework of a Sartrian description of intersubjectivity. But in a recent interview, de Beauvoir was asked about this by Jessica Benjamin "(J.B.)." The question and the reply run as follows:

   > J.B.: So when you wrote in *L'Invitée* that Françoise says what really upsets her about Xavière is that she has to confront in her another consciousness, that is not an idea that particularly came [from] Sartre . . . ?
   >
   > S.B.: It was I who thought about that! It was absolutely not Sartre!
   >
   > J.B.: But that is an idea which it seems to me appears later in *his* work.
   >
   > S.B.: Oh! Maybe! In any case, this problem . . . of the other's consciousness, it was my problem.

   Cited in Margaret A. Simons and Jessica Benjamin, "Simone de Beauvoir: An Interview," *Feminist Studies* 5, No. 2 (Summer 1979), p. 339.
9. Rabil, p. 249.
10. "Le Primat de la perception et ses conséquences philosophiques," p. 134.
11. There are two curious, as well as vexing, features of Merleau-Ponty's consideration of violence throughout all his writings. The first is that he never offers a definition of it, and second, most of his attention rests on the larger context of political and economic (=class) struggle. By contrast, he is only seldom concerned with purely personal violence.
12. "The Last Word: Policy I for Freshmen," *The New York Times Book Review,* September 26, 1971, p. 63. Cited in Joel Feinberg, *Social Philosophy* (Englewood Cliffs: Prentice-Hall, Inc., 1973), p. 3.
13. This is the view defended in *Humanisme et terreur* and later in his article, "Sur la déstalinisation," (1956) reprinted in *Signes* (pp. 366-85). In this latter piece, the author uses the Hungarian Revolution of 1956 as an example of the internal contradictions of contemporary communism because violence was used against the proletariat instead of on its behalf.
14. This argument is essentially an economic variant of those invoked in other contexts of distributive justice. For example, one could consider the much-debated topic of remedying patterns of racial and sexual injustice in professional school admissions and in job-training programs. If henceforth each applicant were to be treated purely as an end in him-or herself, then it would be hard to see how the persisting effects of invidious discrimination could be overcome, since some applicants would have unequal skills and abilities due to past discrimination. Of course Kant could argue, as Merleau-Ponty did, that the capitalist ought to treat each worker as an end in him-or herself and that this policy would entail morally willing the collapse of capitalism. But, so far as I know, Kant never made this argument. See also Chapter VII, n.46.
15. As Frankena points out, egoism as an ethical doctrine is essentially a statement of private interests, or prudentialism, as opposed to satisfying one basic requirement of a moral theory, that it be universal and so *disinterested:* "As Butler said, and as Kant would have agreed, prudentialism is 'by no means . . . the moral institution of life'" (p. 19). Frankena discusses this requirement of the moral point of view in the context of rejecting ethical egoism, a view

which is also inconsistent with the values Merleau-Ponty espouses in his writings on both personal and political situations.

16. A very different picture has begun to emerge with the posthumous publication of some of Sartre's manuscripts although, as noted in Chapter I, their coherence with the early published writings is not yet certain. For an instructive, pertinent summary, see Peter Whitney, "Jean-Paul Sartre's Notebooks," *Journal of the British Society for Phenomenology,* Vol. XV, No. 2, May 1984, pp. 109-22.
17. Maurice Merleau-Ponty, *Sense and Non-Sense,* trans. Hubert and Patricia Dreyfus (Evanston: Northwestern University Press, 1964), p. xxvi.
18. "Creativity in Art and Ethics," *The Journal of Aesthetics and Art Criticism,* Vol. XXXIV, No. 2, Winter 1975, p. 183.
19. For the same kind of thought, in almost exactly the same language, see William James, "The Will to Believe" and "The Moral Philosopher and the Moral Life" in *Essays in Pragmatism* (New York: Haffner Publishing Company, 1948). See especially pp. 95-97.
20. *The Quest for Certainty* (New York: Capricorn Books, 1960), p. 278. It is significant from the point of view of our present discussion that Dewey's chapter here bears the title, "The Construction of the Good." Furthermore, Dewey clearly evidenced his wish to avoid the same kinds of views which Merleau-Ponty rejected: "Without the introduction of operational thinking, we oscillate between a theory that, in order to save the objectivity of judgments of value, isolates them from experience and nature, and a theory that, in order to save their concrete and human significance, reduces them to mere statements about our own feelings" (p. 263).

    Ethics is only one area in which the careful reader can note a variety of similarities between Dewey and Merleau-Ponty. It is all the more interesting, therefore, that Merleau-Ponty told Herbert Spiegelberg that he had never read Dewey. (Private communication from Herbert Spiegelberg.)
21. Rabil, p. 249.
22. Rabil, p. 250.
23. There are important legal ramifications of this problem which are discussed below at VII.1,2.

IV: POLITICS

§1. Merleau-Ponty's Politics and His Contemporary Philosophical Landscape.

Merleau-Ponty never wrote a systematic, coherent politics any more than he did an ethics. This is to say, first, that his own political views changed substantially throughout the course of his philosophical career, some of the details of which we have already charted in the previous chapter. Second, it is also the case that much of what he said at the end of his published remarks on politics failed to answer important questions raised earlier on. We have already seen one example of this fact (III.2) in connection with the possible justifiable role of violence for achieving political ends.

Further, third, Merleau-Ponty consciously committed himself to thinking historically, to following the contingency of political meaning as it revealed itself in the concrete dialectic of the interworld. What he sought to avoid—not altogether successfully in the eyes of his critics[1] and even in his own, as he admits toward the end of *Les Aventures de la dialectique*—was the use of dogma and doctrine to filter our reading of history. And finally, fourth, the absence of a systematic, coherent politics means that one does not find among Merleau-Ponty's texts one major, definitive work. Instead, there are two principal works—*Humanisme et terreur* and *Les Aventures de la dialectique*—which happen not to go together very well—plus many articles and interviews scattered in *Les Temps Modernes, L'Express, Le Monde,* and other places,[2] including fourteen of them reprinted in *Signes* (pp. 309-435).

In spite of, or perhaps because of, this rather disorganized state of affairs, it is precisely Merleau-Ponty's writings on politics which have attracted what is surely the largest amount of commentary and critique of his work by philosophers and non-philosophers alike, beginning with his contemporaries and persisting right down to the present day.[3] These writers disagree, sometimes sharply, about (1) the meanings of certain texts, (2) the significance of disputed passages for the author, (3) how Merleau-Ponty might have extended his thinking on politics in the light of his last writings, (4) the validity of Merleau-Ponty's critique of Marxism, and (5) the tenability of the philosopher's political alternative (the "new liberalism"). Moreover, the reader is not particularly helped in disentangling the main arguments in these debates because most of the disputants ignore, or gloss over, the crucial distinction between a phenomenology of politics—that is, a description of what politics itself is, its essence—and Merleau-Ponty's own politics—his own political judgments and reasons for them.

To some degree, blurring this distinction is entirely understandable, as is the fact that most commentators are more concerned with the latter and only rarely with the former.[4] This is so, first, because Merleau-Ponty himself certainly pays more attention to the latter than to the former, and is much clearer about it, within the limits of such clarity as the texts provide. And second, his view of the nature of politics emerges from both the living history to which he was a witness—terrible, frightening, and sordid as it was—as well as from his phenomenology of the social world generally. It is, thus, even for the author himself, the history of his own political involvement that always tends to come center-stage.

Accordingly, the present chapter will also take up Merleau-Ponty's personal political history, but it will also seek to pay much more attention than is usual in such analyses to his view of the nature of politics. Both are, in fact, relevant to the phenomenon of law—the former because it is the record of Merleau-Ponty's own choices of a certain kind of society and the role of law within it, and the latter because it concerns more general conceptual questions of what politics is and how it *can be* related to law. On the other hand, since the story of Merleau-Ponty's own political commitment has already been told several times and in great detail, I shall provide only a brief synopsis of its essential developments. Spatial constraints prohibit considering many of the differences of interpretation, though I shall point out certain of the major ones in passing. My main concerns will be to show how the events described make Merleau-Ponty's texts more intelligible, as well as to defend his views against some very ill-considered criticisms. Furthermore, for the eventual use value of the story in Part Two below, my principal objective will be to recount only what is most relevant to the phenomenon of law.

§2. *The Beginnings: France, 1945-47*

Merleau-Ponty's politics is continuous with, and indeed emblematic of, the way in which his more general philosophy sought to be a middle path between the Scylla of extreme subjectivism and the Charybdis of extreme objectivism. In the political realm, the latter came to be identified with Marxism, as we shall see below in relevant part. The target represented by the former consisted of the double context of French philosophy and political life before World War II. As noted above, the French philosophical scene was dominated by many interwoven strands of idealism which together reinforced a pattern of extreme individualism in matter of both consciousness and conscience. Even as Europe was collapsing in the chaos of war, Louis Lavelle, for example, spoke for a whole generation (to which Merleau-Ponty reacted with considerable bitterness): "One cannot doubt that, in our country, which is not only that of Descartes, but also of the moralists, everyone considers it to be the supreme ideal of existence to acquire the most lucid consciousness of himself and his place in the world, to transform his opinions into clear and distinct ideas, never to agree to anything nor to act except for good reasons, valid for himself and for all, always to seek for the ultimate basis of his knowledge or his action: this is what is correctly called *philosophy* in the noblest and strongest sense we can give the word."[5]

Such an exaggerated individualism, with its stress on individualistic, atomistic autonomy, had its political counterpart in the classical liberalism of Alain. On his view, (1) politics ought to be merely the application of moral principles, a practical reason directed solely by moral norms (AD 8-9), such that the politician should decide on a certain action or policy according to his or her best moral lights and not worry about the consequences. Moreover, (2) Alain's mind-body dualism entailed for him the view that politics consisted of a struggle to impose what is "spiritual" on what is "body," or "animal." And (3) his exaggerated individualism led to a theory of minimal government so as to maximally encourage individual moral development.

The influence of Alain on the pre-war generation was enormous. As Sonia Kruks points out, "Through his daily 'Propos', appearing year after year in the press, Alain (1868-1951), moulded the opinion of the 'middle' classes in France—the small businessmen, the clerks and minor bureaucrats, the teachers, the more prosperous sections of the peasantry—for several decades. The Radical Party, whose acknowledged theorist he was, was almost continuously in office for the first forty years of this century. For Merleau-Ponty's generation, liberalism *was* Alain."[6] Even so, for Merleau-Ponty, Alain's view was corrupt and hypocritical because it inhabited a heaven of pure principles cut off from, and indifferent to, a considerably different social reality. This effectively Kantian approach to politics was indeed the "terror" that Hegel took to be Kant "put into practice" (HT 160; see above at III.2) because Alain stubbornly maintained his doctrines of excessive individualism and a minimal state, as Kruks also notes, "even at the time of acute economic depression in the 1930's. . . . Small wonder then, that, for Merleau-Ponty, liberalism, as epitomized by Alain, seemed to consist in the subordination of the very real needs of millions of people to a set of abstract principles. In practice, subordination of the 'animal' to the 'spiritual' meant the acceptance of widespread unemployment and misery."[7]

As we have seen above (III.2), it was the experience of the Occupation that shattered these illusions of an optimistic universe of pure morality and which, for Merleau-Ponty, definitively gave the lie to such an exaggerated individualism and the kind of liberalism that embodied it. This is why he wrote that, as cited in the previous chapter, "We were not wrong, in 1939, to want liberty, truth, happiness, and we do not renounce humanism. The war and the occupation have only taught us that values remain nominal, and are not even worth anything, without an economic and political infrastructure which makes them exist. . . . It is not a question of renouncing our values of 1939, but of making them real" (SNS 268).

How, then, were they to be made real? In the aftermath of the war, France was torn between two sorts of political forces—those that wanted a return to "normal," to business as usual, and those that sought a complete change. Not surprisingly, Merleau-Ponty sided with the latter; perhaps not surprising either, it was the former that won out. For the years just after the war saw the start of French colonialist difficulties in Indo-China, domestic economic crises such as a massive workers' strike at the main Renault factory (30 April 1947), the beginnings of the freeze in East-West relationships, and a wave of anti-communism that approached hysteria. Arthur Koestler's books enjoyed a great vogue, especially *Darkness at Noon,* as did Kravchenko's *I Chose Freedom*. It was the ensuing wave of anti-communist paranoia and the failure to achieve any new political order in France that constituted the immediate context for *Humanisme et terreur* and, without taking into account which, that particular work remains very difficult to understand.

For *Humanisme et terreur* is a considerably ambivalent book, a work of philosophical and political hesitation. There is not space here to provide even a synopsis of all the main arguments, as well as anything like a detailed reply to Koestler, but there are two aspects of the essay which have a considerable legal significance. First, as briefly touched on in Chapter III in connection with violence, Merleau-Ponty's political and moral dilemma amounted to an inability to be either a communist or an anti-communist (HT xvii). He could not be a communist because the (distorted) practice of Marxism in the Soviet Union led, not to greater freedom and dignity for the proletariat, but rather to the institutionalization of violence. On the other hand, he could not be an anti-communist because Western liberal democracies were no better. They were, in fact, worse because their violence was fundamentally dishonest. That is, hidden behind the grand slogans of constitutions and legal codes lay in reality an agressive warfare: "Respect for law or liberty has served to justify police repression of strikes in America; it serves today even to justify military repression in Indo-China or in Palestine and the development of the American empire in the Middle East. The moral and material civilization of England rests on the exploitation of colonies. The purity of principles not only tolerates, but actually requires, violence. There is thus a liberal mystification" (HT 9; see also SNS 339-40). Marx was thus correct to want to know, not "what liberals have in their heads, but what the liberal State does in reality" (HT 10). The Marxist distinction is thus upheld between (bourgeois, merely) "formal liberties," on the one hand and, on the other, "real freedom." Thus "a nominally liberal regime can be oppressive in reality" (HT 10) if it neglects the latter to the profit of the former.

As noted in the previous chapter (III.2), for Merleau-Ponty, all regimes are violent, and the only virtue of Soviet violence was its candor. The philosophical and political task of *Humanisme et terreur,* therefore, was "to recall Marxists to their humanist inspiration, [and] to remind democracies of their fundamental hypocrisy" (HT 196). To do this, Merleau-Ponty proposed what Albert Rabil, Jr., has called a "politics of mediation"[8] and which Merleau-Ponty himself was much later to term a "wait-and-see Marxism" (AD 307). That is, he proposed a "third way between the extremes of communism and anti-communism in the form of a three-point political platform. The first plank of this platform declared that all criticisms of the Soviet Union were valid only in context and specifically if placed in tandem with similar criticisms of liberal democracies. Whatever the eventual fate of Marxism or communism, the proletariat was not yet dead and the critique of capitalist exploitation that underlay Western democracies remained valid. Second, preventive war with the U.S.S.R. was ruled out. And third, Merleau-Ponty reminded his readers that France was not at war with the Soviet Union; the latter had committed no aggressive acts towards the former and, until she did, the real political choice was not between giving into her and going to war.

As Rabil also notes,[9] most of Merleau-Ponty's critics failed to understand the proposed "third way"; instead, and surely influenced by the political paranoia of the times, they interpreted it as a justification of Soviet communism. Indeed, Mereau-Ponty acknowledged as much in the "Epilogue" of *Les Aventures de la dialectique:* "Wait-and-see Marxism became communist action" (AD 308).

This misunderstanding was aggravated especially by Merleau-Ponty's analysis of the Moscow Trials of 1936-38, which is the second main legally relevant feature of *Humanisme et terreur.* Stalin initiated this series of "show trials" in 1936; Bukharin's trial, in which Merleau-Ponty was particularly interested, took place in 1938. In these trials, the accused—and mostly condemned and executed—consisted of every member of Lenin's original Politburo except for Trotsky and Stalin himself. In all the trials, as Kruks summarizes them, "the charges made were extremely vague and general: attempts to assassinate leaders, attempts to restore capitalism, spying for 'enemy' countries. In all the trials the main 'evidence' was the confessions of the accused themselves and the trials were so rapid (for example, Bukharin and twenty others were tried together within the space of eleven days) that there could clearly have been no serious attempt to verify the charges according to normal legal procedure."[10]

From the perspective of Western, "bourgeois" justice, the trials were incontrovertibly a farce from beginning to end, and to decide as the tribunals did that the accused' "crimes" were violations of "common law" was to straightforwardly institutionalize violence. And yet, Bukharin, for instance, confessed. Why? Merleau-Ponty considered that it was because, although from a Western point of view the trials comprised a complete travesty of justice, they could only make sense between revolutionaries who judge on the basis of a future to create rather than on a record of past facts—whatever might have been the subjective intentions of the accused. This is to say that Bukharin perceived his "objective guilt," that the objective results of his acts ran counter to the (supposed) interests of the revolution and the proletariat despite what he had intended. Bukharin is thus a tragic figure who could not be for himself what he was for others and he equally could not repudiate the objective reality of his actions (HT 71). It was thus a dilemma of an "unhappy consciousness" that only death could resolve.

Something of the same "predicament of political leaders who make wrong decisions"[11] was present also in the Laval-Pétain trials in France just after the war. It is possible that both men had the best of intentions, as Pétain argued at his trial. However, the objective results of their actions were not to save France, but rather to betray her. But does political responsibility equal, or at least entail, criminal responsibility as well? It does not seem so, Merleau-Ponty says, because the later rested solely on the contingent fact that the Allies won the war. As Rabil phrases it, "their criminal responsibility rested on an accident of history. And history does not guarantee the triumph of morality. Political responsibility transcends both a morality of intentions and the category of criminal responsibility as that is understood in Western jurisprudence."[12]

But despite the analogies between the collaborators' trials and those in Moscow, they are still distinguishable. Although the accused in both cases were judged from the perspective of history, Pétain and Laval are not the tragic figures that Bukharin *et al.* appear to be. For in the case of the collaborators, the subjective and the objective were taken into account and given their due weight. This is so because the collaborators made a deliberate choice to act in such a way as made the German victory more likely. As Kruks indicates correctly, "It is not simply the case that the collaborators made a mistake and misread history. For in the process they also *made* history (HT 39). There can be no such thing as neutral or objective judgments in history, for all judgments entail a position and carry a historical weight. . . . Where, however, the Moscow trials differ from those of the French collaborators is that in the latter case history had already shown the individuals concerned to have been wrong; while in the former, judgement was passed in the name of a still uncertain future."[13]

It cannot be maintained that Merleau-Ponty is overly clear either in his analysis of the Moscow trials or in making his readers comprehend that his principal aim in this part of the text was to understand those trials. That, I think, is one of the reasons that *Humanisme et terreur* is much more obscure than it need be, and certainly one might well wish that its author had worked out his understanding in advance and then published a judgmentally clearer version. But there is a more serious reason for persisting obscurities, and that is that the final import of the book remained a question mark even for the author himself. That is, on the one hand he condemned the Moscow trials because, just as a morality and politics of pure subjectivity—à la Alain, for instance—is to be rejected because we must take into account the consequences of our acts in addition to our intentions, so also a morality of pure objectivity will not do. As against what occurred in Moscow, intentions as well as consequences must count in assessing the morality of political actions. But on the other hand, although we might well expect Merleau-Ponty at this juncture to have unequivocally condemned the Soviet Union and/or denied any relevant difference between Marxism and communism, he draws neither conclusion. Worse still, from the point of view of the clarity of his intentions, he even maintained that, as noted in the previous chapter, regimes without "formal" liberties and which openly admit their violence might have more freedom than those which do have such liberties.

From all that appears, Merleau-Ponty held these positions, however tenuous they may have been, because he still clung to the Marxist conception of the proletariat as the bearer of a universal humanism. But the latter was very far from being manifested on the contemporary political scene and the more remote its chances became, the more a-historical became Merleau-Ponty's wait-and-see Marxism. His commitment became true only in ideas; more and more divorced from reality, it became an unseen ideology. As Rabil puts it, "The truth seems to be that Merleau-Ponty was following his own best insights in emphasizing the contingency of history and in making Marx conform to this view of things, but that in the manner in which he accepted the proletariat he was following Marx; however, this double affirmation of contingency and of the proletariat as a carrier of universal meaning involved an equivocation."[14]

It was also to become clear to Merleau-Ponty that his own "third way," the "politics of mediation" (Rabil), was doomed to being equally a-historical. It had no significant chance in the post-war atmosphere polarized by those who wanted to completely change the social order and those who wished a return to normal. Since it no longer seemed possible for the proletariat to gain any political ground anywhere, Merleau-Ponty's only remaining possibility was to see whether this contradiction between history and Marxist doctrine was not just a matter of Soviet communism, but rather endemic to Marx's theory itself. And that is what he undertook to do in *The Adventures of the Dialectic,* with the results which have already been partly described in the previous chapter.

What lay behind Merleau-Ponty's double hesitation to categorically reject the Soviet Union or to collapse the distinction between Marxism and communism? Certainly part of the answer consisted in his commitment to the moral values at the center of proletarian humanism, but more needs to be said about the political dimensions of this humanism in order to explain the shift from his rejection of liberalism in *Humanism and Terror* to his defense of the "new liberalism" in *The Adventures of the Dialectic.*

Merleau-Ponty's humanism, as Gary Brent Madison has argued convincingly, "was not the dogmatic, rationalist humanism of Marx or Sartre, a humanism which suppresses the absolute only so as to immediately put man in its place."[15] Rather, Merleau-Ponty's view is more like that of Protagoras or Pascal in which man is not an explanation of anything (E 71), but only the "indispensable reference point for all that exists for him."[16] And since, for Merleau-Ponty, humankind is not an explanatory principle, his humanism is fundamentally hostile to any substantive rationalism. It is based instead on a sensitivity to contingency, on the consequent "methodical refusal of explanations" which makes us "incomprehensible to ourselves" (S 306) and, finally, on a scepticism in the face of all doctrines and dogmas—be they Marxist or the grand slogans and ideas of Western democracies.

As Madison also points out, it is "by reason of his skepticism, his humanism, and his anti-rationalist conception of reason"[17] that Merleau-Ponty takes his place in the grand Counter-tradition of French philosophy, a Counter-tradition that includes Pascal and Montaigne, among others. This approach to humanism which one thus find in Merleau-Ponty "could be described in the following words of [Pierre] Charron [the 16th-century sceptic and disciple of Montaigne]: 'It is to maintain modesty and recognize in good faith the human condition full of ignorance, weakness, uncertainty.'"[18]

The link between Merleau-Ponty's being part of the Counter-tradition of French philosophy and his political shift from *Humanism and Terror* to *The Adventures of the Dialectic* consists in the implications of the Counter-tradition for a liberalism in politics. As Madison claims correctly, "A counter-traditionalist thinker can be recognized by the fact that, at one and the same time, he is a skeptic and a humanist, and, having grasped the structure of his thought, one can legitimately expect that—when he turns to politics—his position, if it is coherent with the rest of his thought, will be that of *liberalism.*"[19] This conception of liberalism is not that of Alain, of course, nor that of his historical antecedents. It is, rather, more in the sense that Hayek says that the liberal, as distinct from the conservative, admits his ignorance and how little he knows, and "is fundamentally a skeptic . . . it seems to require a certain degree of diffidence to let others seek their happiness in their own fashion and to adhere consistently to that tolerance which is an essential characteristic of liberalism."[20]

In this light, the key to understanding Merleau-Ponty's shift from *Humanism and Terror* to *The Adventures of the Dialectic* is to be found in his becoming more consistently sceptical and liberal.[21] This is to say that the scepticism and counter-traditionalist sense of humanism which produced the hesitations described above in the earlier work eventually yielded a much more searching, far-reaching critique in the later one, a critique aimed at Marxist foundations themselves. The particular significance of Merleau-Ponty's political change is, therefore, that "it is a development by which, to speak like Nietzsche, he becomes more himself—and more thoroughly counter-traditionalist."[22] Political critique, as we shall see momentarily, became auto-critique.

It is also worthwhile to consider Merleau-Ponty's eventual rejection of structuralism from this perspective of more consistent self-becoming. James M. Edie, for example, remarks that "It *is* intriguing that Merleau-Ponty's theoretical crisis over structural linguistics and his political "crisis" were more or less simultaneous, though, up to now, I see no intrinsic connection between them."[23] It is not clear to me exactly what "intrinsic" means here, but it is significant, as well as consistent, that the abandonments of structuralism and Marxism are closely linked in at least three ways. First, both are situated in the context of the philosophy of history and, within that context, both reject *explanations* of history. Second, both consist of rejections of claims about the nature of reality and of human existence within the framework of nature. And third, both the abandonment of structuralism and that of Marxism are characterized by a substitution of sceptical reaction for such reality claims.

§3. *Beyond Marxism: France, 1948-55*

Merleau-Ponty's decisive break with Marxism did differ, however, in at least one respect from that with structuralism. Namely, when the rupture finally did occur, it was largely due to an external catalyst, the outbreak of the Korean War. It was the decisive turning-point towards Merleau-Ponty's complete disillusionment with the Soviet Union. For, as regards the responsibility for starting the war, although in France the truth was far from clear at the time, Merleau-Ponty adopted the view that, even if Stalin had not commenced hostilities, he could have prevented them or else quickly stopped them. But neither occurred. Therefore, Merleau-Ponty, *qua* political editor of *Les Temps Modernes*—the post he resigned in quitting the journal for good in 1953—imposed an official, sceptical silence on the rest of the editorial staff, Sartre himself included.

The second step towards Merleau-Ponty's disillusionment took place in the face of incontrovertible evidence of the Soviet labor camps—the Gulag. By January 1950, three years after *Humanisme et terreur,* he no longer had any hesitancies about the institutionalization of violence in the Soviet Union or about its possibly having more concrete freedoms than a Western democratic society with only "formal" liberties (see "L'U.R.S.S. et les camps," reprinted in *Signes,* pp. 330-43).

In the aftermath of these sordid events, Merleau-Ponty was led to reflect in *Les Aventures de la dialectique* on the ultimate source of such appalling gaps between, on the one hand, the ideals of proletarian humanism and the putative, historical dialectic of their instantiation, and on the other hand, the stubborn and undeniable facts of recent history. I shall not attempt here anything like a complete summary of his arguments, for that would be neither possible—because of spatial constraints—nor necessary—due to the irrelevance of much of the text to the philosophy of law. Rather, I shall provide only a brief overview of the main features of his effectively counter-traditionalist critique in order to make more intelligible the strategy behind the "new liberalism" which emerges in the "Epilogue" of the text.[24]

Basically what Merleau-Ponty wants to establish is that the dialectic has disintegrated in two radically different ways: by being distorted into pure objectivity in the writings of the later Marx and by becoming pure subjectivity at the hands of Sartre. Merleau-Ponty's critique of the latter will not concern us here, although it has generated a substantial and even partly famous secondary literature,[25] because it has a negligible relevance to legal philosophy. By contrast, as we shall now see, the critique of Marx has a considerable legal significance.

Merleau-Ponty finds that the contradictions of Soviet communism do not constitute a mere lapse from Marxist theory, but rather have their very roots in it. Namely, it is Marx's later writings themselves, he tells us, in which we can find the view that the dialectic exists purely objectively—in things, the course of nature, outside the will of humanity—as an inexorable, impersonal direction which, as we saw above (II.5), Merleau-Ponty joins Weber in rejecting. Moreover, he attempts to establish this conclusion across an interrogation of two Marxist thinkers whose publications as well as their very lives reflected the incongruities of Marxist theory and contemporary history which bothered Merleau-Ponty. These thinkers were Leon Trotsky and Georg Lukács, who was a brilliant student of Weber himself. In both cases, Merleau-Ponty seeks to prove that the equivocations in their versions of Marxism can be traced back to Marx himself.

It was also on the basis of such a view of the dialectic, as having a purely objective reality, that Stalin proceeded with the Moscow trials, for he was effectively pitting his view of the objective course of history and of the dialectic against all other interpretations. Most probably, therefore, Stalin was one person whom Merleau-Ponty had in mind, though whilst speaking of Lenin, when he said that, in the presence of such dogmatic *hubris,* such men would "bring history by iron and fire to express its meaning" (AD 117).[26]

For Merleau-Ponty, on the other hand, the dialectic does not exist in things or nature as a whole, but only in human beings. It exists in and through their free, untrammelled expression of opinions as to how social and political goods can best be attained in a certain historical epoch. Dogmatism, by contrast, always tries to short-circuit this exchange of reasoned viewpoints by a direct appeal to some form of an Absolute—whether it be God, History, or Nature. But Merleau-Ponty's programme of bringing absolutes "down to earth" (see above, II.4), when finally applied consistently in politics, brought it about that, as

Madison observes, "he became a liberal thinker and fully joined up with the Counter-tradition. By his humanism, his skepticism, and his liberalism he makes us think of Protagoras who, at the beginning of the Counter-tradition, denounced the pretensions of the dogmatists so as to guarantee respect for others, and who believed that only the free exchange of opinions by means of rational and peaceful persuasion could make of a society both a just and free one. . . . to insure that the freedom and dignity of men be recognized and respected."[27]

Hence the *raison d'être* for the "new liberalism" with which Merleau-Ponty concludes *Les Aventures de la dialectique:* the dictatorship of the proletariat is rejected for precisely those traditional Western, "bourgeois" institutions, chiefly that of parliament, which were rejected so categoricaly in *Humanisme et terreur.* As noted in the previous chapter (III.3), the programme of the non-communist left relies on democratic, parliamentary action because, as he says, "Parliament is the only known institution that guarantees a minimum of opposition and truth" (AD 304). The key word here is *institution:* it is the institution of parliament which provides the best chance to recognize human freedom and hence to concretize humanistic values (which are no longer based on the supposition of a proletariat). Or, as Merleau-Ponty puts it, it is "the resolution to keep in hand the two ends of the chain, the social problem and liberty" (AD 305). And certainly, as Madison observes, "by liberty Merleau-Ponty understands here liberty in the liberal sense of the word, those 'formal' liberties denounced by the Marxists as 'bourgeois.'"[28]

The programme of the new liberalism, unlike that of its obsolete predecessors—that of Alain, for example—is not an optimistic, superficial philosophy that reduces social history to "speculative con-flicts of opinion, political struggle to exchanges of viewpoint on a clearly posed problem, and human co-existence to the relations of co-citizens in an empyrean politics" (AD 303). On the contrary, class struggle exists and must exist because there are classes in society, and workers have a legal (and moral) right to strike. The working class has the "right to have itself represented, if it wishes, by a party that refuses the rules of the democratic game, because this game disfavors it. The Communist Party is and must be legal" (AD 303).

The legality of the Communist Party is not desired because the new liberalism after all wants secretly to bring about the revolution—that is, because the non-communist left is hypocritical or deceitful—but rather because "Communist action and revolutionary movements are only accepted as a useful danger, as a continual reminder of order. . . . A non-communist left is for us this double part taken of posing the social problem in terms of struggle and of refusing the dictatorship of the proletariat" (AD 303-04).

Nonetheless, struggle can only be for power, and one might well argue, Merleau-Ponty tells us, that the non-communist left is either condemned to exercising power in a "parliamentary and bourgeois sense"— that is, not at all—or else whatever power accrues to the new liberalism will be its onw only provisionally, as a "transition to dictatorship." In that case, the non-communist left would be "crypto-communist" after all (AD 304).

Merleau-Ponty's reply to this argument, in the context of his defense of the formal liberties embodied in parliamentary democracy, runs as follows. First, there is a great difference between the political action of the members of a non-communist left and that of communists because the former, unlike the latter, enjoy a "liberty of criticism" sufficient for adequately posing "the problem of the nature of the Soviet State" (AD 304). Clarifying the social problem "appears impossible in principle in a communist regime but possible in the non-communist world" (AD 306).[29]

Second, as to "the limits of parliamentary and democratic action" (AD 304), Merleau-Ponty candidly admits that the new liberalism is no "solution" to the social problem in the sense of a "crossword puzzle or an elementary problem of arithmetic" (AD 305). No Counter-traditionalist philosopher would make such a claim. Rather, as to the limits of parliamentary action, he first admits that there are some inherent in the institution, and these have to be accepted because, as cited above, "Parliament is the only known institution that guarantees a minimum of opposition and truth" (AD 304). But there are other limitations which consist of certain political "customs and manoeuvres that can be denounced in Parliament itself. Parliamentary mystification consists in not posing true problems or in posing them obliquely or too late. A non-communist left could do much against it" (AD 304).

Merleau-Ponty also tells us that, again reflecting his scepticism and humanism in protesting against dogmatic "solutions," the "only postulate of this attitude is that political liberty not be only or necessarily a defense of capitalism. . . . [There can be a dialectic] only if capitalism has ceased to be a rigid apparatus, with *its* politics, *its* ideologies, *its* imperious laws of functioning and if, instead of its contradictions, another politics than *its* could come to be. A non-communist left is no more tied to free enterprise than to the dictatorship of the proletariat" (AD 305).

Merleau-Ponty reached the conclusions embodied in this political programme through a convergence of many different perspectives, chief among which were the failure of the dialectic as well as a continued reading of concrete history. In continuing to think historically, rather than in the abstract, he considered finally that it was no accident that Marxist revolutions took place only in backward countries—since they were precisely what was needed to sustain the growth of underdeveloped nations—and, correlatively, there being no hope of that sort of revolution in industrial, developed nations, the task of the humanist in such countries was to work within the existing system. It follows, therefore, as Rabil points out, that "there is no reason why a revolutionary in our time should mean one who believes in overturning all existing institutions. In fact, some type of parliamentary framework is necessary inasmuch as we cannot afford to sacrifice *freedom* any more than we can afford to sacrifice order. . . . the question now is not so much one of the mode of appropriation, as it was for Marx, but rather one of social control. We have learned that the dynamics of a society are more decisive than its form."[30] Rabil is correct, in my view, in his summary of Merleau-Ponty's conclusions, but he could have made a much stronger claim: for the Merleau-Ponty of *Les Aventures de la dialectique* and afterwards, freedom is not one thing and order another. Rather, freedom is now understood only as an ordered liberty—in the traditional Tocquevillian sense.

This is not to say that order, institutions, and formal rules constitute a sufficient condition of freedom. We have seen already in Chapter II why that is not so. And in the present context it is perhaps not irrelevant to remember that morgues and cemeteries, like Gulags, are forms of social order. Rather, Merleau-Ponty's claim is that the order incarnated in institutions constitutes a necessary condition of freedom such that the political problem—also a moral and legal one—is "to find institutions which implant in customs this practice of liberty" (S 434). At the same time, we need, as the final sentence of *Les Aventures de la dialectique* urges us, to inspire people "to bear their liberty, to not exchange it cheaply, because it is not only their thing, their secret, their pleasure, and their salvation; it also interests everybody else" (AD 313).

Sonia Kruks remarks about Merleau-Ponty's defense of liberal institutions, chiefly parliament, that "we are back, it seems, on the territory of J.S. Mill and classical liberalism where truth emerges only through the free confrontation of ideas and all opposition is therefore tolerated—as only as it only speaks but does not act. The 'class struggle' is reduced to healthy intellectual opposition, always to be maintained within the *status quo*."[31] She considers that this is the case for two very different reasons. The first of these consists of an interpretation placed on Merleau-Ponty's statement, part of which has already been cited, that according to the new liberalism, workers have the right to strike and the Communist Party ought to be legal, but that "If one speaks of liberalism, it is in this sense that communist action and revolutionary movements are only accepted as a useful danger, *as a continual reminder of order,*[32] that one does not believe in the solution of the social problem by the power of the proletarian class or its representatives. . . . " (AD 303). Kruks interprets this as meaning that the right to strike as well as the right of the Communist Party to legal representation "are to be recognized *only* if they do not threaten to overthrow the liberal order. The role of proletarian politics is to provide a limited opposition *within* the established order, against which liberalism must be able to justify its ideas."[33]

It is certainly an odd construction of Mill's view to think that it tolerates all opposition "as long as it only speaks but does act," unless by action is meant what is inconsistent with the institution of parliamentary democracy itself. But then it would no longer be a question of a proletarian politics so much as an anti-politics—not a position that is funded by, and contributes to, democratic decision making, but rather one that wishes to destroy it. And not only wishes to, for we are not being asked here to consider the thorny problem of tolerating the speech of the intolerant and, therefore, undemocratic members of society, but rather—in some unspecified sense—their political *action*. And if that is Kruks' meaning, then she is correct that both Mill and Merleau-Ponty would be opposed, or at least claim the right to keep such action on a short leash, exactly for the reasons they give and to which she does not speak. And by not speaking to them, her only objection to their position is effectively that they held it. Furthermore, it is unclear in her conclusion whether she means "status quo" to refer to the structure of parliamentary democracy itself or the particular economic and political values of a certain society. I shall come back to this ambiguity, as well as Mill's views, in considering the second reason Kruks gives for her assessment of the new liberalism.

Before doing so, however, there is a more important issue to raise about her first reason. Namely, is Kruks correct in her interpretation of Merleau-Ponty's text, that is, that the right to strike and that of the Communist Party to legal representation are contingent on their not threatening "to overthrow the liberal order?" Certainly the language of the passage cited is not very clear: "communist action and revolutionary movements are only accepted as a useful danger, as a continual reminder of order" ("l'action communiste, les mouvements révolutionnaires ne sont admis que comme utile menace, comme continuel rappel à l'ordre"). Not only is the force of "admis" left unclarified, but Merleau-Ponty also does not specify what the new liberalism would do in the face of a real threat to "overthrow the liberal order." But even so, there is a more important ambiguity in the text which Kruks does not address, and that is whether the threat would originate at the interior of the democratic process itself or from outside it. That is, everything turns on whether "threat" (Merleau-Ponty's "useful danger") refers to the anti-democratic menace mentioned above, proletarian anti-politics, in which the danger might be useful up to a point but is always underlain with a destructive intent—or whether the danger would arise democratically because of electoral popularity, consequent parliamentary success in passing communist legislation, constitutional changes, and so forth. The latter is a more interesting philosophical problem than the former—concerning, as it does, the meaning of democracy and the limits of toleration—and will be taken up again Part Two below (at VII.2). For despite Merleau-Ponty's hopeful language about "useful" dangers, if he is in fact thinking of those within the parliamentary process itself, there is no democratic way to keep opposition limited or (merely) "useful." And if the parliamentary process itself would lead even to its own (legally enacted) demise, then it appears that he would lament and object to it, but have no grounds to contest it.

For, retracing a theme from the previous chapter about the acceptability of violence under the new liberalism in the face of a sustained lack of parliamentary success, Merleau-Ponty can hardly be committed to the institution of parliament only when it is convenient to be so. A "Parlement de convenance"—not unknown as a favorite tool and shield of dictators—like a "marriage de convenance," is not usually thought of as attracting enduring commitments. (It is true, though, that both arrangements sometimes do bring together interesting and surprising bedfellows.) Thus the logic of the new liberalism itself, whatever Merleau-Ponty's unclear intentions, leads to denying Kruks' claims, provided that the "threat" of which she speaks is democratic in origin. And if it is not, as we have seen, her claim is true, but trivially so.

Kruks' second reason for believing that, in the new liberalism, "The 'class struggle' is reduced to healthy intellectual opposition, always to be maintained within the *status quo*", is that she sees Merleau-Ponty as now claiming that capitalism has changed to a more humane system. In support of this view, she cites the statement quoted above, namely, that the dialectic would continue "only if capitalism has ceased to be a rigid apparatus, with *its* policies, *its* ideologies . . . and if another politics than *its* could come to be" (AD 305). To this belief Kruks responds that "The discovery that capitalism is no longer what Merleau-Ponty thought it was is a kind of *deus ex machina* suddenly introduced at the end of the book to further justify the rejection of Marxism, and Merleau-Ponty produces no justifications for this change of opinion."[34]

In my view, Kruks is mistakenly certain that Merleau-Ponty has changed his mind here about capitalism, and hence is also wrong about what she deduces from that mistake. I read the text rather differently in that I not only take seriously his twice-repeated "if," but also the statement following the passage cited by Kruks, namely, "A non-communist left is no more tied to free enterprise than to the dictatorship of the proletariat" (AD 305). The significance of the word "if" is to signal that the claim being made here is a logically consistent extension of Merleau-Ponty's counter-traditionalist scepticism. A hypothetical condition is posited, not a dogmatic assurance that it has been satisfied. This is why, among other things, the new liberalism is the fulfillment, rather than the abandonment, of Merleau-Ponty's scepticism and humanism, and why it is expressly denied to be a definitive solution.

The rest of Kruks' argument seems to me just as weak. It is certainly true that Merleau-Ponty ends up sharing Mill's view that "truth emerges only through the free confrontation of ideas and that opposition is therefore tolerated." Such toleration and the rejection of dogmatic *hubris* are, as we have already seen, characteristic of the sceptical humanism of the Counter-tradition. But the rest of her picture of both Mill and Merleau-Ponty is either false or extremely misleading. For one thing, portraying the new liberalism as mere words which have no practical effect takes no account of the fact that this is the very sort of optimistic and superficial philosophy mentioned above from which Merleau-Ponty expressly wished to distinguish his own view. Kruks fails entirely to consider the latter's arguments to this effect, as they were recounted above. For another thing, there is no reason to believe that Merleau-Ponty thought of the new liberalism as "healthy intellectual opposition, always to be maintained within the *status quo,*" unless by "status quo" she means the continued existence of parliamentary democracy. And in that case, as already shown above, the claim would be true, but trivially so. If, on the other hand, as one suspects from the context of the statement, the expression means (broadly) the existing capitalist economic and political context, then Kruks is wrong, as noted above, as to Merleau-Ponty's intentions. And there is no reason to suppose a parliamentary democracy *must* be tied to capitalism; non-capitalist parliamentary democracies are hardly self-contradictions.

Similarly, there is no reason why we must construe parliament as a theatre of words and intellectual jousts having no real connection with the praxis of daily life. Such a view misses completely the significance of formal institutions for the establishment and maintenance of freedom, and it is this failure above all, it seems to me, which constitutes the source of Kruks' misunderstanding of Merleau-Ponty's defense of the non-communist left.[35]

Furthermore, as regards formal institutions, Merleau-Ponty's ostensive definition of the moral attitude as respect for independence (III.2), and Mill's views, it is worthwhile to remember that, as Ronald Dworkin has pointed out, there are two different concepts of liberty which it is easy, but fatal to clear thinking, to confuse. There is the "idea of license, that is, the degree to which a person is free from social or legal constraint to do what he might wish to do, and liberty as independence, that is, the status of a person as independent and equal rather than subservient. . . . Liberty as license is an indiscriminate concept, because it does not distinguish between forms of behavior. . . . But liberty as independence is not an indiscriminate concept in that way."[36] Rather, liberty as independence is tightly bound up with human dignity and what it means to be a person.

Part of the practical significance of this distinction is that, as Dworkin goes on to point out, "Conservatives confuse these ideas when they use 'permissiveness' to describe both sexual independence and political violence and to suggest that these differ only in degree. Radicals confuse these ideas when they identify liberalism with capitalism, and therefore suppose that individual rights are responsible for social injustice. Mill's collected works are not the source of that confusion, but its antidote."[37] It seems to me that in the way in which Kruks analyses Merleau-Ponty's new liberalism, she comes perilously close to the latter sort of confusion, if she does not actually fall into it.

Such are, in brief outline, the most legally relevant features of the major steps along Merleau-Ponty's own dramatic and turbulent political itinerary. After *Les Aventures de la dialectique,* one does not find any essential changes in his political position except the rising and falling of his hopes for the actualization of the new liberalism. His hopes for the regime of Pierre Mendès-France—whose administration lasted from June 1954 to February 1955, and from January to May of 1956— were dashed when the latter lost power over the Algerian question. Hence Merleau-Ponty's articles in *L'Express,* written in support of the former's program of economic and political reforms, stopped after 1955. And in parts of the "Préface" to *Signes,* one of the last statements he was to make on politics, he oscillated considerably between political despair and hope. On the one side he wrote that "All that one believed thought and well thought—liberty and powers, citizen against powers, the heroism of the citizen, liberal humanism—formal democracy and real democracy, which suppresses and brings about the former, heroism and revolutionary humanism—all that is in ruins" (S 31). But then he also made it clear that the ruins are not conceptual, but rather the historical (im)possibilities up to the time of *Signes* of bringing the new liberalism into being. For his prognosis of the future was not at all as dour: "But watch out. What we call disorder and ruin, others, younger than we, live as natural and perhaps are going to dominate exactly because they do not seek their reference-points where we find them. . . . We are deafened by French events or by the noisy episodes of diplomacy. But underneath the noise, a silence has come about, an expectation. Why could this not be a hope" (S 32)?

On balance, I think, the pendulum finally swings toward hope, in a sense more fully explained in the following section, because the "Préface" of *Signes* ends in the following manner: "The conclusion is not revolt, it is *virtu* without any resignation. . . . There circulates more truth than there was twenty years ago in world capitalism and in world communism and between them. History never confesses, not even its lost illusions, but it does not begin them again" (S 47).

§4. *The Structure of Politics*

At the end of this political itinerary, what can we conclude about Merleau-Ponty's view of the nature of politics itself? That is, if he had written a phenomenology of politics, how would he have described its modes of appearing and what would he have taken to be its essence? Bernard Dauenhauer has argued convincingly that the results of such an enterprise would consist in showing that, just as Merleau-Ponty directs us to think of history according to the model of language—as analysed by de Saussure—so, too, the latter would have us think politics according to the same pattern of structural linguistics.[38] In my opinion, Dauenhauer is entirely correct in this claim, subject only to the limitations of Merleau-Ponty's eventual abandonment of structuralism as detailed above (I.3). In illustrating Dauenhauer's claim, we shall also see that Merleau-Ponty's consideration of the nature of politics ties together many disparate threads of thought traced out in the previous chapters. Thus we shall see how, for Merleau-Ponty, his view of politics is at one stroke exemplary of the deep structure of his more general counter-traditionalist sceptical humanism and illuminative of it.

Dauenhauer's point of departure is not, as one might expect, the discussion of de Saussure and the philosophy of history in the *Éloge de la philosophie* or in *La conscience et l'acquisition du langage,* but rather a much later text which tells us that "We are in the field of history as in the field of language or of being" (S 28). This is to say that we are born into these fields which evidence three important common properties: they are neither completely chaotic nor totally determinate, they manifest previously sedimented structures, and they give us the necessary resources to freely create our own sedimented meanings.

The fact that Merleau-Ponty wants us think politics according to the same pattern "is indicated by the regularity with which his remarks on politics are connected with a discussion of history."[39] Politics is in fact a "special case of history" and of language[40] to the degree that they are all created by situated agents, and whereas thought works on human beings directly and industrial production on material things directly, politics works directly on the intertwining of the two at some historically and geographically precise location. "There is no universal clock," says Merleau-Ponty, "but only local histories" (S 47). And in each of the localities, the object of politics is praxis (see I.2), or at least other forms of praxis, for politics is itself a set of living intersubjective relationships in the life-world.

The central features of this concrete structure of politics and praxis strongly resemble the main elements of Saussurian linguistics: the relations between speech (*la parole*) and language (*la langue*), the distinction between the synchronic and the diachronic, and the inherently intersubjective nature of all language. Considering in turn the political counterparts of each of these distinctions, we can observe first that, just as language comprises the constituted meanings (use values) and syntactical rules on the basis of which any speech comes to be, so, too, the constituted political language of any given historical epoch makes possible new political speech. Any political speech out of *all* relationship with the existing political vocabulary would be literally impractical, cut off from praxis, and would fail to connect with the world like, to use one of Merleau-Ponty's favorite similes, gears engaging one another.

But although language both supplies and limits speech, the former is taken up by the latter in such a way that, as we have already seen (I.3), it can be transcended in creative expression. The past (state of language) does not shackle the present (speech act) into conformity with it, and this is also true in politics in which the analogue of creative expression is *initiative.* Political language and political initiative belong to each other because, as Dauenhauer points out, they form one concrete unity, and each has to be thought in reference to the other. As in creative linguistic expression, so also in politics, there can be a "'coherent deformation' (A. Malraux) of available meanings which orders them into a new sense and makes listeners, *but also the speaking subject,* take a decisive *step*" (S 114-15).

Such was, surely, the way Merleau-Ponty conceived the new liberalism and Mendès-France's program of political and economic reforms. Just as a living language is the concrete, indivisible intertwining of speech and language, so also living politics consists of political initiative and the existing political situation. As Dauenhauer remarks, "Precisely what Merleau-Ponty praises in Machiavelli is the latter's recognition that we need never be mere victims of *fortuna,* of some given political situation. Political action consists in a grasp of the concrete possibilities that the situation presents, coupled with a bold effort to actualize them. Thus genuine politics requires not merely the acknowledgement of the weight of the determinate political situation, the language in which one finds oneself located, but also the risky endeavor to transform that situation, to revivify it by the exercise of *virtù,* the uttering of the new speech."[41]

As Dauenhauer also observes, nothing guarantees in advance that the new political initiative will succeed—any more than it did for Mendès-France—just as one cannot know in advance whether a new genre of linguistic (or artistic) creativity will be successful or appropriate for the particular historical epoch in which it originates. As against the later Marx and subsequent Marxists, as already noted (II.5), there is no privileged objective reading of a logic of history because there is no such logic. There is instead a stubborn and unavoidable contingency in politics as in all other sectors of human history.

Additional consequences of thinking politics according to the Saussurian terms of *la langue* and *la parole* become clear when we situate the above discussion within the latter's distinction between the synchronic and diachronic aspects of language. As already explained (II.5), in the synchronic perspective on language, the perspective of a living language, speakers take up, use, modify to their own purposes, and bequeath to their successors, a given linguistic *system:* "Saussure has shown well that each act of expression only becomes signifying as a modulation of a general system of expression" (S 101). The system has a Gestalt quality about it such that each of its elements is internally related to every other element. No element of the system can preserve its meaning when removed from the system.

In a given synchronic perspective on politics, similar results obtain: "Every element of the political situation is simply a component of the whole. None is self-sustaining with an independent positive meaning. Any responsible political initiative, like any speech, must acknowledge the irreducible complexity of the context against which it arises."[42] Thus, for example, as we saw earlier in this chapter, *Humanism and Terror* argued that all criticisms of communism should be balanced by equally fair criticisms of capitalism. This was not, to be sure, in the spirit of anything like "fair play"—Merleau-Ponty was, as a matter of fact, suspicious of that particular slogan and counselled the necessity of seeing what was hidden beneath it (S 398)—but more importantly because the meaning of each was conditioned by the other. In the usual political condition, there are neither unmixed blessings—in short, salvation—nor absolute evils. And it cannot be supposed correctly that the "new liberal" legislator would be any less sensitive to these demands of fair criticism within parliamentary debates. If anything, for the dialectic in pursuit of social justice to continue successfully in such a format, the new liberal's consciousness of such nuances must be especially heightened. I shall return to this below.

The diachronic perspective on politics, as on language, reminds us that all meanings are subject to change and of the consequent loss of their reference points on the social compass. Were this not so, political initiatives could not come to be at all, but this fact demands the conclusion that "political initiative not attempt either to reverse history or to annihilate the effective weight of anything brought by history to the present situation. Such attempts would be to plan for an imagined world that can no longer exist."[43] This does not mean that a given political initiative, once having failed, must be continued just because it is past. Once again, a proper appreciation of contingency leads to the double conclusions of history teaching negatively—it shows us what will not work and it "never confesses"—and that our attitude should be one of "*virtu* without any resignation" (S 47).

Dauenhauer also notes two other important aspects of political life which are revealed by thinking it synchronically and diachronically. The first of these is that all successful political iniative has to be timely: "Though there is no ideal or perfect moment for imitating some specific action, there are timely and untimely ones. What once could have been a solution to a problem ceases to be one. Or a problem which once had a likely solution no longer does but may in the future again do so."[44]

The second consequence of stressing the synchronic and diachronic aspects of politics is even more important. It is that, as we have seen above at several junctures, it leads to a view of institutions as neither pure objects—inert and cut off from consciousness—nor subjective creations—the expression of public will merely. Rather, an institution is a mélange of objective and subjective aspects. Like a perceptual object, it possesses the paradoxical status of being an "in-itself-for-us." This is true of all living institutions, not only those that are linguistic and political, but also, as we shall see in Part Two (V.2), it is equally the case for legal institutions. Thus Dauenhauer aptly points out that Merleau-Ponty agrees with Marx "that there is a coming-to-be of meaning in institutions. Sartre notwithstanding, institutions, as social apparatuses, are human and cannot be set over against man as something less than human. Rather, institutions endow our experiences with durable dimensions and allow them to form a history. At the same time, they invite us to further experience and thus make possible a future."[45] It thus also follows that, so far from construing institutions as inhibitive or destructive of human liberty and creative political initiative, Merleau-Ponty maintained just the opposite position, Dauenhauer continues, in regard to his programme of parliamentary democracy.[46]

The third key feature of Saussurian linguistics, the intersubjective character of all language, also has its political counterpart. In the interworld of politics, leaders and the rest of the citizenry belong to each other; on Merleau-Ponty's view, no one either completely obeys or totally commands (S 104). Instead, the concrete relationships between political initiatives and institutions come into being in and through a dialectic in principle open to all members of society. Hence the necessity, as we saw above, of tolerance in the face of dogmatic rashness. In line with Merleau-Ponty's counter-traditional scepticism and humanism, a successful political dialectic thus demands opposition and freedom of expression *within* the formal structures of parliamentary democracy.

But to say that the dialectic must remain open conceals a crucial ambiguity. On the one hand, it has the meaning just attributed to it, namely, that no particular person, group of people, or political party rightly may be barred from full participation. (This is to ignore, for the time being, the ambiguity about the Communist Party outlined above, that is, what the new liberalism would argue if the former's danger to the system were no longer "useful" because of its electoral and parliamentary success.) But there is another meaning of the openness of the dialectic which is just as important, and that is that without vigorous participation on the part of the electorate, the very institutions of parliamentary democracy which are taken up, affirmed, and modified by politial speech, will decay. Just as "dead languages" are those which no longer enjoy continued reanimation through creative speech, so, too, political institutions can lose their life in the absence of creative political speech. This is why, among other things, Merleau-Ponty argued against abstention (S 397-401).[47] It is no solution because it merely hands the political initiative to other people. Hence, as Dauenhauer correctly notes, "Unless people risk the revitalizing 'speech' of political initiative, the institutions from which they have drawn their sustenance will either ossify or grant their opportunities to others, others who will be left without the benefit of appropriate opposition."[48]

The last feature of political life which is illuminated by thinking politics according to the Saussurian model of language is the nature of political decision making. As we have seen above (I.3), creative speech can never be merely deduced from the existing synchronic state of language and, in a similar way, as noted earlier in the present chapter, political judgment is not a deduction from pre-existing rules—particularly moral rules. Political judgment, for Merleau-Ponty, will always be different from, to use his own examples, deducing the requirements of the categorical imperative or from the allied reasoning which Alain urged. Political judgment is also, as *Les Aventures de la dialectique* points out, different from scientific judgment—at least in pure science—because the former, unlike the latter, is essentially creative. Political judgments "are neither mere predictions nor mere retrodictions. They are inventive. They issue in actions that modify the prevailing state of affairs."[49]

If political judgments are not reducible to moral judgments in the Kantian sense, this does not mean that, on Merleau-Ponty's view, they have no relation to morality. Structurally, the process of making political decisions resembles that defended in the last section of the previous chapter for a revise, "aesthetic" view of moral decision making. Second, moral values of the sort analysed in the previous chapter provide the regulative ideals at which to aim in politics as well as in morality itself. And third, such values provide what Merleau-Ponty considered that Machiavelli did not possess, namely, in Dauenhauer's words, "a guideline to distinguish between political *virtù,* the excellence in acquiring and wielding power to make the most of the opportunities provided by *fortuna,* and political opportunism, the make-shift accomodation to prevailing pressures aimed merely at survival."[50] Dauenhauer speculates—and, I think, correctly—that "This guideline consists in making the preservation and extension of the dialectic the overarching objective of all political initiatives."[51] Such a conclusion is certainly warranted by the counter-traditional scepticism, humanism, and political liberalism which Merleau-Ponty would bring to such a conclusion.

Now despite the avowedly serious difficulties of respecting such a guideline in practice, Dauenhauer rejoins the theme of hope which emerged above in terms of Merleau-Ponty's last published writings on politics. The latter's conception of politics is construed to be one of hope in the way that it contrasts with many other attitudes abundantly evident in recent history as well as the present—fideism and voluntarism, fanaticism and cynicism, dogmatism, and presumption and despair. It is also important to recognize in this sort of hope not the contradictory, or even the contrary, of scepticism. For it is not a cheapened sort of hope based on the immediate gratification of desires or on the suppression of opposition—attitudes which today certainly apply in more than one way to contemporary variants of capitalism and communism respectively. Nor is it an attitude based on objective calculations of probable success. It is, rather, the prolongation of a commitment announced long ago that "men have immense resources" (SNS 208). Thus, as Dauenhauer says in another essay, "Hope is a double-rayed act (1) whose object is both complex and never fully determinate, but whose complexity is ordered with priority given to the person or persons in whose efficacy one hopes over the state of affairs for which one hopes, and (2) which is inseparable from the conviction that the future is open to efficacious activity in which he who hopes, by the very fact of hoping, either does or can participate. . . . Hope, then, is essentially an act of a self-acknowledged finite agent acknowledging his intersubjective, historical involvement with some other agent or agents in a world and comporting himself with courage and confidence toward the future taken as open."[52]

Hope is thus a commitment to a certain kind of programme in the belief that there is no credible alternative, but always on condition of reserving judgment and adjusting one's course. In a historical epoch in which the threat of nuclear destruction is always on the agenda—the threat that history will eliminate the irrational by finally eliminating itself—and an epoch of so many disappointments and discredited political ideologies—ideas that, as e.e. cummings once said in a different context, "like Gillette Razor Blades having been used and reused to the mystical moment of dullness emphatically are Not to Be Resharpened"[53]—Merleau-Ponty's politics of hope has much to recommend it. His view of politics also has, more immediately, a decisive importance for understanding the phenomenon of law, to which we now turn.

NOTES

1. Even Merleau-Ponty's most sympathetic critics, some of whom are cited below, generally agree that, in *Humanisme et terreur,* he was blind to his own ideological commitment to the proletariat as the bearer of a universal humanism. It was precisely this ideology which, as we shall see below, he was to admit in *Les Aventures de la dialectique* and in *Signes* (see especially the "Préface").
2. For a listing of some of these articles, see below under Works Consulted.
3. See particularly Barry Cooper, *Merleau-Ponty and Marxism: from terror to reform* (Toronto: University of Toronto Press, 1979); Sonia Kruks, *The Political Philosophy of Merleau-Ponty* (Sussex: The Harvester Press, 1981; published simultaneously by the Humanities Press, Inc. [Atlantic Highlands, N.J.]); Garry Brent Madison, *The Phenomenology of Merleau-Ponty* (Athens, Ohio: Ohio University Press, 1981); and Albert Rabil, Jr., *Merleau-Ponty: Existentialist of the Social World* (New York and London: Columbia University Press, 1967).
4. A singular exception, to which I shall return in §4 below, is Bernard F. Dauenhauer's insightful essay, "Merleau-Ponty's Political Thought: Its Nature and Its Challenge," in *Phenomenology in a Pluralistic Context,* eds. William L. McBride and Calvin O. Schrag (Albany: State University of New York Press, 1984), pp. 14-25.
5. Kruks, p. 23, n.1.
6. Kruks, pp. 67-68.
7. Kruks, p. 68.
8. Rabil, p. 94.
9. Rabil, p. 95.
10. Kruks, p. 41, n.2.
11. Rabil, p. 99. "Pierre Laval (1883-1945), headed the 'Vichy' government, in the Southern part of France, in 1942. He was tried and executed for collaboration in 1945. Philippe Pétain (1856-1951), was France's foremost military hero from World War One. However, he agreed to

become 'Head of State' during the German occupation, from 1940-1944. He was also condemned to death in 1945, but his sentence was reduced to life imprisonment."—Kruks, p. 97, n.2.

12. Rabil, p. 99.
13. Kruks, p. 89.
14. Rabil, pp. 101-02.
15. Madison, p. 304. See also above at I.3 and I n.22 which concern Merleau-Ponty's rejection of "dogmatic" rationalism for one that is "methodological."
16. Madison, p. 304.
17. Madison, p. 305.
18. Madison, p. 305.
19. Madison, p. 307.
20. F. Hayek, "Why I Am Not a Conservative," in *The Constitution of Liberty* (South Bend, Ind.: Gateway Editions, 1972), p. 416. Cited in Madison at p. 339, n.32. Compare Merleau-Ponty's ostensive definition of the moral attitude cited above (at III.2), which concerns the rights of third-world countries to self-determination as against European colonization (S 409).
21. As Madison quite rightly observes, "This is to say that humanism, skepticism, and liberalism are part of the same structure of thought; indeed, no genuine liberalism can exist without skepticism" (p. 339, n.32). Merleau-Ponty's commitment to liberalism is thus an extension of sceptical method. Alain's liberalism, by contrast, consisted of a dogma of extreme individualism.
22. Madison, p. 307. This is part of the answer to Kruks who (at pp. 103-04) can find no connecting thread between *Humanism and Terror* and *The Adventures of the Dialectic,* and argues that the latter "as a whole remains incoherent and unsatisfactory, a weak case for the abandonment of Marxism and a still weaker one for the advocacy of liberalism as the alternative" (p. 104). The present section deals with the first half of her critique; the latter half will be considered below in terms of the signficance of institutions for human freedom.

    Kruks also argues (pp. 72-75) that, in *Humanism and Terror,* Merleau-Ponty's critique of liberalism was unfairly a-historical in that the latter did not consider many historical variants of Western liberalism, some of which professed and sought to actualize the very values he would have done. It is true that Merleau-Ponty did not canvas the history of Western liberalism(s) very carefully in his writings. But Kruks' argument strikes me as an ironic example itself of thinking a-historically. For, as *Humanism and Terror* is composed of articles that originally appeared in *Les Temps Modernes,* plus certain additions, and since, as Kruks herself points out, for Merleau-Ponty's generation in France "liberalism *was* Alain," it hardly should be surprising that Alain's thought is tacitly assumed by both author and readers as the definitive example of liberalism under critical discussion. It would have been very odd if Merleau-Ponty had confined his attention to the Reform Act of 1832 or the principles of Jeffersonian democracy (though he certainly would not have missed the significance of the latter owning slaves).
23. "Merleau-Ponty: The Triumph of Dialectics Over Structuralism," *Man and World* 17: 299-312 (1984), cited in J.N. Mohanty, ed. *Phenomenology and the Human Sciences* (Dordrecht: Martinus Nijhoff Publishers, 1985), p. 72, n.16.
24. Readers interested in the finer details of the buried substructures of Merleau-Ponty's critique of Marxism, instead of just the more visible outcroppings sketched here, should consider especially the relevant parts of Cooper and Kruks' works. In the latter, see particularly pp. 101-33, Part 3 of her book, which is entitled "Retreat." For the reasons given above in the

previous note as well as in the text to which the note refers, I cannot consider this a happy title.

25. I have in mind principally Simone de Beauvoir's famous reply, "Merleau-Ponty et le pseudo-sartrisme," which appeared in *Les Temps Modernes,* Nos. 114-15, May 1955. Rabil (at pp. 130-33) has an interesting commentary on this article that deserves careful consideration. In part of his remarks, he sets off against de Beauvoir's sharp criticisms of Merleau-Ponty in the above article an earlier, very favorable review of the *Phénoménologie de la perception* which she had written for *Les Temps Modernes,* in Volume I, November 1945. As Rabil points out, in 1945 de Beauvoir believed that both Sartre and Merleau-Ponty had the same intentions, and that the latter provided a "necessary complement" to the former's "strong contrasts" between being and freedom, the in-itself and the for-itself, and so on. But by 1955, her conclusion about Merleau-Ponty's divergence from Sartre was that he (Merleau-Ponty) really did not agree with Sartre in 1945 either. However, as Rabil points out, "the truth of the matter seems to be that Mlle de Beauvoir did not hold Sartre's view of freedom in the early post-war period" (p. 133). Considering that her book, *The Ethics of Ambiguity,* is much more congenial to Merleau-Ponty's view of freedom than to that of Sartre, Rabil concludes: "It appears, then, that Mlle de Beauvoir regarded Merleau-Ponty's approach as the more fruitful, but that her allegiance to Sartre outweighed her agreement with Merleau-Ponty when the two came into conflict with each other" (p. 133).

    There are many possible interpretations of this triadic relationship, not all of which are complimentary to the principals. Madison, for example, notes that, "in his rejection of Marxism, Merleau-Ponty's attitude is identical with that of Camus. . . . And, just as after the publication of Camus's systematic critique of Marxist mystification in *L'homme révolté* in 1951 Sartre instigated a vicious tirade against Camus, so also after the publication of *Adventures of the Dialectic* Sartre commissioned his friend, Simone de Beauvoir, to publish a scathing attack on Merleau-Ponty" (p. 340, n.41).

26. Once again, the word used for "meaning" is "sens," and here the ambiguous double meaning of "sense" and "direction" is especially pronounced.
27. Madison, pp. 311-12.
28. Madison footnotes this sentence as follows: "I am using the word 'liberal' in the traditional, European, and specifically Tocquevillian sense of the term" (p. 340, n.41). It is interesting that Kruks (at p. 73) names de Tocqueville as one of the liberals to whose thought Merleau-Ponty in *Humanism and Terror* was not properly sensitized in his putative a-historical critique of liberalism.
29. Had he lived, it is doubtful that the recent history of Czeckoslovakia and Poland would have given Merleau-Ponty any reason to change this statement. What is now happening in those countries, as well as what will soon occur in countries such as Yugoslavia, is much more ambiguous.
30. Rabil, p. 114, citing S 397-401.
31. Kruks, p. 124.
32. The clause italicized here, hardly unimportant for her argument, Kruks mistakenly leaves out of her citation (that is, there are ellipsis marks to note a purposeful omission). My translation differs from the one she employs, by Joseph Bien (London: Heinemann, 1974), p. 226, who renders "comme continuel rappel à l'ordre" as "as a continual call to order". See Kruks, p. 123.
33. Kruks, p. 123.
34. Kruks, p. 124. Kruks concludes about the "new liberalism" that "Indeed, it seems to me, the main failing of Merleau-Ponty's new political position is that he arrives at it deductively, as a logical consequences of the unity of Being, and not from the study of history and society" (p.

124). I find this conclusion amazing both in what it affirms and in what it denies. As for the latter, it suffices to say that one could hardly find a philosopher more obsessed with "the study of history and society" than was Merleau-Ponty—to say nothing of that terrible, frightening, and sordid history through which he lived. As for the first part of Kruks' conclusion, there is very little in *The Adventures of the Dialectic* that even resembles such language or reasoning. As described above in the Introduction, talk about "the unity of Being" is much more typical of Merleau-Ponty's last, posthumously published writings.

35. Accordingly, it is astonishing to find James Edie saying of Kruks' research that, "Though her work on this subject is much more extensive than mine, I am happy to ssee that it does not *essentially* differ from mine. I also find myself in agreement with her analysis and assessment of Merleau-Ponty's two major political works, namely *Humanism and Terror* and *The Adventures of the Dialectic"* (p. 72, n.16; italics in the original text).

Throughout her book, Kruks severely criticizes Merleau-Ponty's political philosophy for being unble to provide answers to crucial questions. Thus it is stupefying to read in her "Concluding Remarks" the following conciliatory statements that his failure to give answers to "most of the important questions he raises" "is not, however, a weakness of his work. Perhaps the main lesson to be drawn from Merleau-Ponty's political philosophy is that the debate can never be definitely closed" (p. 134). Were this failure to give answers which earlier engendered so many criticisms not a failure on Merleau-Ponty's part, Kruks surely would have ended up with a much shorter book.

By contrast, what she does find of value in Merleau-Ponty is a certain way of *"perceiving* politics" (at p. 134) as placed "within the broader dialectic of human existence" (p. 135). Such a broad focus would include the concrete relationships of politics to family life, language, and other areas of life "traditionally labelled as 'non-political'" (p. 135). I have attempted to sketch out some of these broader relationships in "Language and Abnormal Behavior: Merleau-Ponty, Hart, and Laing," *Review of Existential Psychology and Psychiatry,* Volume XVIII, Nos. 1,2, &3, 1982-83 (but actually published in 1985), pp. 181-203.

36. Ronald Dworkin, *Taking Rights Seriously* (Cambridge: Harvard University Press, 1977), pp. 262, 263.
37. Dworkin, p. 265.
38. The essay in which the following argument is developed is that listed above at note 4.
39. It is also indicated by a direct quotation in the last paragraph of "Indirect Language and the Voices of Silence." Writing about language, Merleau-Ponty calls our attention to the fact that "We install ourselves, with our apparatus of expression, in a situation to which it is sensitive, we confront this apparatus with the situation, and our statements are only the final balance-sheet of these exchanges. Political thought itself is of this order: it is always the elucidation of a historical perception in which all our knowledge, experience, and values are simultaneously at work, and of which our theses are only the schematic formulation" (S 104).
40. Dauenhauer, p. 14. Throughout his article, the author systematically uses "parlance" instead of *langage.* For reasons given above in Chapter I, and for consistency throughout the present chapter, I shall keep the original Saussurian terms which Merleau-Ponty employs, namely, *la langue* (language) and *la parole* (speech).
41. Dauenhauer, pp. 15-16.
42. Dauenhauer, p. 16.
43. Dauenhauer, p. 17.
44. Dauenhauer, pp. 17-18.
45. Dauenhauer, p. 18.
46. Dauenhauer, p. 18.

47. In considering the story that André Gide refused to vote because "the voice of his concierge counted as much as his own" (S 397), Merleau-Ponty reproaches Gide for the view, if he held it, that educated people ought to have more than one vote. "He knew better than anyone that culture is not a guarantee of judgment" (S 397). Sartre relates another pertinent story involving Merleau-Ponty's attitude toward intellectuals: "He told me that the communists were right to distrust intellectuals. They were always seduced by the particular action proposed, badly equipped to undertake it and above all to make it come to an end. They were quickly enamoured of it and even more quickly disenchanted, thus in the same breath abandoning the common enterprise and returning implacably to their precious studies." "Merleau-Ponty [I]," trans. William S. Hamrick, *Journal of the British Society for Phenomenology,* Vol. 15, No. 2, May 1984, p. 140. In such a situation, one might well have more confidence in the "voice of the concierge."
48. Dauenhauer, p. 19. In another essay, the author tells us that his view "is consonant with Michael Oakeshott's claim that every mode of utterance, including poetic utterance, is properly construed in the context of a society of conversationalists rather than in a society devoted to scientific inquiry or one engaged in practical enterprise. For Oakeshott, politics is a conversation and political education involves learning how to be a participant in a conversation." "Hope and its Ramifications for Politics," *Man and World* 17: 453-76 (1984), cited in J.N. Mohanty, ed. *Phenomenology and the Human Sciences,* p. 465. The reference to Oakeshott is his "The Voice of Poetry in the Conversation of Mankind," in his *Rationalism in Politics and Other Essays* (New York: Basic Books Publishing Co., 1962), pp. 243-247.
49. Dauenhauer, "Merleau-Ponty's Political Thought: Its Nature and Its Challenge," p. 21.
50. Dauenhauer, p. 21.
51. Dauenhauer, p.21.
52. Dauenhauer, "Hope and its Ramifications for Politics," p. 459.
53. "Poem, Or Beauty Hurts Mr. Vinal," in *100 Selected Poems* (New York: The Grove Press, Inc., 1959), p. 19.

PART TWO:
THE PHENOMENON OF LAW

Home is where one starts from. As we grow older
The world becomes stranger, the pattern more complicated
Of dead and living. Not the intense moment
Isolated, with no before or after,
But a lifetime burning in every moment
And not in the lifetime of one man only
But of old stones that cannot be deciphered.

—T.S. Eliot, *East Coker*

V: THE ORIGINS OF LAW AND ITS ESSENTIAL STRUCURES

We have now traversed, across the Introduction and the first four chapters of this work, the main features of Merleau-Ponty's phenomenology of the social world as they are expressed in the cultural mediation of nature, intersubjectivity, history and the origin of meaning, ethics, and politics. Running through all these themes and connecting them at various junctures is the notion of language analysed according to de Saussure's distinctions of *la langue* and *la parole,* on the one hand, and the synchronic and the diachronic, on the other. Following the interplay of these perspectives on language, we have seen how Merleau-Ponty finds them illuminative of the bonds of intersubjective communication, creative expression in the origin and change of meaning, the nature of history (at least up to a point), and politics.

Now we intend to pry out of these phenomenological evidences an account of the phenomenon of law. What follows will be to a large extent an exercise in creative expression as Merleau-Ponty himself understood it. That is, it will consist of an interrogation in which speech takes up a given body of language or a cultural work, gives us the illusion that what is said is already contained in the former, and yet infuses it with a new life for which it already had the capacity. It will make this cultural work say, therefore, more than it has said, but at the same time, what it already had the capability of saying.

Although the way that law stands forth as a phenomenon in the social world has been largely implicit throughout the preceding pages, it has not been wholly so. We have seen explicit and clear references to law in certain of Merleau-Ponty's texts, and we shall start from these and others in this chapter. The very nature of these references, we shall see, is such that they provide us with the means to go farther in the consideration of law than do the texts themselves, and they will allow us to construct deductive arguments to relate more effectively what is said about law to the rest of Merleau-Ponty's general philosophy. Thus the full picture of the phenomenon of law will be constructed both from the texts themselves and from what can be deductively derived from them.

§1. The Origin of Law

Law, it is clear for Merleau-Ponty, originates and is rooted in power relationships, chiefly those that are political. This does not mean this or that political vision which its proponents seek to enforce at law, but rather politics itself as a human enterprise. Not only is it politics that forms the immediate context for almost all of Merleau-Ponty's comments about law, but also—and much more importantly in his eyes—the war. That is, before any theoretical development of a phenomenology of the social world, the experience of the war showed him plainly how a given legal system—the Vichy government—could be emptied of all validity and replaced, in the context of different political power, by another legal order. It is not only particular moral and legal values that remain purely nominal in the absence of an effective political and economic infrastructure, but entire legal systems as well. Thus, in Merleau-Ponty's view, the efficacy of a legal system as a whole is a necessary condition of validity.

This systemic claim does not imply that within the system the validity of any particular law is equivalent to its efficacy—a subject to which I shall return below. But in terms of a legal system itself, it is also the case for Merleau-Ponty that its efficacy is not a sufficient condition of its validity. That is, efficacy, or the power of enforcement, is a necessary but not sufficient condition of the validity of a legal system because law is more than power, a legal order more than mere force. Rather, it is a matter of societal choice as to the way we live: "Man can define himself by this power that he has to conceive or in any case to respect what he is not and what he has not. It suffices to make some men live together and to associate in the same task just as soon as basic rules and a beginning of law are pried out of their life in common" (SNS 208).

The choice by at least the majority of society's members of how to live together in the world, and what kind of legal system will be incarnated in such a choice, is global rather than restricted to isolated sectors of social life, because it embraces all relevant aspects of the life-world. The unity and coherence of this common vision, in Merleau-Ponty's view, stem from the fact that one particular dimension—say, the legal, the religious, or the economic—is not tacked on to the others. Rather, as explained above (I.2), they form interdependent parts of a single Gestalt and a single history of a given society. Moreover, since they are inextricable parts of a single web of relationships, they interpenetrate to the extent that one cannot be in any simple sense caused by, or reduced to, another: "The conception of law, morality, religion, and the economic structure signify each other in the Unity of the social event as the parts of the body imply each other in the Unity of a gesture or as 'physiological,' 'psychological' and 'moral' motives are tied together in the Unity of an action, and it is impossible to reduce interhuman life either to economic relations or to juridicial and moral relationships thought by men, just as it is impossible to reduce individual life to bodily functions or to the consciousness that we have of this life" (PhP 202).

Although one of the orders of meaning within the Gestalt can become dominant at a given time and place of social life (PhP 202)—occupying the position of focal-point as against others that remain in the background—it is still the case that all the orders of meaning are *essentially* interwoven such that an examination of any one of them reveals the presence of the others. Thus in his 1953-54 course at the Collège de France, "On a Theory of History," Merleau-Ponty wrote of "the solidarity of the economic order, the political order, the juridicial order, the moral or religious order, starting from the moment in which even the economic fact is treated as a choice of a relationship with men and the world and takes its place in the logic of choices" (RC 50). This is why Max Weber was right to point out the *Vielseitigkeit* of historical facts, as explained above (II.4), which "permits us to read in a religious fact the first outline of an economic system, in an economic system the positions taken up with regard to the absolute. Religion, law, and the economy make up one sole history because each fact of one of these three orders recovers in a sense those of the two others, and that stems from the fact that they are all inserted into a single web of human choices" (AD 28).

Since law forms an inextricable aspect of this web, its close similarities with, and differences from, other orders of meaning in the social world create two interesting and symmetrically different problems for a phenomenology of law. On the one hand, the evident similarities prevent any sort of traditional eidetic analysis, the aim of which is to disengage an essence of law from the structures of other social phenomena. Thus, for instance, Merleau-Ponty could not have subscribed to the sort of project that John Austin undertook in *The Province of Jurisprudence Determined,* in which he laboriously sought to disentangle the "province" of law from all other social phenomena. Nor, to take two other examples of legal philosophy of varying prominence, would Merleau-Ponty ever have followed the lead of Hans Kelsen's perhaps Kantian-inspired "pure theory of law"[1] or Paul Amselek's similarly motivated treatment of the subject.[2] Of course, all these thinkers are patently aware of causal relationships between law and morality or politics. But what Merleau-Ponty is anxious to assert is fundamentally different: namely, that the interpenetration of law and other orders of social meaning is such that when, for the purpose of analysis—Austinian or otherwise—law is stripped of all reference to the rest of the social Gestalt, its very identity cannot survive the distortion. I shall come back to this below (VI.1) in the context of legal rules in their social setting.

The situation of law within the social Gestalt also gives rise to a different and diametrically opposite sort of problem for the philosophy of law, namely, how to properly distinguish law from other law-like objects such as customs, mores, taboos, positive morality, and the like. Since the bent of Merleau-Ponty's phenomenology is on unity and coherence—arguing, like Marx, within a certain context for particular reasons—and since he was a philosopher rather than a jurist, one does not find much within his writings to answer this question. There are, however, scattered comments, hints of what kind of answer he might have given, which I shall attempt to flesh out in a plausible answer in the following section of this chapter and in the second section of Chapter VI.

To do this, however, requires another step of the argument, and that is that one main function of the various orders of meaning within the social Gestalt is expression: expression of a social aim, of a common vision of a certain way to live. These several orders of meaning consist of expressions of values reflected by and in the entire network of social relationships. Law, then, appears as a particular mode of expressing values. This is not to say, of course, that there need be any sort of unanimity in choosing what values do get expressed in a certain legal system. Since there is no uniform "collective consciousness," but only an "intersubjectivity" (SNS 157) representing a variety of interests—sometimes overlapping, sometimes identical, but also very often irresolvably conflicting—law is presented as expresing both a common texture of social values, what is necessary to maintain the unity of a particular society, as well as certain ways of handling conflicts.

To say that law appears as a certain mode of expression of values,which is tightly bound up with other forms of expression, immediately raises the important question of the relation of law and morality. However, this question, owing to its complexity, can only be raised *en passant* in the present context; it will be addressed at length in Chapter VII. On the other hand, since the matter also will be of some importance for the understanding of law in society, it is appropriate to note here that, on Merleau-Ponty's view, law and morality consist of interdependent aspects of a global choice of social values—but this does not imply that one is reducible to the other. Correlatively, he would not argue for a fusion of the idea of law as it is with that of law as it ought to be.[3]

This distinction is illustrated effectively in two very different sorts of contexts in his writings. First, in the "Epilogue" of *Les Aventures de la dialectique,* the insistence that the new liberalism's sanction of parliamentary democracy is free of any *a priori* commitment to either the triumph of the proletariat or free enterprise would be impossible if, to be law at all, it had to endorse a certain set of moral values. The second context, which contains much stronger evidence denying a fusion of law as it is and law as it ought to be, consists of those passages in *Humanisme et terreur, Signes,* and elsewhere, which condemn both the Soviet institutionalization of violence and Western democratic hypocrisy (see III.2,3; IV.3). For, to consider only the latter, Merleau-Ponty never suggests that the laws under which took place the economic practices and policies which he condemned, were not for that reason valid laws. In saying that everyone knows that "the world as it is is unacceptable" (E 49), Merleau-Ponty certainly had in mind legal systems as well as the socio-political and economic forms of life which the former both reflect and help to create. Law thus manifests and in a particular way helps to mould a society's values—both moral, non-moral, and sometimes, immoral.[4]

Law, then, appears as a type of expression, both reflecting and reinforcing other orders of meaning in the social world which are, themselves, expressions of a network of values seen from other points of view and which, in spite of a lack of a "collective consciousness," is unified enough to justify us saying that a given social group constitutes *one* society. And it is precisely this expressive quality about law which allows us to go much farther in relating what has been said above to Merleau-Ponty's general philosophy. For, as already noted (at III.4), there is an "intimacy between all forms of expression" because of "their common belonging to one sole order" of meaning, a fact "which brings about the link between the individual and the universal" (S 91) as well as close structural similarities from one form of expression to another. Furthermore, the particular forms of expression most referred to and actually used in Merleau-Ponty's writings to illuminate other forms are those of language and painting, and it is in fact language that is continually appealed to in order to clarify other forms of expression—even, on occasion, painting itself (S 94). Thus it appears entirely reasonable to conclude that, had Merleau-Ponty chosen to work out a phenomenology of law, he would have followed the same model of language. Moreover, since politics is to be thought according to the pattern of language, and since of all of the phenomena which comprise the social world it is politics that most often serves as the immediate context for Merleau-Ponty's remarks on law, it is no great leap of reasoning to believe that he would think of law according to the same model.

Accordingly, the balance of this as well as the following two chapters will develop a phenomenology of law according to the model of language which Merleau-Ponty employed—that based on Saussurian linguistics. We shall follow out the legal counterparts of language just as we did in the relevant parts of Chapter IV for politics. Here, in roughly the same way, we shall be concerned with the relationships between *la parole* and *la langue,* and the synchronic and the diachronic, in order to speak to the nature of legal rules. The following chapter will deal with the intersubjective context of rules and judicial decision making, whilst the final chapter will consider, as noted above, the relation of law and morality. In each case, we shall see that law is, like history or politics, structurally similar to language and that living a legal system—equivalently, living (in) a legal world—will also present features of experience analogous to those of living a language.

Here the emphasis falls on structural similarity, not identity. The claim to be worked out and defended is that, in its essential features, law consists of a structure, some main aspects of which are closely analogous to those of language as de Saussure described them. I do not assert that, on Merleau-Ponty's view, law *is* a language. One reason for this is that Merleau-Ponty never made or implied such a statement. Another reason is that the claim is false. For, among a great many other things, there are important differences in kind, rather than just in degree, between legal and linguistic rules in what concerns their modes of origin, manifestation of authoritativeness, and loss of validity. There are also no officials in a linguistic system—except in a very loose sense and exception perhaps being made for the Académie Française—although there are authoritative texts. But for all that, it does appear correct to say that Merleau-Ponty would have sought in his descriptions of language, and in his derivative phenomenological descriptions in which he used the former, the keys to describing the phenomenon of law.

I shall also try to show, using as well other conceptual tools from Part One to fill in areas of the emerging picture to which language will lead us, what such a view of law will imply in terms of a variety of traditional and contemporary questions within the philosophy of law. The result will be, "by the same will to seize the meaning of the world or of history" to make Merleau-Ponty's own philosophy more fully "merge with the effort of modern thought" (PhP xvi). It is not asserted that conceiving law according to the model of language, or even with all the remaining resources of Merleau-Ponty's phenomenology, will illuminate all aspects of law. On some points, in fact, there could be only unjustifiable speculation about what he might say. But it is still the case that thinking law on a linguistic model, together with other phenomenological evidences from Part One above, will suffice to illuminate much of what is most central to law—its essence—and how that essence is existentially anchored in the life-world.

§2. *The Legal Analogues of Speech and Language*

Let us begin, then, with some main relationships between speech and language and their legal equivalents which will prepare us for the examination of legal rules in the following section. First, law appears, as does language, as a source of constituted objectivity in society. It is always presented as more than the will of society's members, and this would still be true even if the latter consisted of a "collective consciousness" instead of an "intersubjectivity." For law also consists of an ensemble of sedimented meanings and the locus of founded traditions: an *institution* which "endows our experiences with durable dimensions, in relation to which a whole series of other experiences will be meaningful, and will form a thinkable continuation or a history" (RC 61). As Neil MacCormick points out, the *"persistence through time"* "is the basic reason for lawyer's conceptions of 'things' or institutions."[5]

Law appears in a number of different ways as a constituted system within any given society. For instance, actions of officials within the system are presented as in principle relatable to each other in the coherent unity of one objective legal order. This does not mean that any given official acts with this systemic unity in view, that he or she is even explicitly aware of it, or that any given member of a society must reflectively posit such an attitude in order to experience a legal system. Since one is constantly involved with the experience of law, and since, as we shall see momentarily, this experience partly resembles that of the craftsman, certain aspects of law can appear to us as familiar tools, and it is this very familiarity which obviates the necessity of reflective, positing acts of a legal consciousness. For as Amselek says whilst citing Bergson—words that Merleau-Ponty would remember later in his descriptions of the habitual body (see II.1)—"'The workman's tool is an extension of his arm'; it is, so to speak, part of himself, like 'an artificial limb which is an extension of the human organism.' It follows that such a workman ceases to be conscious of the presence of the tool used by him; it merges into his own subjectivity. A phenomenon of this kind manifests itself in our relationship with law and legal tools; our contact with them is normally more lived out than thought out."[6] I shall return to this below in terms of the synchronic perspective on language and its legal analogues.

What is meant, rather, by the assertion that actions of officials are presented as relatable to each other within the unity of one coherent system—where such a system exists—is that various official functions can be connected to each other through the same rule structure that validates them. The system itself appears, as does a perceptual object (see I.1), as a whole object given incompletely from a certain perspective. But as a system of possible perspectives, it is always given with the open invitation to further exploration. This is because its "hidden sides" that shade off into indeterminacy are present-as-absent, but this absence is not nothing. It is a particular mode of appearing, an able-to-be-seen. Thus the official actions of officials in the system can stand out as focal points against a background of indeterminacy which is the rest of the system, and like any "part" of a Gestalt, such actions both reflect the whole Gestalt-context to which they can lead us to explore, are internally related to the other "parts" of the meaning structure, and finally, lose their experiential identity when removed from this context. Just as a linguistic act of expression is a modulation of a given language system (S 101), so too, in law, actions on the part of officials as well as, say, particular positive laws do not exist out of all relation to the rest of the legal system. They can instead be made to refer back to some criterion of validity as expressed in an anterior code, constitution, or similar legal instrument.[7] I shall come back to this in the following section, in connection with H.L.A. Hart's concept of rules.

Another way in which law appears, as does language, as an objectively constituted system, consists of precisely the ways in which it serves as tools for the "craftsman." That is, law, like language, presents itself to us as a system of expressive possibilities for the crafts of speech and the concretization of values. It is in this sense that the notion of a language as a cultural "treasure" of sedimented meanings which provide the possibilities for expression (see I.3) is equally true of the legal language of codes, constitutions, positive law, evolving bodies of case law in the courts, and even in common-law traditions that lie submerged in the backgrounds of the origins and evolution of some legal systems. In each case, such cultural achievements sediment crucial social meanings, the history of which they help in turn to prolong and further establish. As Geoffrey Sawer has observed, through all the stages of legal evolution "there was a growing body of stored, enduring knowledge and experience, and an increasing capacity for managing legal administration and for stating substantive legal rules so as to cover a wide or a changing set of social circumstances."[8]

The historical, objective weight of legal language, then, brings to legal rules as well as to law as a functioning whole an incontestable and unavoidable reality. As there can be no speech out of all relation to language, so, too, does the constituted language of law make possible legal speech. The institution of law thus performs for the legal counterpart of speech a double function: it supplies as well as limits it. As far as the latter is concerned, this is to say that the liberty of expression referred to above—the ability to relate to law as a system of expressive possibilities—is, like any human freedom, situated and conditioned by its past without being bound to conform to it. (Certain unique limitations placed on judicial expression will be considered below, at VI.3.) Institutions comprise objective, sedimented contours of our life-worlds, but in law as elsewhere, institutions also invite us to further experience and thus, according to Merleau-Ponty's definition of "institution," help make possible a future. As the latter stated in *Signes,* "Husserl used the nice word *Stiftung*—foundation or establishment—in order to designate first the unlimited fertility of each present which, exactly because it is singular and it passes, will never cease to have been and thus to be universally—but above all that fertility of the products of culture which continue to count after their appearance and open a field of research where they perpetually relive" (S 73-74).[9] In new legal speech, then, as in the closely associated political realm, creativity and inventiveness are clearly possible, although, as we shall see below in both the following section and chapter, how much creativity is possible depends on the context and on one's position within the system.

Pursuing the notion that a legal system, like language, is a system of expressive possibilities, leads us both to the consideration of the legal equivalent of *la parole* as well as to additional perspectives on the institution of law as such. For legal speech consists very broadly of all the daily and complex ways in which a community of legal subjects make use of law in the regulation of their daily lives. Accordingly, law as a system of expressive possibilities can be made to express different values in different ways. For example, through the use of the criminal law, society as a whole—or at least as the majority of a stable legal and social system—expresses certain moral values by defining a minimally acceptable floor of behavior, falling beneath which would expose an offender to the risk of punishment. In the employment of the civil law, on the other hand, individual citizens can express their self-determination through the making of marriages and wills, through the making of contracts for various purposes, through application to adjudicative agencies such as courts or arbitration agencies for relief in settling disputes, and so forth. In addition, officials in a given legal system can make a much more complex and creative use of a constituted legal language through a *parole* which aims at creating new law. Officials thus enjoy in a privileged way the fact that the institution of law is not independent and self-contained but rather, like all institutions (see II.2), is open to a subsequent coming-to-be of meaning.

There are at least two different perspectives from which officials within a given legal system may interrogate the language of law, manipulate it, and put it in the service of expressing particular social values. These two perspectives consist of seeing law as a tool of "social administration," the aim of which is social control, and "lawyer's law," which amounts to "special techniques *as applied to particular areas of legal regulation.*"[10] In the former, which is mainly, but not exclusively, the province of a legislature or other law-making authorities, "the dominating considerations are questions of policy and of social purpose, directly apprehended as such."[11] Law of this sort is subject to frequent amendment, but such changes are not usually viewed as "law reform," but rather as policy changes, the impetus for which usually stems from changes in society at large with consequent changes in political vision (see VI.2). Thus, as Sawer indicates, "Typical problems in the law of social administration likely to arise in English-speaking parliaments are: Should the age at which persons qualify for retirement pensions be reduced?. . . . [and] By what combination of measures concerning motor vehicles, roads, and road users can deaths and injuries caused by traffic accidents be reduced?"[12] Conversely, a typical activity on the part of ordinary citizens in relation to the law of social administration would be applying for a driver's license. No lawyers are apt to be consulted nor, still less, litigation engaged in. Rather, the applicant's legal activities will be almost wholly passive and concerned with officials who administer the relevant provisions of the motor-vehicle code.

"Lawyers' law," on the other hand, is a considerably different perspective on law which is more nearly concerned with social order than with social control, is usually the province ofjudges and lawyers, and constitutes a considerably different use of legal language. Here the main concern is not with social purpose and policy; these recede into the background of the focus on definitions of basic terms and consistency of reasoning. Insofar as social purposes are relevant to such arguments, "they tend to be very generalized or long-term in character, and to be congealed in propositions so that inferences from the propositions rather than directly from the purposes are usual."[13] Characteristic problems in this area of the law which are likewise discussed in English-speaking parliaments are: "Should the doctrine of consideration be retained in the law of contracts?. . . . [and] Should the requirement of non-natural user be retained under the rule in *Rylands v. Fletcher*?"[14] Other questions apt to arise in this area of the law concern the basic functioning of the criminal law, family law, laws dealing with property, the structure and functioning of the judicial system, and so forth.

Changes in this area of the law do not usually occur with the same speed or frequency as those of social administration. When they do, they are usually thought of as "law reform." At least part of the reason that such change tends to be slower and less frequent is that this area of the law is presented as a cultural treasure in a different fashion than is the law of administration. Precisely because in a stable system of government the former is presented as the accumulation of experience over generations—the sedimentation of a considerable number of complex legal meanings—it comes to be identified with what is most enduring about the social order itself, which it is usually thought wise not to tamper with too frequently. Lawyers' law thus performs approximately the same function in legal experience as does the knowledge of *technique* in that of the artist—at least when functioning under existing paradigms (see above at III.4).

In most modern legal systems, there is a subtle and pervasive dialectic between the law of social administration and lawyers' law, as well as certain prominent overlaps between the two—for example, in constitutional law. I shall return to these dialectical relationships below (at VI.2). Here, though, it is necessary to extend the descriptions of language and speech by a slight change of perspective to take into account the synchronic view on the legal world.

For with this shift of perspective, more particulars become clear about the relationship between the legal counterparts of language and speech. To begin with, in terms of the essentially intersubjective character of language, we have seen that, if speech is what one says and language constitutes the treasure in which the speaking subject can speak, it is equally true that language belongs to no particular speaker. Language belongs to the whole community of speaking subjects, and the speaker unites in him- or herself both the will to understand and the will to be understood (CAL 257). From the synchronic point of view, language mediates the individual and the social, the particular and the universal, the objective and the subjective, and the external and the internal.

The same is the case for law: there is no private law[15] any more than there is a private language, and law is the medium *par excellence* in which one can see, across the economic, political, and other dimensions of the social world, both the presence of individuals to institutions and to each other through those institutions. We legally mediate each other, within a given legal system as a whole, throughout a vast range of daily actions—from buying a candy bar (on which we pay taxes) to driving a car, renting an apartment, electing to pay a supplement to our utility bills in order to subsidize the heat of those who cannot afford to pay, to the specification of certain rights and obligations within the family—in short, throughout the length and breadth of not only what Tönnies labelled *Gesellschaft,* but also what he called *Gemeinschaft* as well (see above, I.2).

Furthermore, we saw in the last chapter that an important political implication of this mutual presence consisted in the fact that leaders and other citizens all belong to each other, such that no one either commands or obeys absolutely. Political tolerance, freedom of expression, and an open dialectic were to be encouraged and legally protected for that reason. Now there is another important legal implication of the same belongingness, and that is that it gives us another reason why Merleau-Ponty would not have been tempted to endorse Austin's positivism. For, on the latter's view, law amounts to a sovereign's publicized commands, as distinct from private wishes, backed up by the threat of coercive force, so that, as Hart summarizes it, "the foundations of a legal system consist of the situation in which the majority of a social group habitually obey the orders backed by threats of the sovereign person or persons, who themselves habitually obey no one. This social situation is, for this theory, both a necessary and a sufficient condition of the existence of law."[16]

In Austin's view, then, (i) law appears as a command which is (ii) issued by a sovereign (ruler, oligarchy, people as a whole, etc.), and the distinctive feature of which is (iii) a threat of hostile reaction in the absence of obedience. And this view survives down to this day in the consciousness of someone who sees an obligation to pay his income tax or to stop at a stop sign only as a means to stay out of harm's way. In Merleau-Ponty's view, on the contrary, the intersubjective character of law (on the linguistic model) argues against (ii),[17] whilst the fact that force is a necessary, but not sufficient, condition of the existence of law makes (iii) equally unacceptable. Moreover, we shall see in the following section in connection with legal rules why he would reject (i) as well. But we can already note that there is little if anything in lawyer's law that could be correctly described as the attempt of some person or social group to command others. And although some aspects of the law of social administration may take on the cast of commands, they do not all do so. For example, laws governing deductions from federal income taxes in the United States attempt to control behavior by (as a typical instance) establishing a substantial minimal floor that must be reached before claiming a deduction for money lost to theft. The aim is clearly to discourage carelessness, and/or not to allow the law to be used as an instrument for profiting from carelessness. But it is doubtful whether anyone who ever benefitted from, or was frustrated by, such a requirement perceived it or the deduction option as a whole as a command. Thus even without yet considering the concept of legal rules, where the discussion of commands will again be relevant, we can perceive already that there is much of the phenomen of law that a careful phenomenological description shows to be incompatible with the Austinian model.[18]

The synchronic perspective on language also gives us additional purchase on the way that a legal system is taken up, modulated, and employed fruitfully as tools for expression. Merleau-Ponty tells us, be it recalled (I.3), that for speakers within a given linguistic community, language has a "use value" more than fixed definitions, "in the sense in which one speaks of the value of a piece of change that one could exchange for an infinite number of objects" (CAL 257). The fact that language is given to us in this way is not only a considerable source of inspiration for continued inventiveness and creativity, but also, as we have seen above, it points to the kinds of non-conscious activities in and through which speech takes up and appropriates language, namely as an internalized working familiarity with a linguistic system, or a "knowledge by acquaintance."

This kind of knowledge, however, is radically different from a theoretically constituted knowledge because in the former, unlike the latter, the structure of language is taken up in speech acts as a kind of "anonymous presence," that is, as a more or less unarticulated, vague set of social rules—now forgotten or perhaps never clearly framed in the consciousness of the speaking subject. Since both creative and non-creative speech acts—"originary speech" and "secondary speech" (PhP 446)—can take place in the absence of a theoretical knowledge of the rules, it follows that "the meanings of speech are always ideas in the Kantian sense, poles of a certain number of convergent acts of expression which animate discourse without being properly given for their own sake" (S 112).

By contrast, it is only if one stands outside the synchronic perspective of a functioning linguistic community that a theoretical knowledge of the rules is necessary to constitute the sense of expression. In this detached position, like that of students learning foreign languages, a theoretical grasp of a language is usually built up piece by explicitly constituted piece.

Now the legal analogues of these non-thematic ways in which speech synchronically appropriates language are as follows. First, the complex "syntax" of legal rules and other aspects of a legal system are also presented non-thematically in that they manifest themselves as a rather anonymous, vague background of objective, social regulation, only some of which is clearly in focus at any given time. In addition, the range and intensity of the clarity depends to some degree upon one's position within the legal system itself. For the reasons given above, officials in the system tend to attain a considerably more theoretical knowledge of the rules than do laypersons for whom, say, buying a railway ticket is a legal act, but which can and usually is accomplished with no special legal consciousness of one's obligations or, still less, laws that govern fares, penalties for non-payment, or negligence which results in injury to passengers.

Instead of confronting the whole ensemble of legal rules directly, we focus only on certain ones, if at all, when immediately relating to official signs and warnings, actions of officials and, if we inhabit a stable society, the similarly governed behavior of at least the majority of our fellow citizens. Throughout the range of possible legal experiences which incarnate the various ways that legal speech expresses values, this speech works within the system in such a way that a theoretically constituted knowledge of the rules is neither sufficient nor necessary. It is not sufficient because it could not account for the creative use of rules; it would provide their "fixed meanings," but not their synchronic "use value." And it is not necessary because, as in the railway example noted above, theoretical statements of rules provide far more than is required to account for either one's consciousness of being bound by a given rule (feeling obligated) or the awareness of having the obligation. (The difference between these will appear in the following section.) Thus, to take another example, a red traffic light can appear to a motorist as a reason for stopping without the additional requirements that he or she know all of the provisions of the motor-vehicle code, or even all those that just concern traffic signals.

The inverse of this non-necessity of theoretical knowledge is that, in complex, fully developed legal systems, a certain ignorance of the law is unavoidable. The knowledge by acquaintance operative in the way that legal speech takes up and modulates a given legal system thus parallels and extends Bergson's description of the familiar tool which is the unreflective extension of the worker. Like the experienced pianist who settles in at his or her instrument to play a piece of music, it is more a question of a "communication with a manner of being" than of "the position of an object" (SNS 163). The well-known phrase, "Ignorance of the law is no excuse" does not mean, then, that we are all legally bound to have a comprehensive thematic knowledge of our particular legal systems. Rather, what is impeached is the opposite of the internal working familiarity with the system which characterizes the consciousness of those members of society who do accept the rules for doing or abstaining from doing certain things. In other words, what is found unacceptable is the reverse of the "manner of being" in which legal subjects thus situated take up their legal situations in a more or less clarified rule-governed framework and see the rules as reasons for doing so.

Before turning to the concept of rules itself, let us note in passing one final reason why a theoretical knowledge of legal rules is not necessary to establish their use value for legal speech. That is, in certain legal systems there are some rules which are never, or only very exceptionally, relevant or clearly articulated. These are so-called "obsolete" rules which correspond to archaic uses of words.

Just as there can be worn-out forms of expression (E 74), as well as whole dead languages—that is, those no longer animated by speech—evidencing the phenomenon of decay, so also, particular laws as well as entire legal systems can lose their expressive capacity and use value. To consider only particular laws within an ongoing legal system, when all their use value has evaporated, they are damped to the fringes of our consciousness, if they are there at all, so as to be practically (in both senses) non-existent.

Thus, for example, in England archery is illegal on Sunday. In the United States, it is illegal in the city of Indianapolis to sneeze in a post office (because, in the 19th-century, such an unhappy event during a flu epidemic ended by killing all the customers then present). The State of Kentucky, for reasons that are nothing if not arcane, prohibits men from marrying their wives' grandmothers. (Doubtless this is a violation of federal equal protection laws as well, since no similar restrictions appear to have been enacted for women. Surely only egalitarian maniacs, however, would press such a complaint.) And in the State of South Dakota, it is illegal for elderly women to speak to young married men in the street (though apparently not against the law to marry young eligible ones). I shall return to obsolete rules below, in terms of the issue of legal validity, a subject that forms an important part of the nature of legal rules themselves.

§3. *Legal Rules*

Thinking law according to the model of language also requires an account of legal rules not as an abstraction, as a set of pure concepts, but rather as situated in the context of living legal relationships—the synchronic perspective in which legal speech takes up, modulates, and interprets a syntax of rules. Just as abstract legal words such as "rights," "citizen," and "democracy," have a (living, synchronic) meaning only in terms of the tissue of living social relationships to which they refer (PhP 200), and just as grand constitutional slogans and moralisms must be similarly understood—as we saw in the previous chapter—so, too, legal rules must be seen as mediating the internal and the external, the subjective and the objective, the individual and the social. In articulating how this mediation takes place in rules-as-lived, such an account must specify both what sort of existence rules have, how they appear to consciousness, as well as what kinds of rules there are.

When we consider the existence of rules as incarnating and reflecting the interrelationships of legal counterparts of speech and language, we can begin to see why they are not purely objective entities within the framework of a constituted legal system. They cannot be purely objective precisely because, as we have noted above several times, in a synchronic perspective no living institution of a society is closed and purely objective. Like language, the institution of law and legal rules which help constitute it remain open to the creative interpretation of legal speech such that, in rules-as-lived, there is also a "coming-to-be of meaning" (IV.5).

Merleau-Ponty would have joined thinkers such as Roscoe Pound, Rudolf von JHering, and François Gény, in rejecting a concept of law as a system of pure concepts—a *Begriffsjurisprudenz*. As Sawer summarizes their collective reaction, which typifies proponents of "sociological jurisprudence," "What the writers of this 'school' do share is *rejection* of the 'jurisprudence of concepts' against which Ihering inveighed, and *acceptance* of the view that law can and should be developed, by judges as well as by parliaments, in order to meet changing social needs. A jurisprudence of concepts is one which attempts to treat the law as a closed system of definitions, rules of operation, and substantive major premisses such that any specific legal problem can be solved by deductive reasoning from the propositional system so established."[19]

But this does not mean, to parallel an earlier discussion in the previous section, that rules are purely subjective either or that, correspondingly, their validity and our obligation to obey them are reducible to the subjective wills of society's members. On this "psychological" account, which is one that Austin wanted to discredit, having an obligation is misinterpreted in terms of "feelings" of obligation. But not only is there no absurdity in someone's saying that he or she does not feel any obligation to do something, or abstain from doing something, whilst all the while that person does in fact have such an obligation, but also such a "psychological" account more generally fails to appreciate the objective reality of legal rules as they form part of the constituted legal system.

A rule, then, possesses a structure like that of the perceiver and the perceived, or the speaker and the spoken. Neither a pure in-itself nor a pure for-itself, its concrete unity of the subjective and the objective casts it in the form of the "in-itself—for-us." Its living reality—its being a rule-as-lived, synchronically—makes it appear to a legal consciousness as usable cultural equipment: as words to speakers in a linguistic community, less with determinate meanings than with concrete use values. And the multiplicity of possible uses, some of which were described above, that make up legal speech determine in turn the ways that rules appear to us and what kinds of rules there are.

How, then, can we best understand these modes of appearing and types of rules which are at once sedimented, objective sense and always open to new dimensions of meaningfulness in legal speech acts? A considerable amount of progress in this area has already been made by Hart in his seminal work, *The Concept of Law*. His descriptions of legal rules are, in very large measure, exceptionally congenial to the result at which one arrives by thinking law according to the model of language,[20] as the reader will easily perceive in the following brief summary of the most relevant aspects of Hart's views. Merleau-Ponty's phenomenology thus provides a foundation for Hart's account of rules and also, as we shall see below, ways to strengthen certain of his arguments. (It will also provide us in the following chapter with a vantage-point from which we may criticize other features of Hart's programmme that are closely related to certain contemporary assessments of what *The Concept of Law* achieved.)

Hart's principal object is to explain the main features of a mature legal system which is made up of different kinds of rules. To do this, he contrasts his own theory with that of Austin, seeking to arrive at a more sophisticated positivism as against the too-simple sort of his 19th-century predecessor. On Hart's view, Austin's theory is an instructive failure, and the main reason is that "the elements out of which the theory was constructed, viz. the ideas of orders, obedience, habits, and threats, do not include, and cannot by their combination yield, the idea of a rule, without which we cannot hope to elucidate even the most elementary forms of law."[21]

In the central fifth chapter of *The Concept of Law,* "Law as the Union of Primary and Secondary Rules," Hart characterizes these two types of rules as follows. Those that are "primary" require people "to do or abstain from certain actions, whether they wish to or not."[22] These rules are common to primitive legal systems (Hart occasionally calls them "pre-legal regimes") and to those that are fully developed, or "mature." "Secondary" rules, on the other hand, which are found only in fully developed legal systems, are "in a sense parasitic upon or secondary to the first; for they provide that human beings may by doing or saying certain things introduce new rules of the primary type, extinguish or modify old ones, or in various ways determine their incidence or control their operations. Rules of the first type impose duties; rules of the second type confer powers, public or private."[23]

A legal structure composed merely of primary rules would be suitable only for small groups closely bound together by family ties, common beliefs, and not subject to upheavals of an unstable environment. Modern complex societies, on the other hand, need a far richer rule structure because such a simple system would expose them to three serious legal defects. First, there would be no official, authoritative way for settling doubts or uncertainties about what counts as a rule in the system. Second, the rules would be static such that changes in the rules would be limited to slow growth of optional behavior becoming obligatory and, inversely, what was once obligatory—and the infractions thereof consistently punished—slips into non-observance (and the violations of which are no longer noticed). And the third defect of the simple form of life for modern complex societies is the inefficiency of enforcement of the rules. What is lacking here, and what complex societies need, is some agency, such as courts, which are specifically authorized to determine finally and definitively deviations from the rules.

Thus the role of secondary rules which confer public powers is to remedy these three defects. Secondary rules "specify the ways in which the primary rules may be conclusively ascertained, introduced, eliminated, varied, and the fact of their violation conclusively determined."[24] The first defect, that of uncertainty, is remedied by a "rule of recognition"[25] which may vary from the rather simple example of an authoritative list to the more sophisticated variants of mature legal systems which specify "some general characteristic possessed by the primary rules" which gives us "the germ of the idea of legal validity."[26] (See above in the discussion of the ways that the legal counterpart of language is presented to consciousness as a *system*).

The second general defect, the static character of the rules, is remedied by introducing "rules of change" which obviously are very tightly related to rules of recognition.[27] And the third defect, the inefficiency of the maintenance and enforcement of rules, is remedied by the introduction of closely connected "rules of adjudication" which confer on courts or other official agencies the right to make authoritative judgments as to whether rules have been broken.[28]

As we have seen, the notion of use value is tightly related to the modes of appearing of law in consciousness—in terms of the various and complex forms of expression of which legal speech is capable. This fact is closely tied to another distinction Hart makes about rules, and that is that both primary and secondary rules have internal and external aspects. The external aspects of rules are those that present themselves to an observer who is outside the system and does not accept the rules as binding on him- or herself. Such an observer can utter many types of statements about the given legal system: he or she may "assert that the group accepts the rules, and thus may from outside refer to the way in which *they* are concerned with them from the internal point of view."[29] He or she may again "merely record the regularities of behaviour on the part of those who comply with the rules as if they were mere habits, without referring to the fact that these patterns are regarded by members of the society as standards of correct behaviour."[30] And finally, such an observer might also "record the regular hostile reactions to deviations from the usual pattern of behaviour as something habitual, again without referring to the fact that such deviations are regarded by members of the society as reasons and justifications for such reactions."[31]

For Hart, the result of these kinds of utterances is that the external point of view on rules does not really yield the concept of rules at all, and so also not "the rule-dependent notions of obligation or duty. Instead, it will be in terms of observable regularities of conduct, prediction, probabilities, and signs. For such an observer, deviations by a member of the group from normal conduct will be a sign that hostile reaction is likely to follow, and nothing more."[32]

What this means is that, from the external point of view which yields probability statements and predictions about people's behavior patterns and correlations between particular events and actions, when one has already established a correlation between X and Y—say, a traffic light turning red and motorists stopping their cars—X will be no more than a sign that Y will probably follow, "a natural *sign that* people will behave in certain ways, as clouds are a *sign that* rain will come."[33] For Hart, the central failing of Austin's theory is that it treats legal phenomena, including validity and obligation, only predictively or, what amounts to the same thing, only from the external point of view. We shall return to this below.

For Hart, rules of law have an internal aspect which is indispensable for them to be rules at all because, beyond behaviour patterns which an external observer can record and on the basis of which make predictions, the internal aspect of rules refers to the ways that the members of society who accept the rules as a common standard judge their own and others' behavior critically and reflectively. The internal aspect of rules thus refers to "the way in which the rules function in the lives of those who normally are the majority of the society. These are the officials, lawyers, or private persons who use them, in one situation after another, as guides to the conduct of social life, as the basis for claims, demands, admissions, criticism, or punishment, viz., in all the familiar transactions of life according to rules. For them the violation of a rule is not merely a basis for the prediction that a hostile reaction will follow but a *reason* for hostility."[34]

Thus in the traffic-light example mentioned above, the red light is "not merely a sign that others will stop: they look upon it as a *signal for* them to stop, and so a reason for stopping in conformity to rules which make stopping when the light is red a standard of behaviour and an obligation."[35] Consequently, the concepts of duty and obligation are rule-dependent, which entails being internal-aspect-dependent, because rules are seen as justificatory reasons for obeying them and for hostile social reactions in the absence of obedience.

It is just for this reason, then, that a predictive account of legal obligation will not suffice. This theory which, for Hart, Austin correctly preferred to usually irrelevant utterances about people's beliefs or fears,[36] considers claims of obligation not as psychological claims, but rather as predictions of suffering punishments, or "sanctions." What is fundamentally wrong with such a view is that it "obscures the fact that, where rules exist, deviations from them are not merely grounds for the prediction that hostile reactions will follow or that a court will apply sanctions to those who break them, but are also a reason or justification for such reaction and for applying the sanctions."[37]

In this respect, the stability of a particular society depends directly on the fact that a majority of its citizens accept its rules from the internal point of view. But of course most societies, if not all, display a certain tension—in some, rather pronounced—between those who accept the rules and those who do not. Whether in the case of, say, hardened criminals or alienated minority groups, the external point of view on rules may very nearly capture their relationship to rules. For their situation would be not unlike that of Holmes' famous "bad man": they would only be concerned with rules "when and because they judge that unpleasant consequences are likely to follow violation. Their point of view will need for its expression, 'I was obliged to do it,' 'I am likely to suffer for it if . . .', 'They will do that to you if . . .'. But they will not need forms of expression like 'I had an obligation' or 'You have an obligation' for these are required only by those who see their own and other persons' conduct from the internal point of view."[38]

The exact way in which one relates internally to rules depends very much on whether the rules concerned are primary or secondary, for the latter brings complexities not often found in the former. Here new meaning has to be attached to concepts such as validity, legislation, and a substantial range of legal powers, both public and private. Describing all these activities in fact-stating, predictive language can only give us the external facade of the law-as-lived. To grasp them from within, we need the internal aspect of rules as well in order to do justice to the way that legislative or judicial operations or the exercise of private powers by ordinary citizens relate to secondary rules.

Whilst obligation is primarily, though not entirely, related to primary rules, validity stands in a similar relationship to the secondary rules that confer public powers, chiefly that of recognition. And here, for Hart, Austin's analysis falls short of the mark for the same reason as did that of obligation, namely, the predictive account leaves no room for the internal aspects of rules. That is, from the internal point of view one decides whether a particular rule is valid by referring to a secondary rule of recognition, or perhaps even to the ultimate rule in the system such as (in England) "What the Queen enacts in Parliament is law." Although as noted in the previous section there is usually no need to cite such a rule or adopt such a thematic, positing consciousness, articulation is still always theoretically possible, should it be necessary. But, as Hart tells us, "When we move from saying that a particular enactment is valid, because it satisfies the rule that what the Queen in Parliament enacts is law, to saying that in England this last rule is used by courts, officials, and private persons as the ultimate rule of recognition, we have moved from an internal statement of law asserting the validity of a rule of the system to an external statement of fact which an observer of the system might make even if he did not accept it."[39] From the external point of view, one could predictively assess the validity of a rule on the basis of the behavior patterns of private citizens and officials and, in particular, whether it will be enforced by the courts. One would then arrive merely at the efficacy of certain rules as well as that of the whole system.

But as in the case of obligation, the predictive theory of validity also fails and, along with it, the false equivalence of validity and efficacy. For, as we have already seen above, "there is no necessary connexion between the validity of any particular rule and its efficacy, unless the rule of recognition of the system includes among its criteria, as some do, the provision (sometimes referred to as a rule of obsolescence) that no rule is to count as a rule of the system if it has long ceased to be efficacious."[40] And, on the other hand, as we have also seen in the preceding section, the efficacy of the entire system is a necessary condition of the validity of a certain rule, rather than its meaning. This is particularly clear, as Hart points out, in the way that a "judge's own statement that a particular rule is valid functions in judicial decision; for though here too, in making such a statement, the judge presupposes but does not state the general efficacy of the system, he plainly is not concerned to predict his own or others' official action. His statement that a rule is valid is an internal statement recognizing that the rule satisfies the tests for identifying what is to count as law in his court, and constitutes not a prophecy of but part of the *reason* for his decision."[41]

We shall return to Hart's theory of rules and its implications for judicial decision making in the following chapter. Here, rather, let us consider how well his account coheres with thinking law on the model of language. First, the external aspects of rules correspond to either the synchronic or diachronic contemplated as an object in itself. The former, which is effectively the primary object of Hart's external observer, presents, among other things, the legal experiences of the system's participants considered as purely objective data rather than as lived. And just as in the experience of the outsider who is inserted into a foreign language system, the system gradually comes to manifest enough coherence such that he or she can make predictions about the behavior of the participants and, in the case of law, the system's officials.

In the external point of view on the diachronic aspects of a linguistic or legal system, on the contrary, no such coherence is assured because in both cases their historical development is far from unfolding a single, unbroken logic. (We shall see in the following chapter how both Jhering and Holmes criticized the advocates of *Begriffsjurisprudenz* for just such a view.) For even within stable constitutional systems—as, for example, in the United States—judicial interpretations of the meanings of certain words, clauses, or amendments can and do vary widely from one historical epoch to another. But in law as in language, de Saussure's distinction between the synchronic and the diachronic offers the possibility of an intelligible history as we come to understand how the former—with its stress on concrete use values rather than on fixed definitions—stands to the latter as order in disorder, reason in unreason, and logic amidst contingency.

The internal aspects of primary and secondary rules may be perceived either (i) synchronically, the most common case, or (ii) diachronically. With (i) we are concerned with the ways in which primary and secondary rules exist to give full range to the expressiveness of legal speech and how the internal aspects of rules answer to the ways that participants in a legal system who accept the rules take up the constituted legal order and find in it a complex mesh of use values. In other words, the modes in which legal speech functions as an internal working familiarity with the system in order to use it as a guide in following rules in all the relevant and familiar actions of the life-world corresponds to the synchronic perspective on language in which speech copies, manipulates, and changes the received system.

The internal point of view on the diachronic (ii) would amount to the rarer perspectives of the revolutionary and those passively caught up in the significant wrenchings of history in which one legal order is emptied of validity and another takes its place. Diachrony, let us remember, is only a succession of synchronies. Thus, whether it is a question of a Sartre or Merleau-Ponty witnessing the demise of Vichy, or of Robbespierre that of the French aristocracy, there is a decentering and recentering of meanings, as described above, and an urgent search for new legal use values and a legal "truth to be made" (see II.4, 5). One could also say that the difference between the internal point of view on (i) the synchronic and (ii) the diachronic uses of legal meanings is the same difference noted by Thomas Kuhn between doing "normal" science under a prevailing paradigm and "crisis" science when the prevailing paradigm has been toppled (see II.2).

The internal and external points of view on the diachronic, supplemented by the internal perspective on the synchronic, would appear to be of most use to not only philosophers of science, but also to linguists, philologists, and in what concerns law, to legal historians. Indeed, Merleau-Ponty himself ties together language and law in talking about the history of both. The context is the substitution of use values for fixed definitions, and he observes that "Michel Breal compares the word[42] with the institution in history. Example: Parliament, which was in the beginning a court of justice, acquired progressively, beginning with the right of recording royal edicts, the right of protest and even became an organ of political opposition in the 18th-century. In the same way, the word which has been introduced in order to signify something loses its original meaning and acquires another one. At each moment, the meaning is an element of a total configuration: one can consider language thus understood as an aspect of what '*culturalist*' sociologists call *culture*. When Saussure speaks of the 'conventional' character of language, he expresses in another vocabulary this idea that language is '*cultural*', not '*natural*'" (CAL 257).[43]

Focussing more closely on the internal point of view in the synchronic use of a legal system, we find as in the case of language a richness of different types of expression for various purposes, some of which have already been described above. As we have seen, a legal system, like that of language, offers us a multiplicity of use values, and a careful phenomenology of diverse forms of legal expression would pay particular attention to the modes of appearing of each kind of experience in consciousness in order to preserve the experiential identity of the phenomena. Therefore, one would not be tempted to reduce types of legal experiences to each other unless evidence at the interior of those experiences gave one ample reason for doing so.

This conclusion is singularly important for a certain sector of legal theory, in consequence of which Hart is at some pains to insist on the variety of types of laws. And he does so primarily because he considers reductivist theories as inadequate accounts of the ways in which rules are lived or, in other words, as bad phenomenologies.[44] The reductivist view at issue here contends that all laws, no matter how phrased or what powers of expression they make available to legal subjects, are "really" just coercive orders. In the more extreme form, represented by Hans Kelsen (*General Theory of Law and State,* p. 63), all genuine laws "are conditional orders to officials to apply sanctions. They are all of the form, 'If anything of a kind X is done or omitted or happens, then apply sanctions of the kind Y.'"[45] Thus, for instance, there is no law forbidding murder, but there is a law "directing officials to apply certain sanctions in certain circumstances to those who do murder."[46]

This theory is not quite the same as the command theory defended by Austin—that is, laws seen as orders issued by a sovereign and backed up by the threat of force. Instead, "the central conception now is that of orders to officials to apply sanctions. On this view it is not necessary that a sanction be prescribed for the *breach* of every law; it is only necessary that every 'genuine' law shall direct the application of some sanction."[47] Even on a more moderate version of this theory, power-conferring rules—such as those secondary rules that confer private powers to make wills, marriages, or other contracts—will be seen as mere parts of rules ordering certain persons to do certain things. On the more moderate view, then, "Power-conferring rules are represented by the antecedents or if-clauses of rules ordering ordinary citizens, under threat of sanctions, to do things and not merely (as in the more extreme theory), as the if-clauses of directions to officials to apply sanctions."[48]

Thus, for example, rules permitting people to marry after having satisfactorily passed pre-marital blood tests would be viewed as veiled orders to officials to apply the sanction of annulment (plus perhaps other sanctions as well) in the absence of such test results. Or, rules governing wills which require two witnesses would be interpreted as "really" orders to officials to apply the sanction of not admitting the will to probate if such a condition were not fulfilled.

Yet, as Hart observes, what is wrong with both the extreme and the moderate versions of this reductivist theory is that they provide the happy uniformity of a single pattern to which all laws are reduced at the price of distorting the various social functions of various kinds of legal rules. This distortion clarifies many different aspects of law when we consider what it cannot account for, and this is perhaps most visibly the case for criminal law. For, as we have seen above, the latter functions primarily as a guide for setting minimum standards of behavior for ordinary citizens, who are expected to conform to them without the intervention of officials. Officials are concerned only secondarily, when there has been a breach of the rules and sanctions become relevant.

The cardinal problem for the reductivist theory is, then, that it makes what is really secondary primary, and vice-versa. Holmes' "bad man," whose concern for law is limited (by the author's definition) to staying out of harm's way, should not be thought a paradigm of legal consciousness. For "Why should not law be equally if not more concerned with the 'puzzled man' or 'ignorant man' who is willing to do what is required, if only he can be told what it is? Or with the 'man who wishes to arrange his affairs' if only he can be told how to do it?. . . . The principal functions of the law as a means of social control are not to be seen in private litigation or prosecutions, which represent vital but still ancillary provisions for the failure of the system. It is to be seen in the diverse ways in which law is used to control, to guide, and to plan life out of court."[49]

By analogy with the reductivist theory, whether it is a question of Austin's (or anyone else's) command theory or Kelsen's view of law as veiled threats, Hart points out that one might just as well say that, hidden under the rules of a certain game, lies the uniformity that all the rules are "really" complex directions to the officials of the game. In baseball, for example, certain motions after a hit has occurred would constitute a "run" and this would *mean* a direction to a scorer to record a run on his or her book. But there is no reason to believe that such a thematic awareness of a hit or a run has to arise in the consciousness of any given player to play the game successfully, and there is similarly no reason to believe that, in the internal point of view on rules, legal speech must be restricted to such a narrow modulation of a system of rules. Thus Hart argues that "the uniformity imposed on the rules by this transformation of them conceals the ways in which the rules operate, and the manner in which the players use them in guiding purposive activities, and so obscures their function in the co-operative, though competitive, social enterprise which is the game."[50]

Such reasoning also serves as a useful criticism of Paul Amselek's description of law which both retains as well as rejects important parts of Austin and Kelsen's views. In his account, the *eidos* of law reveals itself as having "1. Generic eidetic elements: law presents itself in its most essential state as a set of *norms;* it belongs to the eidetic genus of the normative."[51] These norms are neither mental representations nor a system of pure concepts as described by a *Begriffsjurisprudenz*. Rather, they are "*models with existential content*"[52] because they engage the life-world by allowing law to serve certain social purposes. As noted in the previous section, Amselek considers law to be a tool and, following Heidegger's conception of a tool as being "a tool for" something, he takes law to be a tool for measuring. In other words, legal rules or norms (he expressly uses these words interchangeably) provide standards or models of what is expected in social behavior. They are models of "evental patterns," "*models of the unfolding of facts of human activity*[53] *in the course of things, models of the occurrence of human things in the evental flux* . . . they represent models of the unfolding of human history."[54]

The *eidos* of law further reveals itself as having "2. Specific eidetic elements: the norms which constitute law present themselves more precisely as *ethical* norms; and even more precisely, as *ethical norms with the function of commands*."[55] By "ethical," Amselek does not mean to denote any particular ethical doctrine or to suggest a fusion of law and morality of the sort that Austin, Hart, and Kelsen protest. Rather, he is concerned to make a distinction between human existence which is capable of self-direction and inanimate nature which is not. In much the same vein of thought as we saw above in Chapter III—particularly about an instrumental concept of rules and moral decision making—Amselek tells us that "ethics, in its most fundamental sense, is defined as *the art of directing conduct*. Thus ethical norms represent the ideal technique for this art: they are norms which have the special instrumental fashion of guiding or directing human conduct."[56]

This "guiding or directing" is based on, among other things, a situated and conditioned freedom to culturally mediate nature in ways which Merleau-Ponty describes in detail, and Amselek also says of man that, "Within the limits of his finitude, in the context of the mechanisms which form the pattern of his constitution, there is room for some movement or liberty—a sort of *marginal liberty* (which is different from the 'total liberty' invoked by Sartre and which is in effect meaningless since it implies the nonfinitude of man). . . . Thus ethical norms are the type of instrument invented by the human intelligence in reply to the challenge of nature, which left man at least partially to be the master of his 'fate.'"[57]

Ethical norms differ essentially from scientific norms, the main concern of which is fact-stating predictability, and since legal norms are a subset of the ethical, Amselek jettisons Austin's predictive account of legal validity and obligation.[58] He also rejects, as we saw earlier, the theory of sovereignty, but he keeps the notion of legal rules as commands. In specifying how this is so, he first makes a distinction which is practically identical to Hart's division of primary from secondary rules, namely, that between "imperative norms" and "permissive norms."[59] There is, in the case of both, as against Hart, no effective difference between having an obligation and being obliged to do or refrain from doing something. For even "permissive norms," which express powers and rights and, in general, imply "that something *ought to be able* to happen or not to happen"[60]—are presented as commands. Both types of norms thus manifest the essential nature of a command, namely to be "*orders, instructions, injunctions,* or *decisions* in the strong sense. . . . This is also what is meant by legal theorists when they invoke in relation to legal norms the ideas of *constraint, necessity, coercion,* or *coercibility, the obligatory,* and other similar concepts."[61]

On the other hand, Amselek wishes to distinguish the idea of command from Kelsen's view of law as orders to officials to apply sanctions for breaches of law. A legal norm does not manifest itself as coercion, compulsion, or as a threat of sanctions, but it is nonetheless still present to consciousness as compulsory. It is compulsory because all legal rules are commands of public officials. Thus they manifest "3. Particular eidetic elements: these commands which constitute law *are part of the function of the public direction of human behavior.*"[62] Further, "Commands are given as ethical norms with the function of constituting measures to be *compulsorily* followed and reproduced, to be *compulsorily* used as supports or guides for the realizations of the individuals concerned."[63]

In addition, Amselek insists that even permissive norms can be framed as compulsory commands: "In this case one would be confronted by a human evental pattern model to be compulsorily observed, a pattern implying the possibility of the occurrence or the nonoccurrence of such and such a thing."[64] He does admit that "a certain effort is necessary to be able to conceive clearly a permissive command and how it is distinguished from a recommendation. . . . [but that] On the other hand, it is true that one could be tempted to think that at first sight there is scarcely any noticeable practical difference to the individual between receiving a command granting him the power to do a certain thing and receiving a recommendation expressing the obligation or the power to do the same thing."[65]

It is the case that "a certain effort is required to conceive clearly a permissive command," and it might well be true that there is little practical difference of the sort that Amselek has in mind, but the main problem with this argument lies elsewhere. It consists, rather, in the assumption that permissive norms—and much else in law as well—are presented as commands. Certainly there is *an aspect* of compulsoriness or objective necessity about legal rules, in the sense of indicating non-arbitrary or non-optional patterns to follow in order to give effect to particular values. Thus Hart's "puzzled man" or the "man who wishes to arrange his affairs" wants to be told what the law requires. He does not want a (mere) recommendation, it is true, but it does not follow that he must experience, say, permissive norms (or secondary rules) as commands. This is so because the contradictory of recommendations is not commands, but non-recommendations which includes the many modes of functioning of norms as Hart has described them. To reduce all these to commands does conceal effectively the manifold ways in which rules function in the law and how legal subjects use them for guidance. Thus using permissive norms (or secondary rules) to make a will need never give rise to the consciousness of being commanded to do anything; the type of self-expression operative here through the distribution and transmission of property is phenomenologically distinct from that of being commanded. Permissive norms can function in legal experience as language does in speech acts: as sets of expressive possibilities, a quality equally present, as demonstrated in the previous section, in lawyers' law and much of the law of social adminstration.

The upshot is, therefore, that, although Amselek is correct to locate legal norms within the ambit of the ethical, as he defines it, and equally right to disengage the concept of commands from both a doctrine of sovereignty as well as from the threat of sanctions (or orders to officials to apply sanctions) for breaches of the law, he has not gone far enough. His critique needs to be radicalized in two related ways: first by giving up a "pure" theory of law in favor of seeing law as interwoven in the Gestalt structure of other orders of meaning in society, as Merleau-Ponty has described it; and second by unhinging the concept of a norm or rule from that of a command by properly distinguishing between the latter and what is compulsory. Thus commands cannot form part of the essence of law in the way he thinks they do.

Although it is plainly the case that Hart's concept of rules is much more congenial to thinking law as structurally similar to language than is Amselek's view, it is still true that his account of the ways in which the players use the rules of the legal "game" does not answer all the questions which one might raise about at least three issues on which Merleau-Ponty's phenomenology can shed light. These consist of the validity of obsolete rules, the coherence of a legal system, and the significance of legal rules in the wider social context. I shall take up the first two problems in the remaining discussion of the present chapter, and the third in the following chapter.

The issue of the validity of obsolete rules—in legal systems with no rule of obsolescence—emerges from the fact that, in the internal point of view, rules are presented to consciousness as "reasons for. . . ." In part this means that, as in the relationship of speech to language, consciousness is seldom in the position of reasoning from the particular rule appearing to the legally indicated course of conduct. Of course, one might be in the position of "the puzzled man" who wants to fulfill his legal obligations and either does not understand the relevant rules and/or how to apply them. (The linguistic analogue would be someone who has something to say and is searching for the proper way to say it.) But even here there is a (pre-)disposition to accept the rules as reasons. Thus, as we saw in the previous section, reasoning from a certain situation to its legal status does not tell the whole story, or even what is most important about the legal consciousness of the internal point of view.

But obsolete rules are not only not seen as reasons for doing or refraining from doing something; they are not usually seen at all. Thus, unlike rules-as-lived, we ordinarily do need reflective acts of a positing consciousness in order to apprehend them. They are more or less permanently irrelevant to the conduct of social life. One has to add "or less" because, in systems with no specific rule of obsolescence, such rules may be temporarily resurrected by prosecutors who are either mad or perhaps looking for an effective means unavailable elsewhere for coping with some particular problem. As a possible example of the former, Hart tells us that "In 1944 a woman was prosecuted in England and convicted for telling fortunes in violation of the Witchcraft Act, 1735."[66] And as a potential case of the latter, *The Sunday Times* reported recently (20 January 1985, p. 5) on a 19-year-old Dane who was determined to ride his motor-scooter "across the now frozen Oresund Channel between Denmark and Sweden. In last week's attempt, he not only went through the ice but also got arrested for 'driving on the sea without permission', a law that few realized was on the statute books."

Normally, however, consciousness takes up the internal point of view in such a way that rules present themselves as having a more permanently living use value. We thus expect that such rules will be more enduringly fruitful and relevant for providing guidance in playing the legal "game." This fact about legal consciousness has much to do with the distinction between "real rules" and "paper rules" advanced by the American Legal Realists,[67] and ends up arguing against part of Hart's view on the validity-efficacy relationship, though not, because of the objective aspects of rules, in favor of the "rule scepticism" of the former group.

For, on Hart's view, let us recall, (i) there is no necessary connection between a law's validity and its efficacy, (ii) the efficacy of the system as a whole is a necessary condition, rather than the meaning, of the validity of a particular law, and finally (iii) "having an obligation" is essentially different from "being obliged." Now if we take these claims, together with his distinction between the internal and the external aspects of rules, and situate them in the context of the synchronic and the diachronic, it becomes plain that what Hart says is much more applicable to the former than to the latter. Validity thus becomes a rule-bound concept in a synchronic system (a tautology) which is efficacious and utilized from the internal point of view through all those legal activities which correspond to the way that speech uses language. The external observer, on the contrary, examines the system synchronically in order to predict behavior patterns, to reason from them to the efficacy of a certain rule, and thence to conclude that this efficacy constitutes the validity of the rule in question.

But although from the synchronic perspective it is always possible to disentangle validity from efficacy in this way—in theory, if not always in practice—when it is a question of the diachronic, the question becomes murkier. This is precisely the problem with obsolete laws (in systems with no rule of obsolescence) which are so far on the horizons of our legal consciousness—if they are there at all, which is most doubtful—as to be completely inefficacious. And that there is some real sense in which such laws are not valid can be seen plainly when the matter is phrased in terms of obligations. For, in the diachronic perspective, *desuetudo,* the continued and constant disuse of a rule, tends to blur together the senses of "having an obligation" and "being obliged." That is, there is here a genuine sense in which such obsolete, "paper" rules are not law because, to consider only the simpler case of primary rules, they no longer impose any duties. What meaningful obligation, after all, can there be today for men to always wear pants upon entering the city of Tucson, Arizona, or in Hawaii to abstain from putting pennies in their ears?

Hart would not accept such a view, since for him rules do not retain their validity on the grounds of habits of obedience alone. For instance, the 1944 prosecution and conviction of the woman for telling fortunes in violation of the Witchcraft Act of 1735 can hardly be understood in terms of habitual obedience to George II and his Parliament. In this he is quite correct. But from the diachronic perspective, rules are not just habitual behavior. Diachrony is primarily and for the most part a succession of synchronies, each of which is systematically coherent and revolves around a valid rule structure as Hart has described so well. As a result, we may claim consistently such a concept of validity, as distinct from that of efficacy, when it is a question of the synchronic perspective, and yet blur this distinction from the diachronic aspects of the system.

On the other hand, since in systems with no rule of obsolescence obsolete rules do belong objectively to a constituted legal order, they are not purely subjective either and consequently, as Joseph Raz points out, the attitudes of the participants in the system are irrelevant to the *existence* of such rules.[68] Furthermore, as Merleau-Ponty observes of language, and the same is true of law, a detail of a system fallen into *desuetudo* may be picked up and systematized (again) (CAL 258). Thus we should say that obsolete rules are formally valid, but in a purely "empty" sense (pure form) of being mere vestiges of the past now buried under contemporary social life. Their validity is thus, from the internal point of view, potential rather than actual because for all practical purposes—which is to say effectively the legal life of the society from the internal point of view—they ought to be disregarded, in the unlikely event that they are known at all. This is to say that they ought to be treated as invalid unless and until they are accepted and acted upon by the law-applying entities of society, such as the courts.[69] After such authoritative new life has been breathed into them, they pass from the state of being historical relics to an operative part of the legal vocabulary which, if enforcement is consistent enough to establish a pattern, can impose obligations, create rights, and so forth. Of course, whether courts would do so would depend upon a variety of factors, including the way that legal rules are situated in the wider context of society, which is the topic of the following chapter. Before proceeding to that subject, however, let us look briefly at the second unresolved problem in Hart's account of rules, that of the coherence of a legal system.

The problem of the coherence of a legal system arises from Hart's contentions that (1) a mature legal system is composed of both primary and secondary rules, (2) the internal point of view on rules is really necessary for there to be rules at all, and the acknowledged fact that (3) it is largely only officials in the system who have anything to do with that class of secondary rules conferring public powers. As we have seen above, it is primarily officials who enjoy the greatest creativity of legal speech—because for them the system has a much greater range of use values than for laypersons. But the result of this set-up is that, from the internal point of view, only a tiny fraction of a legal population would be situated such that they could relate to that considerable body of secondary rules that confer public powers, or indeed, to have much knowledge of them (they are usually in the domain of lawyers' law). For the vast majority of legal subjects, therefore, in this two-tiered arrangement, secondary rules that confer public powers are likely to play little role, if any, in their legal consciousnesses.

At least part of the answer to how this sort of arrangement can be coherent, and perhaps enough of an answer after all, is to be found in further precision of the way that these secondary rules are actually presented to those who do not deal with them directly. That is, we have seen that the rule structure as a whole is given to consciousness (from the internal point of view) as a rather anonymous, vague background of social order and control, only certain aspects of which are focussed on at a particular time. This is to say that, as detailed in the previous section, the phenomenon of rules evidences the same Gestalt structure of focal-point and horizons as does the perceptual object. The unity of the appearing legal system from within the internal point of view is not threatened by the necessity to thematically constitute secondary rules which provide for public powers (because they are usually given only indirectly, through the actions of officials) because the whole objective rule structure is already given pre-reflectively in consciousness, and what is not given directly is still given indeterminately. Like the hidden sides of a perceptual object, therefore, even secondary rules conferring public powers are to non-officials present-as-absent, but this absence is not nothing. It is a particular mode of appearing, an able-to-be-seen if desired.

In the manner of their being present-as-absent, however, such secondary rules are the inverse of obsolete rules. For the latter are not given at all, except through a certain specific legal act which resurrects them. The former, however, make up the continuously presupposed context of whatever part of the legal system is illuminated. They would thus not present the same "empty" sort of experience of validity as do obsolete rules—whenever the latter happen to come into focus at all—except in the case of particular legal acts effecting changes in one or another secondary rule.

The subject of changes in legal rules generally, however, demands consideration of the environing social context of rules in order to appreciate the motivation of such changes, their relation to changes in society at large, and the reverse influence of law on the wider context of the social flux. These topics, together with a cluster of issues about judicial decision making, will form the subject of the following chapter. But before going that far, let us step back from what has been said in the present chapter and try to summarize what exactly law is for Merleau-Ponty.

From all that appears, law in his view is a social structure, or order of meaning, which is a form of praxis, of living intersubjective relationships. As a structure, it has its objective aspects—the institution of social order—and those that are subjective. The latter are the expressive activities of legal consciousness in and through which legal subjects take up the constituted legal system of a given society—which broadly includes not only its rule structure of positive laws but also environing contexts of common law traditions, if any—modulates them, and adds (sediments) new meanings in the system. Since like all orders of meaning in society law has as its prime purpose the expression of meaning, and since all forms of expression have the same structural features, and since it is language as analysed in Saussurian linguistics that Merleau-Ponty mostly uses as the paradigm of all expression, and since finally he thinks politics—the immediate context for most of his references to law—according to the model of language, it follows that he would see law also as a similar form of expression. Accordingly, the Saussurian distinctions between *la parole* and *la langue,* on the one hand, and the synchronic and diachronic aspects of language, on the other, have been employed to illuminate their legal analogues in a system of living rules, or law-as-lived.

Further, since law—like other social institutions, and chiefly language—serves as a system of expressive possibilities for concretizing values, it is interwoven with other orders of meaning in society as "parts" of a Gestalt—a "structure of structures" (S 147). This is to say that all the "parts" of the Gestalt are internally related such that each reflects the whole unified network of social choices expressed in the political, economic, or religious regions of the life-world, and each is robbed of its experiential identity when removed from the internal relation of this Gestalt structure. This means that, among other things, law reflects and is involved in all other orders of meaning within a given society, but is neither identical to nor determined by them. (The consequences of these last two statements will be explored more fully in Chapters VI and VII, respectively, in terms of an analysis of law in the wider social context and that of law and morality.)

The situation of law within the social Gestalt has the additional consequence that it is impossible to carry out a Husserlian sort of eidetic analysis of law, in which the *eidos* of law would be abstracted from (purified of) other orders of social meaning. It also means, inversely, that in addition to the similarities of law with other social phenomena or "law-like objects," some way must be found to distinguish law from those other phenomena. Phenomenological description must therefore pay attention to differences as well as similarities. Merleau-Ponty, who (like Marx) was arguing within a special context for particular reasons, paid much more attention to the latter than to the former. Thus the differences, or at least some main ones, have to be added to his texts by reasonable conjectures, which is in part what the following chapter will attempt.

NOTES

1. See particularly his *General Theory of Law and State* (New York: Russell and Russell, 1961) and *The Pure Theory of Law* (Berkeley and Los Angeles: The University of California Press, 1967).

   Austin's *The Province of Jurisprudence Determined* appeared in 1832; it was also published by the Noonday Press (New York: 1954).
2. In his "The Phenomenological Description of Law," trans. Raoul Mortley, in Maurice Natanson, ed. *Phenomenology and the Social Sciences* (Evanston: Northwestern University Press, 1973), II: 367-449, at 381ff., Amselek labels approaches to law such as that of Merleau-Ponty "syncretism." Instead, he prefers the "methodological principles" of Hans Kelsen's "pure theory of law" "which bear a fundamental relationship to those defined by Edmund Husserl" (p. 382). Accordingly, Amselek wishes to work out a purely eidetic analysis of the essence of law, disentangled from all other social phenomena. He considers that Kelsen's intentions were pure, even if his results were not, and views him as "speaking the real language of phenomenology" when he (Kelsen) writes of the envisaged pure science, "The fundamental principle of its method is thus to eliminate from the science of law all elements which are foreign to it." Merleau-Ponty would be much more inclined to endorse the view that "law reaches into nearly all social ativities but only as a part (of varying importance) of each such activity. . . . " Geoffrey Sawer, *Law in Society* (Oxford: The Clarendon Press, 1965; reprinted 1973), p. 13. As a result, law cannot be disentangled from other aspects of the social Gestalt without distorting its experiential identity. I shall return to this in the last section of this chapter.

   Amselek, be it noted in passing, is not only critical of Kelsen's results—for rendering law "obscure by certain doctrinal considerations, in particular by a fairly marked Kantian influence" (p. 383)—but also takes issue with Austin's positivism and theory of sovereignty, whilst keeping a "command theory" of law. See below in section 3. The former claim is all the more interesting because it is far from clear that Kelsen ever read Kant.
3. This issue, which has a considerable history, will be addressed in the final chapter. In our own times, perhaps the most illustrious contribution, also discussed below, is the celebrated debate between H.L.A. Hart and Lon L. Fuller. For the former, see, among other things, "Positivism and the Separation of Law and Morals," 71 *Harvard Law Review* 593-629 (1958), *Law, Liberty, and Morality* (Oxford: Oxford University Press, 1963), and *Essays in Jurisprudence and Philosophy* (Oxford: Oxford University Press, 1983) (in which, by the way, the first article is reprinted). For the latter, again among many texts, see "Positivism and Fidelity to Law—A Reply to Professor Hart," 71 *Harvard Law Review* 630-73 (1958), and *The Morality of Law* (New Haven: Yale University Press, 1963). This debate is only the tip of a much vaster iceberg, but it is a splendid tip.
4. Hart observes, *à propos* of Mark Twain's *Huckleberry Finn,* that it is "a profound study of the moral dilemma created by the existence of a social morality which runs counter to the sympathies of an individual and to humanitarianism. It is a valuable corrective of the identification of all morality with the latter." *The Concept of Law* (Oxford University Press, 1961), p. 254n. The passage to which this note is attached is as follows: "Huckleberry Finn, when asked if the explosion of a steamboat boiler had hurt anyone, replied, "No'm: killed a nigger.' Aunt Sally's comment 'Well it's lucky because sometimes people do get hurt' sums up a whole morality which has often prevailed among men" (p. 196).

5. Neil MacCormick, "Law as Institutional Fact," 90 *Law Quarterly Review* 102 (1974), at pp. 106, 110. Cited in John Finnis, *Natural Law and Natural Rights* (Oxford: The Clarendon Press, 1980), p. 227n.
6. Amselek, p. 369. The references to Bergson are, respectively, *The Two Sources of Morality and Religion,* trans. R. Ashley Audra and Cloudesley Brereton, with W. Horsfall Carter (New York: Holt, 1935), p. 298 (translation slightly modified by Raoul Mortley); and *Creative Evolution,* trans. Arthur Mitchell (New York: Holt, 1911), p. 141.
7. "Expressed" is used here in the widest possible sense to cover rules that are explicitly written out as well as those which are implicitly revealed in actions or interpreting texts. Not all criteria of validity are explicitly formulated, and not all constitutions or codified systems provide specifically mentioned criteria (or ultimate criterion) of validity in the system.
8. Sawer, pp. 64-65.
9. This passage repeats an earlier, more interesting, but posthumously published version at PM 95-96: "Husserl employed the nice word *Stiftung* to designate first this indefinite fertility of each moment of time, which exactly because it is singular and passes, will never be able to cease having been or to be universally—and, what is more, the fertility, derived from the former one, of the operations of culture which open a tradition, continue to count after their historical appearance, and demand beyond themselves the same and other operations."
10. Sawer, p. 127. (Italics in the original text.)
11. Sawer, p. 128.
12. Sawer, p. 128.
13. Sawer, p. 127.
14. Sawer, p. 127.
15. There is, however, a puzzle over the precise legal status of private administrative orders in systems which allow for them. For example, presidents of the United States can issue "executive orders" without any requirement to publicize them. At certain times, as in the case of Richard Nixon during the Watergate era, such secrecy is of acute legal importance.
16. Hart, *The Concept of Law,* p. 97.
17. Amselek (pp. 433-34) argues for some of the same reasons against Austin's theory of sovereignty whilst keeping a command theory of law as conceptually distinct from the question of positions of superiors and inferiors. This is so in part because "commands and recommendations can be set up on the basis of joint agreement between two or more individuals concerned (e.g., legal contracts)" (p. 434).
18. Kelsen follows Austin here in large part, but Amselek rejects the conceptual link between commands and compulsion, and yet maintains that it is part of the essence of law to appear as a command (pp. 426-49).

    It is perhaps wise to remember as well that the fact that force (enforceability or the likelihood thereof) is a necessary condition of a valid legal order implies as well that particular laws in the system cannot be purely subjective either. They cannot merely project the state of mind of officials in the system, but rather must have some objective weight. Hence the oddity of Parisian traffic signs which say, "Parking Tolerated But Not Advised" ("Stationnement Toléré Mais Pas Conseillé"). Parisian drivers, always alert to the possibility of even the most infintesimal parking place, if not to the subtleties of a legal consciousness, are not overwhelmed by the subjective wishes of their officials. In New York City, near the World Trade Center, social control functions a bit differently. For, although there is a hugely prominent warning that reads, "Don't Even Think of Parking Here," the latter sign is posted underneath a more prosaic threat to tow away the automobiles of offending drivers and to subject the latter to Draconian fines. In any case, the former sign could hardly have any legal force before the arrival of the Thought Police of *1984*.

19. Sawer, p. 17. (Italics in the original text.) Amselek also rejects the fundamental tenets of a *Begriffsjurisprudenz,* for reasons that will appear in the following section.
20. For an earlier version of the following remarks, see William S. Hamrick, "Towards a Phenomenology of Legal Rules," *Journal of the British Society for Phenomenology,* Vol. X, No. 1 (January 1979), pp. 9-22.
21. Hart, *The Concept of Law,* p. 78.
22. Hart, pp. 78-79.
23. Hart, pp. 78-79.
24. Hart, p. 92.
25. Hart, p. 92.
26. Hart, pp. 92, 93.
27. Hart, p. 93.
28. Hart, p. 94.
29. Hart, p. 87.
30. Hart, p. 244.
31. Hart, p. 244.
32. Hart, p. 87.
33. Hart, p. 87. (Italics in the original text.)
34. Hart, p. 88.
35. Hart, p. 88. (Italics in the original text.)
36. This view refers to the psychological theory of obligation mentioned above, as well as to Hart's distinction between "being obliged" to do something and "having an obligation" to do it. The conditions for the former are satisfied if coercive force is applied and recognized as such. For example (Hart's own), if a gunman demanded my wallet or my life, I would "be obliged" to hand it over. But I would clearly have no obligation to do so. In Hart's view, the Austinian analysis makes law into "the gunman writ large" *(The Concept of Law,* pp. 6ff.). Alf Ross also analyses validity and obligation in terms of both whether a given rule is really effective and whether it is generally perceived to be motivating or socially required. See Chapters I and II of his *On Law and Justice* (Berkeley and Los Angeles: The University of California Press, 1959).
37. Hart, p. 82.
38. Hart, p. 88. The same situation can apply in various ways to different classes of people, and not just to "bad men." One could consider, for example, the accounts by R.D. Laing and A. Esterton of the ways that children try to cope with parentally imposed "obligations"—actually, the state of "being obliged"—and rules which are perceived as absurd obstacles. One way of describing the resultant schizophrenia is to say that the children concerned could never reach the stage of "having obligations," but were rather always "being obliged" to follow inconsistent and mystifying commands. Emptied of all internal sense, the rules were reduced to mere expedients for staying out of harm's way. They were not accepted from the internal point of view as reasons for doing or abstaining from doing certain things. Rather, they were mere problems, but horrifying ones, of calculating the path of least resistance. See Laing and Esterton's *Sanity, Madness and the Family* (London: Penguin Books, 1970) and William S. Hamrick, "Language and Abnormal Behavior: Merleau-Ponty, Hart, and Laing," *Review of Existential Psychology and Psychiatry,* Volume XVIII, Nos. 1, 2, & 3, 1982-83 (but actually published in 1985), pp. 181-203.
39. Hart, p. 104.
40. Hart, p. 100.
41. Hart, p. 102.

42. "Word" here is "le mot," in the sense of a dictionary word which is part of the linguistic equipment belonging to *la langue* rather than "the spoken word" which pertains to *la parole.*
43. Italics are in the original text. Pierre Bourdieu, one of the leading figures in socio-criticism in France today, has recently expressed almost the same ideas in his "Le champ littéraire: Préalables critiques et principes de méthode," *Lendemains* 36, 1984, p. 5.
44. The "Preface" to *The Concept of Law* tells us that, "Notwithstanding its concern with analysis the book may also be regarded as an essay in descriptive sociology." He is also influenced in this respect by J.L. Austin's "linguistic phenomenology" in the sense that, in doing a descriptive sociology, "it is particularly true that we may use, as J.L. Austin said, 'a sharpened awareness of words to sharpen our perception of the phenomena'" (*The Concept of Law,* p. vii). By contrast, one might say that in Merleau-Ponty's phenomenology, one finds a sharpened awareness of the phenomena which can help us comprehend better our use of words, and the internal and external aspects of rules form a particularly interesting case in point. And in fact, precisely in the context of the internal aspects of rules, Neil MacCormick points out a possible reason why Hart's account of the internal aspects of rules converges with Merleau-Ponty's view of the relation of speech to language and of the place of language amongst other orders of social meaning. MacCormick underlines the fact that Hart was influenced substantially by Max Weber, especially through Peter Winch's *The Idea of a Social Science and its Relation to Philosophy* (London, 1958), especially Chapter 2. MacCormick's references to this influence on Hart are located in his *Legal Reasoning and Legal Theory* (Oxford: The Clarendon Press, 1978), pp. 278-79.
45. Hart, p. 35.
46. Hart, p. 35.
47. Hart, p. 36.
48. Hart, p. 37.
49. Hart, p. 39.
50. Hart, p. 40.
51. Amselek, p. 384. (Italics in the original text.)
52. Amselek, p. 408. (Italics in the original text.)
53. This expression is borrowed from Georges Hostelet, *L'Investigation scientifique des fait d'activité humaine* (Paris: Rivière, 1960); cited by Amselek at p. 411.
54. Amselek, p. 411. (Italics in the original text.)
55. Amselek, p. 384. (Italics in the original text.)
56. Amselek, p. 417. (Italics in the original text.)
57. Amselek, pp. 418-19. (Italics in the original text.)
58. Amselek, pp. 422-25.
59. Amselek, pp. 414-15.
60. Amselek, p. 416. (Italics in the original text.)
61. Amselek, p. 429. (Italics in the original text.)
62. Amselek, p. 384. (Italics in the original text.)
63. Amselek, p. 432. (Italics in the original text.)
64. Amselek, p. 436.
65. Amselek, p. 437, n.129.
66. Hart, p. 60.
67. See, for example, Joseph Bingham, "What is the Law?", 11 *Michigan Law Review,* 2-15, 22-23 (1912). See also Hart, "Positivism and the Separation of Law and Morals." At n. 40, Hart points out that one legal realist, Karl Llewellyn, recanted an early, extreme form of the doctrine which had appeared in his *The Bramble Bush.* In the second edition of that work, which appeared in 1951, Llewellyn described his earlier formulations as "unhappy words when

not more fully developed, and they are plainly at best a very partial statement of the whole truth" (p. 9).

Roscoe Pound classified phenomenology as the fifth of six "social philosophical schools of the philosophy of law." See his *Outlines of Lectures on Jurisprudence* (Cambridge: Harvard University Press, 1943), p. 20. Pound argues for the relative jurisprudential unimportance of phenomenology in America, since its goals had already been reached by the Legal Realists. In terms of the concept of legal rules, Pound was mistakenly certain that this is the case, as the present chapter has made abundantly clear—at least for the existential phenomenology of Merleau-Ponty. (I am grateful to Mr. Neil Duxbury of the Faculty of Law, London School of Economics, for calling my attention to this reference. It is to be found in his unpublished undergraduate thesis in the University of Hull, 1984, "In What Way Might We Move Towards a Phenomenological Approach to Law?", p. 64, n.1. Mr. Duxbury currently is completing his doctoral dissertation on Reinach's phenomenology of law.

68. What Raz actually says is that the fact that obsolete rules "are disregarded by the population is irrelevant to their existence." *The Concept of a Legal System* (Oxford: Oxford University Press, 1970), p. 201. But this subtly misdescribes the situation, because we cannot disregard something unless we first notice it, and it is most improbable that the majority of participants in a legal system are aware of most obsolete rules in the first place.
69. This is Raz's own conclusion, except for the claim that obsolete rules ought to be treated as invalid whenever met with.

VI: LAW AND SOCIETY

In connection with working out Merleau-Ponty's probable view of law according to the model of language as a system of expressive possibilities, the last chapter dwelt at length on H.L.A. Hart's theory of rules. This was not due to the fact that Merleau-Ponty was influenced by Hart; in fact, there is no evidence that the former had ever read his Oxford contemporary. Nor was it owing to any sort of reverse influence, for Hart has stated explicitly that he has never read Merleau-Ponty.[1] It is, rather, because it would be difficult to overestimate the importance of Hart's contributions to the philosophy of law, and the impressiveness of his work makes all the more significant the close similarity of his thought to conceiving law according to the model of language. In the best sense of the traditional task of philosophers to "save the phenomena," he has managed to save that of law from its distortions at the hands of earlier positivists, the American Legal Realists, and pure formalists of various stripes. And he has done so with such lucidity and persuasiveness that his work certainly constitutes a "decisive sedimentation" (S 194), back beyond which it will not be possible to go in the philosophy of law.[2]

This does not mean, however, that Hart's approach to law cannot, and has not, been criticized. On the contrary, searching criticism has existed for some time on the relationship of law and morality, which we shall explore in the following chapter; on the differences between primary and secondary, as well as between duty-conferring versus power-conferring rules; on the similarities and differences between mature legal systems and "pre-legal regimes"; and on the relation of principles and rules.[3] Most of these questions, interesting and important as they are in their own right, entail further precisions of Hart's work and raise issues about which Merleau-Ponty wrote nothing. Therefore, we cannot go beyond merely mentioning them here, with the exceptions of a certain aspect of the relationship of principles and rules, which will be considered in the last section of this chapter, and the subject matter of the following section.

§1. Legal Rules, Words, and the Wider Social Context

Hart's work has been substantially criticized in a way in which Merleau-Ponty would do himself, based on what he wrote about the situation of law in the whole tissue of the social Gestalt. This line of criticism, which has been argued in an interesting and convincing fashion by J.R. Lucas,[4] holds that legal rules are much more tightly related to other phenomena in the social world than Hart claimed in *The Concept of Law* and elsewhere. As noted at the beginning of the last section of Chapter V, grounding a discussion of law in the concrete means accounting for legal rules as they are situated in living legal relationships in one's life-world. Lucas contends that, although Hart in principle shares this aim by stressing the internal aspect of rules which is really necessary for there to be rules at all, Hart's account remains too abstract because not enough significance is attached to, nor place left for, the ways that rules function in the wider social context. In Merleau-Ponty's idiom, Hart's descriptions of rules would be "less false than abstract." Thus Lucas advises that "We should, rather, see law as a social phenomenon, to be distinguished from other social phenomena, but intelligible only in a social context, and not—as lawyers are too ready to suppose—an autonomous discipline which can be explained and understood entirely in its own terms."[5]

Lucas argues that this untoward abstraction stems from Hart's desire to emphasize the differences between a mature legal system and a "pre-legal regime" via the addition of secondary rules. The effect of this distinction is to play down the ways that mature and primitive legal systems are really connected and thus to consider the rules of the former as having much more abstractness and autonomy than they actually possess. Thus marriage as an institution existed in both primitive legal systems as well as in our own, but the secondary rules governing marriage came after, and therefore do not constitute it. Consequently, for Lucas, "Marriage is not, as one might suppose from *The Concept of Law,* an institution created by law, nor do wills exist because Henry VIII passed an Act enabling us to make them. Rather, marriage is a social institution, and laws about marriage do not so much *constitute* the state of matrimony as *specify* the procedure for getting married and the rights and duties of husband and wife."[6]

This same line of criticism is picked up by Geoffrey Sawer, but in a much more extended and radicalized way. This is so because, in dealing with the means by which law is grounded in society, he points out how not only whole areas of law but also the meanings of basic legal terms themselves are formed on the basis of a prior social understanding and thus effectively reflect all these other orders of meaning within the social order. Thus "lawyers and judges also have and cannot do without general views about the structure of a society and of particular social groups; constitutional law depends on some theory of the relations between government and governed, family law on some theory of domestic relations; even so abstract a legal concept as property derives much of its content at a particular time from the social values of that time."[7]

In so saying, Sawer thus joins Merleau-Ponty's concern (at PhP 220-21) for translating legal vocabulary in terms of the living social relationships which (synchronically) fund it with meaning in a given historical epoch. By way of further illustration, he considers certain similarities between primitive societies and our own, with which Lucas was partly concerned, and he underlines in the former four kinds of "normative observances" which correspond to law in modern societies—and which Merleau-Ponty would have considered, like *mana,* forms of intersubjective relationships constitutive of praxis. These four types are (1) rules which define sub-groups within a particular culture, (2) marriage and exogamy, (3) religion established in a particular culture, and (4) what we would call property.[8] At the end of his descriptions of these "normative observances," he takes certain writers to task for anachronistic interpretations of primitive societies which view the latter through a filter of modern legal terminology, and in particular through the classic matrix of eight correlative but contrasting legal relationships between rights, liberties, or privileges; powers, and immunities worked out by Wesley N. Hohfeld.[9] It is certain that Merleau-Ponty would applaud such a critique of anachronistic interpretation. But it is equally clear that he would appreciate even more Sawer's contention, if it is ultimately valid, that Hohfeld's scheme, isolated as it is from changing social conceptions of its basic terms, cannot adequately account for the process of legal development.

As an instructive example, one which also coheres well with the protests of Merleau-Ponty's new liberalism, Sawer writes that "much modern legal development depends on an ambiguous use of the word 'right.' If we find that at a particular time a man's ability to earn a living is protected only in an indirect fashion and that the activities of capitalist monopolizers on the one hand and of trade union monopolizers on the other do not come within the ban of existing law, then we tend to inhibit the creation of further remedies which the times may demand if we insist that there is no 'right' but only a 'privilege' or 'liberty' to earn a living."[10]

Moreover, as Merleau-Ponty clearly also would agree, tables of abstract relations give a misleading impression of the concrete relationships between law and other social structures. "Actually," Sawer concludes (as did Lucas), "social life is a phenomenon largely independent of the law, having a complexity and fluidity which cannot be expressed in legal categories. From it we abstract for legal purposes certain aspects of activity and subject them to legal categorization."[11] By "independent" Sawer does not mean to deny his claim, noted in the previous chapter (at n.2), that law extends into almost all social activities, though not in the same degree in each, but rather to indicate that social institutions antedate their legal formalization, that the modes of law and other social activities are different and distinct, and that an interface of law with these activities does not amount to reducing the latter to exclusively legal categories.[12]

Social institutions, therefore, tend to develop first, whilst law comes after as a way of resolving unclarities and disputes which stem from them (and other sources). Legal rules come into being to provide guidance and precision, and once these are fairly settled, no additional legislation or other law-making activities are required until social change warrants them. (Legal speech can then draw on such rules as part of the constituted legal "syntax" with no necessary additional specification.) Thus, as Lucas phrases it, "The function of law is not to initiate forms of life but to obviate and resolve disputes. It does not create institutions, but gives them definition. . . . The law provides a skeleton, which needs to be fleshed out by the social arrangements of our everyday life. It is reasonable for professional purposes to abstract this skeleton, and study the law without overmuch concern with its social setting: but for a philosophical understanding of law, we shall misconstrue it if we abstract too much."[13]

§2. *Legal Evolution and Social Evolution*

Sawer also joins Lucas' reasoning here by providing a number of illuminating examples of the ways in which social evolution has generated a corresponding legal evolution—all of which are illustrative of Merleau-Ponty's descriptions of law as a "part" of the social Gestalt. For instance, compensation came to be substituted for revenge after a growth of social wealth, and it "first becomes wide-spread in communities where cattle-owning is common because payment in cattle is easy for the offender and tempting to the injured. Social stratification causes compensation to be calculated on scales which reflect the social distinctions."[14] Second, economic motives of rulers can be shown to lie behind changes in legal institutions. Throughout medieval Europe, kings asserted special interests in certain kinds of offenses, such as murdering a Frenchman in Norman England, and denoted certain places, such as the royal roads, under their special jurisdiction. Thus, as Sawer notes, "The holding of courts tends to be a profitable business; there are fees as well as penalties, and there are Royal officials as well as their masters wanting to encourage, if necessary by legal fictions, the use of Royal courts when a lower feudal court should be employed."[15]

Further, many of the forms of social relationships, or praxis, to use Merleau-Ponty's idiom, have come to be regulated by contracts instead of informal custom, and this is in large part because of social evolution to complex industrial societies. Thus "The area open for negotiation and agreement is much larger . . . partly because social mobility is great, and partly because the opportunities for buying, selling, hiring, borrowing, lending, pledging, entering associations, and associated legal transactions depending in some degree on *choice* have become so much more numerous with increase and spread of wealth and education."[16]

Finally, fourth, Sawer remarks[17] how American law reform in what concerns the judicial system tends to reflect a stress on business management techniques derived from the environing capitalist, technological culture. And he also cites with approval Jerome Frank's observation in *Courts on Trial* (1949)—based on a chilling American Bar Association handbook for trial lawyers—that American courts serve as theatrical substitutes for private battles and "relates the prominence of battle in the courts of the U.S.A. to the values of competitive private enterprise."[18]

On the other hand, as we have seen above in Part One (I.2), society is a structure of interrelated structures in which there is no necessary simplistic correspondence of one structure to another—the legal to the economic or the political, for instance. Rather than any too-simple isomorphism, the relation of one structure to another is "subtle and variable"; there is on occasion a "homology," but at other times "one structure is the counterpart and antagonist of the other" (S 148). Correspondingly, Sawer points out a number of instances, of which three may be briefly sketched here, in which the structure and functioning of a legal system do not correlate simplistically to the economic or political environment of the society concerned. (Other examples will be given in the following section, in terms of the functioning of the courts.)

The first example concerns the way that Roscoe Pound managed to refute an over-simple economic interpretation of the "fellow servant" rule laid down in *Priestly v. Fowler* (1837). "This case," as Sawer explains, "established that a master is not liable to his servant for injuries caused by the carelessness of a fellow-servant, and it has often been relied on by social historians to show how law is influenced by the economic bias of judges."[19] Pound showed why, in terms of the way the issue was presented in court, received legal doctrines antedating industrial capitalism were really responsible for the outcome of the case. (But it is also true, as Sawer goes on to mention, that the subsequent acceptance and generalization of the decision in England and in the United States owed much to the mores of capitalism at that time in which there was little concern for workers' conditions of employment.)

A second example concerns law reform. Despite Frank's observations cited above, law reform need not be thought of as bound so closely to prevailing social values or to the political commitments of the reformers. Changes in lawyers' law can and have been effected without regard to the conservative or liberal preferences of officials concerned to make such changes, and "This is also the kind of law with which the American Law Institute has been mainly concerned since its foundation in 1923."[20]

Finally, third, both modern capitalist and communistic societies share at least four features important for the study of law which are much older than the economic forms of life in those societies. These are (i) specialized law-making institutions, (ii) courts of law, (iii) a police force, and (iv) a developed legal profession. In Sawer's view, one of the main functions of (i)-(iv) is "sharing in the exercise of power within the society. Indeed, this way of regarding them is much more congenial to much juristic thought than is the sociological view that they perform a designated 'role' as institutions."[21]

Sawer's descriptions of law in society are also pertinent to the second of the two problems outlined above (V.1) concerning the essence of law. That is, the situation of law within the Gestalt structure of various orders of social meaning posed both the impossibility of a traditional eidetic analysis of law—which would entail disentangling the phenomenon of law from all other phenomena—as well as the opposite sort of problem, to which Sawer's remarks are connected, of saying what distinguishes law from other similar phenomena such as mores, customs, habits, taboos, and so forth. If we recast this latter problem in terms of thinking law according to the model of language, it becomes a question of knowing how law as a means of speaking and instituting certain values differs from other social means of doing so. Of course, the complexity of this topic is enormous, in partial testimony to which a vast quantity of books and articles have been written in the domain of sociological jurisprudence and elsewhere (a substantial number of which are vague, ambiguous, and confusing). And as explained above (V.1), Merleau-Ponty's phenomenology gives us very little guidance at this point since he was most often concerned to stress the unity and similarity of various forms of expression in the life-world. As a result, only a brief sketch of an answer relevant to his texts can be attempted here.

Effectively there appear to be at least three salient differences between the ways that law and other orders of meaning, including language, serve as systems of expressive possibilities. The first of these, the discussion of which has already begun in the previous section, is that law usually works with a different rhythm and slower pace than other changes of meaning in society. Legal changes tend to come after other social changes to formally validate them, settle disputes, and as Lucas pointed out, otherwise regulate existing forms of life. Moreover, for the reasons given in the previous chapter (V.2), changes in lawyers' law, the law of social order, tend to move more slowly and be less frequent than those of the law of social administration—the law of social control—which respond to other social changes.

It is true that there can be judge-made law (a claim defended in the following section)—about which the majority of a population are ignorant and sometimes, even if fully informed, would be completely indifferent—which sets in motion other social changes.[22] More portentiously, law may also be occasionally at the forefront of an evolving social vision, the unity of which would eventually come to be reflected, if it succeeds at all, across a variety of different strata of meaning in the life-world—in economics, politics, religion, and so forth, as

Weber argued—for the majority of participants in the system who come to accept this vision. One might well argue, for example, that this was the case in the United States for the Warren Court's famous school-desegregation case of *Brown v. Board of Education,* 347 U.S. 483 (1954).[23] Certainly one can see from this distance how much that decision was out of step with the times: it is not only a question of the rumblings of constitutional crisis it provoked when it was handed down, but also of its long, bitter, grudging acceptance by the majority of society. And there are still American school systems and their circumambient communities which behave as though they have never heard of *Brown,* and there are still citizens who relate to that landmark decision from the estranged perspective resembling the external point of view on rules. Even so, it is still the case that the attitudes of most American citizens have been shaped definitively by *Brown* and the social upheavals it set in motion, such that it is now impossible for American society to return to a pre-*Brown* consciousness. It is another example of a decisive sedimentation of meaning.

But although law may be occasionally on the cutting edge of an evolving social vision which it helps to shape, and other modes of value expression, such as positive morality, take their shape in the light of an advanced state of the law, this situation remains a-typical. The more usual situation in the eyes of most social historians, sociologists, and lawyers,[24] is the mirror-image of this one. Social institutions develop, movements in positive morality spring up, rapid advances in technology occur, none of which requires a legal spearhead. Law then follows, as Lucas pointed out, to obviate or solve problems and to ratify what has already been accomplished. Thus law and other media of social value expression exist in an ongoing dialectic. In the time-structure of our legal consciousness, moral or technological changes occur within the existing framework of the received legal system, but the creativity of our past projects sometimes cannot be accomodated within the structure as it is constituted. Changes are then necessary in the legal system—as a living institution, it is always in principle *open* to such changes—and with these new sedimentations of meaning the altered state of the system is projected towards a future. Our successors will then take up the system themselves and invest it with their own particular use values, and so forth.

The recent history of American and, to some extent, English law offers three different sorts of clear examples of this dialectic. First, the women's movement over the last twenty-five years or so has managed to raise the consciousness of enough of the population such that women in business as well as in private life can never be systematically demeaned as they were previously. This does not mean, of course, that female workers in America (or anywhere else) are now generally safe from job-discrimination, sexual harrassment on the job, or in general are now treated as equals. Such is hardly the case, especially in the area of unjustly unequal salaries. But even so, in the wake of this development in popular morality, laws were passed and decisions handed down in courts (some of which are discussed in the following section) which in turn formally ratified women's social gains. And it is to be hoped that this altered legal structure will, in turn, be a positive factor in shaping attitudes of succeeding generations who may then not grow up with the prejudices of their forefathers.[25]

The second and third examples of the way that law interlocks with other social phenomena have to do with recent rapid advances in technology. The advent of the computer industry within the last ten years has compelled an important change in the law of social administration, if not in lawyers' law as well, in what concerns privacy. For it developed that previous definitions of privacy which were formulated largely with print media in mind were in many ways inadequate to protect the privacy required for data in electronic storage and retrieval systems. Thus law had to respond to a (very quickly) changed social situation.

The third example is in many ways much more interesting than the first two, because it is considerably more complex, more fluid, and has much less of a firm foundation in either substantive principles of the common law or in positive law, case law, or even in constitutional provisions. This example concerns bio-medical research over the last several years which has produced not only a breathtaking series of discoveries, but also in the process has seriously outpaced the abilities of the legal system as well as positive morality itself to keep up with it. An enormous literature in both ethics and law, as well as a major research institution (The Institute of Society, Ethics, and the Life Sciences at Hastings-on-Hudson, New York), have all come into being because of this research.

Some of the legal (and moral) questions raised by these scientific advances have proved to be of a rather traditional sort posed in an unfamiliar laboratory setting. But others, in fields such as genetic engineering—especially recombinant DNA research[26]—*in vitro* fertilization, and other reproductive technologies, have been more novel and harder to deal with. To take only some of a myriad of examples, in France recently, a Presidential decree had to be issued authorizing a widow to withdraw from a sperm bank semen deposited by her husband before his unexpected demise, for the purpose of having his child. It is not only a philosopher's puzzle as to whether the child has a father and if so, in what sense, but also a matter for law-making authorities when legitimacy, the transmissibility of names, and inheritance rights are at stake.

In quite a different region of reproductive technologies, one could ask whether fetal research ought to be legally (and morally) permissible when there is no intention of attempting implantation in a woman's uterus? That is, the blastocyst would be maintained in its petri dish culture—not, as popularly supposed, in a test-tube—for as long as possible for experimental purposes. Is it consistent with evolving legal (and moral) conceptions of justice to do *in vitro* fertilizations, since it necessarily subjects the (eventual) fetus to unknown risks to which it cannot consent? Or one could ask whether, if an artificial womb is developed, ought it to be legally (and morally) obligatory to use it, since the "quality control" of the developing fetus would be much higher than in the uncertain (because only intermittently monitored) environment of the mother's womb? Even if not obligatory, should women who give birth in the usual way be subject to negligence suits by their children born with birth defects which could have have been detected and repaired in the laboratory?

Further, courts and moral theorists as well have wrestled with knotty problems associated with artificial insemination. Is "artificial insemination by donor" (AID), for example, simply adultery in a different form? Or consider various scenarios attached to "artificial insemination by husband" (AIH) when a surrogate mother is employed. If the husband's wife is able to produce an egg but not able (or want to) bear a child to term, conception may occur in the laboratory via AIH and the embryo implanted in the uterus of a surrogate mother. The latter, providing no genetic material herself, effectively provides an incubating service and a delivery system. Or, the surrogate mother may provide half the genetic material herself if the wife cannot produce an ovum or does not want to—say, because of the risk of transmitting genetic defects. In the present state of technology, conception would occur via AIH as before, and the embryo implanted in the surrogate mother's womb.

Now, some interesting legal (and moral) difficulties are strewn along the way of these reproductive technologies. In the case in which the surrogate mother contributes no genetic material of her own, what would be legally indicated if she decided to have an abortion during the pregnancy and for reasons that did not contravene any law in her jurisdiction? Could she be prevented from doing so by the genetic parents? If she did abort, could she be sued by the genetic parents, and for what? If a written contract existed, would it be enforced in the courts over her subsequent desire to be rid of the fetus?

The abortion question might also be posed in the case in which the surrogate mother does contribute her own ovum, since her claim to be subsequently free of the fetus might be thought a stronger one. And interesting questions about the enforceability of a contract—together with the question of what "consideration" there is here—have also been raised. But we could equally well consider the inverse situation in which, say, part of a contract stipulated an abortion in case the relevant genetic tests disclosed specified birth defects. Suppose that after such tests are positive, and are considered reliable, the surrogate mother decides not to abort. Ought the contract to be then enforceable at law? If so, how? Would the State be placed in the position of enforcing abortions? Or would damages for breach of contract be sought at trial in a new version of a "wrongful life" suit? If the contract would not be enforceable, could tort law be invoked against the surrogate mother for willful negligence in producing a damaged product?

Further legal obscurities surround these cases in which surrogate mothers contribute their own genetic material to the embryo. Some new legal definitions of legitimacy will have to be worked out, for one thing, for it is a conceptually and legally different situation from that of adoption. Can a man adopt his own child? Can a couple adopt half its child? In addition, can a surrogate mother legally (and morally) sell her child without being guilty of slavery? Can she rightly be said to be selling only half a child and, if that is meaningful, is selling half a child slavery? (Some State courts in the United States have ruled that it does somehow make sense and that selling half a child is slavery.) Or again, if the genetic father dies before the child is born, ought the surrogate mother be able to retain possession, even in the face of a suit by the non-genetic mother? (This strikes me as a more interesting puzzle than the one Solomon was called upon to solve.)

The list of such questions and their legal and moral ramifications is almost endless, and as interesting and socially important as they are in their own right, I have detailed only a small slice of them here because they offer us a paradigm case of the usual ways in which law interlocks with other modes of social change. Technology has raced ahead of our moral preparedness to deal with the possibilities that such scientific research has opened up, and whilst positive morality struggles to adjust, there have already been a multiplicity of public and socially important results demanding legal regulation and corresponding changes in the legal system itself. Or again, as Lucas phrases it, "The function of law is not to initiate forms of life but to obviate and resolve disputes. It does not create institutions, but gives them definition."[27]

The interrelations of law and other social changes often tend to stimulate a dialectic of changes within law itself—between lawyers' law and the law of social administration—and I shall say more about this momentarily. For now, let us consider the other two main differences between the ways that law and other social orders of meaning serve as systems of expressive possibilities. The second difference consists of the (formally) non-optional quality of law, as opposed to customs, mores, and traditions—which can, to be sure, exercise an intense pressure on people to conform to some received view, but this coercion by itself will be only informal. As noted above (V.1), for Merleau-Ponty, formal enforceability is a necessary, but not sufficient, condition of a valid legal system. And we have also already met with the formally compulsory quality of law in Paul Amselek's mistranslation of it as commands (V.3).

But it is still the case that, despite Amselek's mistranslation, there is an unavoidable compulsory element about law. If I do not follow the custom of sending the appropriate card on Mother's Day, no one will put me in jail. On the other hand, suppose I am always observant myself but like, say, Robespierre, I cannot give my conscience a rest and stay home. Thus I manage to have my unfaithful neighbor pilloried in the newspapers. Then I can be taken to court because, as we have seen, primary rules (or imperative norms) impose obligations regardless of whether we wish them to or not. And even with secondary rules (or permissive norms), as also pointed out above (V.3), there is still an atmosphere of force attached which, although far from constituting their meaning in the internal point of view on law, still constrains the expressive possibilities of legal speech by means of the spectre of sufficiently unpleasant consequences for not adhering to the observance of the prescribed ways to make use of such norms. A will, for example, may be declared invalid in England if the testator correctly signs it, but at the top of the first page rather than at the bottom of the last one (an example of Hart's).[28] Or, a marriage may be declared invalid in the absence of following the legally prescribed form—no matter how creative the parties want to be or what personal principles they want to defend—as, for instance, in homosexual "marriages." Law, then, like *mana,* language, or capital, manifests itself to consciousness as a form of praxis in the broad sense—a type of exchange or intercourse amongst the members of society—with the distinguishing characteristics of different kinds of constraints and corresponding consequences.

The unavoidability, or non-arbitrariness, of these constraints is also connected to the third major difference between the phenomenon of law and other social phenomena, and that is that, at least in mature legal systems, law gets established formally rather than informally. Unlike law, customs, habits, mores, taboos, and the like, all tends to grow up informally, without being the outcome of decisions by identifiable persons or bodies of persons such as kings, legislators, or judges. Also, again in contrast to a mature legal system, customs, mores, and the rest, do not emerge in accordance with any secondary rule, such as that of recognition, by means of which law becomes formally sedimented in the history of a given society. Thus law does not simply grow up or emerge anonymously from the general background of the social context, but is formally instituted. Nor can it be changed in the same way, as Merleau-Ponty clearly realized.[29]

Correspondingly, the circumstances of their disappearance are also dissimilar. Customs, taboos, and mores, can all "die off" and disappear. They present themselves to consciousness as the dead letter of a past now submerged and transcended. Of course, they may be all taken up by a present-day consciousness "*à la recherche du temps perdu*" with a variety of values attached—nostalgia, curiosity, desperation, and so forth. Nevertheless, they still are gone. But obsolete laws, in legal systems with no rule of obsolescence, do not simply go away. They may not be enforced any longer, and so for all practical purposes do not count, but that fact does not undo their formal reality. Thus, whilst a considerable amount of ink has been spilled over the validity of obsolete or "paper" rules, no similar controversy exists for informal means of social control. For customs, mores, taboos, and the like, their validity *is* their efficacy, and although in practice it might be difficult to determine the degree of efficacy at a given moment in a changing society, it is still usually not difficult to recognize a certain custom or taboo which is rejected definitively.[30]

I mentioned earlier that the dialectic between legal and other social changes tends to set in motion another within the law, namely, that between the law of social order, lawyers' law, and that of social control, the law of social administration. One way in which this happens is that social pressure for some type of legally relevant change, if strong enough, usually attracts political attention and then takes the form of legislation concerned with social control. But it can also occur that, in societies with enduring or rigid constitutions, the provisions of the latter may frustrate the desires of political leaders. Questions of lawyers' law then attract political attention, perhaps changes in the former are then effected, and afterwards, as part of the social order, it lapses into a datum taken-for-granted rather than an instrument of social control. This is one main reason why, as mentioned above (V.2), constitutional law often serves as a bridge between the law of social order and that of social control. Geoffrey Sawer, who argues this point, provides a clear example of this constantly shifting relationship that succeeded in effecting changes in the law of social administration in England during the 19th-century. It happened that "the general law governing the structure of business corporations was a matter of political dispute and difference in England from 1825 until 1862, and in the early 1850s, the press was still cursing the principle of limited liability as an instrument of fraud. But the general principles of the 1862 Act were generally accepted, and a considerable number of lawyers' law questions began to arise, of the sort which empty the House of Commons if anyone tries to explain them or solve them by appropriate legislation."[31]

On the other hand, another example that did *not* work, to which Merleau-Ponty's new liberalism certainly would be sensitized, concerns an attempt to apply a law which is not accepted by the general population. "Thus," explains Sawer, "during the first two-thirds of the nineteenth century, over the greater part of the English-speaking world, the capital-owning and employing classes attempted through their influence with enforcement agencies or by private prosecution (which at that time was widely available) to prevent the growth and activity of trade unions of employees, using for this purpose common law and statutory provisions concerning conspiracies in restraint of trade. It was an attempt at social control which failed, and the failure was due to social changes which had to be accomodated by such changes in the law as the English Trade Union Act, 1871."[32] As Merleau-Ponty would phrase it, the relationships between the various social structures involved here were subtle and variable enough so that one did not simply become the product of the other, and finally, that changes in the legal structure reflected previous, independent changes in society at large as opposed to the desire for social control manifested by powerful politicians and capitalists. This anchorage of law in wider social life is equally visible in judicial decision making, the subject to which we now turn.

§3. *La Parole Juridique and Its Similarities to other Speech Acts*

No consideration of law in society, however incomplete, could fail at least to touch on the significance of courts and the nature of judicial decision making. For one thing, as Sawer quite rightly claims, "Law is not clearly distinguished from other aspects of social order until courts of law come into existence."[33] For another, law must have at the same time a certain stability but also fluidity—an institution always open (synchronically) to the coming-to-be of new meaning. Law, therefore, like language, must be a "moving equilibrium" (S 108), and it is very often the case that, especially in legal systems such as those of England or of English derivation, it is the judiciary that have played the role of prime mover in bringing about changes in the law—and sometimes, as in *Brown,* in society at large. Courts thus perform the crucial double function of maintaining, or helping to maintain, a legal and social equilibrium as well as serving as a fulcrum of new expression and sedimentation of meaning.

Now Merleau-Ponty never wrote a coherent, systematic philosophy of law, let alone a comprehensive theory of legal reasoning: he was, after all, a philosopher, not a jurist. On the other hand, thinking law according to the model of language, coupled with other parts of his philosophy, does provide us insights into certain aspects of judicial decision making both in terms of the way that courts embody a fundamental continuity with other orders of meaning in society, in terms of illuminating the decision-making process itself, and finally in speaking to certain contemporary issues within the philosophy of law. In considering each of these in turn, what follows is not intended in the least to be a complete treatment of the subject, or even part of it. For every subject touched on here, there are many more that there is not space to consider and which are detailed in countless books in legal philosophy. But exhaustiveness is not my object: the purpose of this essay imposes the limitation of only considering what Merleau-Ponty's phenomenology of the social world would lead him to say about these matters. Thus the following sketch aims at being an exercise in creative expression as the latter understood it, in the sense of staying within the limits of his own texts and adding meaning to them which they already had the capacity to generate.

To begin with, the ways that judicial speech (i) takes up a constituted legal language—of statutes or codes, constitutional provisions, relevant precedents, common law traditions, and the like, depending on what sort of legal system is at issue—(ii) modulates it, and (iii) adds new meaning to it, are similar to other exercises of speech throughout the social world in at least seven ways. First, it shares with other forms of expression the structure of freedom operating in a settled order of social institutions. Second, it shares with ethical and political decision making (III.4, IV.4) an ineradicable contingency, or lack of certitude, in attempting to make the best decision possible in a particular case situation. As in both the ethical and political aspects of life, there is in judicial expression an unavoidable ambiguity or indeterminacy attached which undermines an absolute certainty in arriving at the best solution. Judicial decision making is, from this point of view, only a special case of a general and persistent need to get on with things and be content with a lack of total assurance as to the concreteness of the course chosen (see III.4). I shall come back to this at the end of this section.

Third, as in other areas of social expression, judicial decision making evidences a distinction between "originary speech" which is creative, and "secondary speech" which is a more passive, copying mode (PhP 446). Almost all interesting cases—whether in codified Continental systems descended from Roman law, or in statute-based systems such as those of England or the United States which have evolved in the light of the common law—may be grouped under "originary speech." And all "hard cases," in which there is no fixed and settled law which determines the outcome either way, would be included by definition. By contrast, "secondary speech" would embrace, not necessarily trivial, but certainly uncontroversial decisions in which there are no particular difficulties in determining the facts and finding a clearly indicated provision of a code or a statute to apply. In general, there are many different ways in which judicial speech can make use of the language of law to bring a determination of the facts of a particular case into organized juxtaposition with the applicable rules of law. I shall return to this subject below in terms of the import of judicial creativity for the concept of rules.

Fourth, in legal systems such as that of England or those of English origin, in which judicial decisions are controlled or at least influenced by precedent, judicial speech usually takes the form of reasoning by analogy. This is so because of the fundamental principle of justice (known at least since Aristotle) that like cases are to be treated alike. Sawer shows effectively how legal analogical reasoning is rooted in a more general social understanding, and a reference to the social purpose of law concerned, by means of ascertaining the aspects of the precedents which are supposed to be pertinent to the instant case. In other words, there is some freedom of decision here, as elsewhere, as to what particular linguistic tools will be used and how. To take a simple and undistinguished example—but for that reason a very clear one—in *Ellis v. Johnstone*, 2 Q.B. 9 (1963), the question was, "are dogs to be treated in the same way as horses and cattle under the principles exempting animal owners from liability for collision between animal and vehicle in a highway? A majority of the Court of Appeal said yes, with the result that the dog-owner was not held liable to the car-driver."[34] In making this decision, attributes of dogs and those of cattle and horses (animals previously involved in such cases) were compared. But how did the judges determine which were the relevant characteristics? "They considered earlier decisions and information about the legal history of the matter, and from these sources concluded that the relevant characteristics were *being a domestic animal* and *having a propensity to wander.*"[35] These were hardly the only logically possible characteristics to consider, of course, and the appellate decision was not unanimous. Thus the decision-making situation clearly underlines the presence of choice in such creative speech which effectively links it to other such exercises throughout the life-world.

A fifth way in which judicial speech is continuous with the structure and functioning of other orders of expression is in terms of the way that it interlocks with other modes of expression. Thus the discussion in the previous section about the subtle and variable relations of social structures and the fact that one is not likely to be a simplistic copy of, or caused by, another, has its counterpart in judicial expression as well. For instance, although there have been in the past prominent and even flagrant attempts to politicize courts,[36] and although judges' political (and other) values are certainly relevant to the decisions they hand down, it still does not follow that a justice's opinions will necessarily and directly reflect his or her political (and other) values. For example, President Eisenhower made this discovery when the Warren Court, whose Chief Justice he had appointed under supposedly more conservative colors, handed down the landmark decision in *Brown v. Board of Education.* And there are many other examples of this lack of a simplistic causal theory of behavior, one of the most recent of which has been that the Supreme Court under Chief Justice Warren Burger has been in some ways more activist than that of his predecessor whose activism President Nixon wished to halt with his Burger nomination.

Or again, as Sawer points out, "It has become a commonplace that A.V. Dicey was wrong when in his *Law of the Constitution* (1885) he assumed that Continental-type systems of administrative courts would be biased in favour of governments and civil servants; on the contrary, they provide more effective and flexible remedies against governments and their servants than do the Anglo-American systems, yet their judges have usually had an even closer association with administration in their early training than men who specialize in other types of jurisdiction."[37]

One prominent jurist who did believe that there was a direct causal link betwee a judge's beliefs—especially those that are subconscious—and his or her decisions, was the late Jerome Frank. On his view, expressed in *Law and the Modern Mind* (1930) and *Courts on Trial* (1949), judges should be psychoanalysed in order to expose those hidden beliefs. Similarly, in the former text, as Hart expresses it, "the belief that there could be legal rules binding on judges and applied by them, not made by them, in concrete cases is stigmatized as an immature form of fetishism or father fixation calling for psychoanalysis."[38] We have seen above (II.2) that Merleau-Ponty rejects such subconscious causal explanations, although he does not deny the sub-(or un-) conscious entirely. Rather, it is a certain "latency" in experience which always *could* be relevant to what is on the conscious agenda. But it would not follow that whatever personal factors incline a judge to make a decision—even in the presence of no particular guidance from a controlling statute or precedent or section of a code—are necessarily buried in the depths of the subconscious and "silently" determine the judge's thought processes and linguistic expression.

On the other hand, there clearly are hidden subjective factors somehow at work in judges' decision making, funding the perception of formal rules with other social meanings, as there are throughout the entire spectrum of expression in the life-world. A body of statutes and precedents, or codes and their judicial interpretations, are not pure objects closed in on themselves, but rather the correlates of a judicial consciousness. And this basic fact about living institutions is joined to another feature of the social world as a whole, namely that the judiciary is not, any more than any other group or society as such, a "collective conscience," but is rather "intersubjectivity" (I.2, V.1). The truth of these assertions can be illustrated in a variety of legal contexts, and is especially evident in a series of related cases in the same field. A particularly illuminating set is to be found in certain United States Supreme Court decisions during the 1970's concerning sex discrimination.[39] The following brief résumé is by no means all that could be (or has been) said about these cases, but it will suffice to clearly exemplify Merleau-Ponty's descriptions of speech and language, the openness of institutions to new meaning, and of "intersubjectivity" instead of a "collective conscience."

As a necessary, but short, preface to these cases, it should be pointed out that American sex discrimination law, as well as the whole of the equal protection law of which it forms an important part, are chiefly rooted in the Fifth and Fourteenth Amendments to the Constitution. The former provides in relevant part that no one shall "be deprived of life, liberty, or property, without due process of law," and the latter requires that "No State shall make or enforce any law which shall abridge the privileges or immunities of citizens of the United States; nor shall any State deprive any person of life, liberty, or property, without due process of law; nor deny to any person within its jurisdiction the equal protection of the laws."

Now despite these clear, unambiguous statements, there remain stubborn difficulties in locating a coherent and principled intervention in equal protection cases by the U.S. Supreme Court. For a long time, the Court had interpreted the Equal Protection Clause of the Fourteenth Amendment as requiring only a "very deferential rationality" review. As Gerald Gunther clearly explains it, "That 'old' variety of equal protection scrutiny focused solely on the means used by the legislature: it insisted merely that the classification in the statute reasonably relate to the legislative purpose. Unlike substantive due process, equal protection scrutiny was not typically concerned with second-guessing and restraining legislative ends. And usually that rational classification requirement was satisfied fairly readily: the courts did not demand a close fit between classification and purpose; perfect congruence between means and end was not required. . . . Only in special, limited contexts was equal protection found to have a deeper bite during most of its history—most notably in racial discrimination cases."[40]

Now during the Warren Court era, as Gunther goes on to show, this "old" equal protection came to be combined with a "new" variety. A clearly defined two-tiered approach evolved in which the "new" equal protection entailed a more intensive, strict scrutiny. (This phrase was first used in a Vinson Court decison, *Korematsu v. United States,* 323 U.S. 214 (1944), where it was promptly not followed.) Strict scrutiny was addressed to ends as well as means and hence "required a far closer fit between classification and statutory purpose, a far closer congruence between means and ends, than the rough and ready flexibility traditionally tolerated by the old equal protection. Moreover, equal protection became a source of ends scrutiny as well: legislation in the areas of the new equal protection had to be justified by 'compelling' state interests."[41] The Warren Court established that strict scrutiny would fall on "suspect classifications"—mostly racial in nature—and laws affecting "fundamental" rights. The latter included voting, criminal appeals, and certain others, but as Gunther notes—and which Merleau-Ponty would find an illuminating example of legally creative speech—" in the extraordinary amount of commentary that followed, analysts searching for justifications for those enshrinements were understandably tempted to ponder analogous zones that might similarly qualify. Welfare benefits, exclusionary zoning, municipal services and school financing came to be the most inviting frontiers."[42]

In the Burger Court, the locus of the sex discrimination cases at issue here, there has emerged a "newer" shape of equal protection law in which the best established aspects of the "new" equal protection law remained intact, but in which also the Court has proved reluctant to expand its frontiers. Strict scrutiny for racial classifications has been preserved and a number of sex-based classifications have been overturned, although a majority of the Court have not yet ruled that sex is a suspect classification. And in terms of a search for an elusive coherent and principled intervention protocol, several Justices have wrestled with various formulae which would blur the rigid two-tiered distinctions inherited from the Warren era. This is particularly so of Justice Marshall who argued in his dissents in *Dandridge v. Williams,* 397 U.S. 471 (1970), and especially in *San Antonio Ind. School District v. Rodriguez,* 411 U.S. 1 (1973), that there is no coherent, principled scheme for judicial interventions in equal protection law. Instead, he insisted in *Rodriguez*—in a way most interesting from Merleau-

Ponty's point of view—that the Court applies a "sliding scale" (his phrase in *Dandridge*) of standards depending on what the majority perceive to be the "constitutional and societal importance of the interest adversely affected and the recognized invidiousness of the basis upon which the particular classification is drawn."

There were two additional elements of the Burger Court's intervention in equal protection cases during the 1970's. The first was that a sexual or racial classification had to have some rational relationship with a "legitimate, *articulated* state purpose," as Justice Powell wrote for the Court in *McGinnis v. Royster,* 410 U.S. 263 (1973), rather than with a purely speculative or illusory purpose. The second criterion, which was that a sexual or racial classification had to further materially the objective of the statute in which it was located, was expressed in a sex discrimination case, *Reed v. Reed, Administrator,* 404 U.S. 71 (1971).[43] But what principle controlled the Court's intervention here, "old," "new," or "newer" equal protection? As Gunther points out, it is not easy to understand the result in *Reed* "without an assumption that some special sensitivity to sex as a classifying factor entered into the analysis. . . . Only by importing some special suspicion of sex-related means from the new equal protection area can the result be made entirely persuasive. Yet application of new equal protection criteria is precisely what Reed v. Reed purported to avoid."[44] And in fact, as Justice Marshall complained in his *Rodriguez* dissent, "[*Reed*] can only be understood as [an instance] in which the particularly invidious character of the classification caused the Court to pause and scrutinize with more than traditional care the rationality of state discrimination."

Further, the Court decided two years after *Reed* in *Frontiero v. Richardson,* 411 U.S. 677 (1973), that military dependents' benefits programs were unconstitutional in which, as Justice Brennan announced the decision of the Court, "a serviceman may claim his wife as a 'dependent' without regard to whether she is in fact dependent upon him for any part of her support. A servicewoman, on the other hand, may not claim her husband as a 'dependent' under these programs unless he is in fact dependent upon her for over one-half of his support." The programs were declared unconstitutional because, as with the Idaho statute in *Reed,* they contravened the Due Process Clause of the Fifth Amendment. In *Frontiero* this was so because women alone had to prove the dependency of their spouses—thus being required to overcome a greater obstacle to receiving benefits. In *Reed* this was so because women had to prove that they were as qualified as men to administer an estate, but not vice-versa.

Although most people today would agree that these cases do put the law on a rational basis, problems of interpretation still remain. For in *Frontiero,* Justice Brennan found "at least implicit support" in *Reed* for his view—also shared by three other Justices—that gender was an "inherently suspect" classification "and must therefore be subjected to strict judicial scrutiny." As Justice Brennan saw it, *Reed* was a justified "departure from 'traditional' rational-basis analysis," but as we have just seen, this is at best a controversial claim.[45] (The phrase, "rational-basis", refers here to the "old" equal protection law, rather than the more general meaning employed in the first sentence of this paragraph.)

Now considering Merleau-Ponty's descriptions of expression in what concerns its "subterranean logic," its frequent necessity to solve problems indirectly in order to concretize values "indirectly" (see II.2), he would have also found illuminating the attempts by certain Justices to avoid the interpretive perplexities sketched above by adopting the strategem of "irrebuttable presumptions." Proponents of this doctrine argued that it avoided the equal protection route entirely, although certain other Justices sharply disagreed. The gist of the strategy is to discern the vice of "irrebuttable presumptions" in a given statute or administrative scheme, the presence of which prevents an individual from making a well-founded claim, and this reasoning appears in cases such as *Vlandis v. Kline*, 412 U.S. 441 (1973); *United States Dept. of Agriculture v. Murray*, 413 U.S. 508 (1973); *Bell v. Burson*, 402 U.S. 535 (1971); and *Cleveland Board of Education v. LaFleur*, 414 U.S. 632 (1974).

In the latter case, which is a particularly clear example, pregnant school teachers won their case against the school board's policy which required an unpaid maternity leave beginning five months before the anticipated birth and lasting until "the beginning of the next regular school semester which follows the date when her child attains the age of three months." The Board had argued for the policy on the grounds of preserving continuous teaching and to exclude physically disabled women from the classroom. But in the judgment of the Court, the obligatory dates did not satisfy the test of mere rationality and, since the Board's policy contained no provisions for individualized testing of teachers who wanted to continue working within the proscribed time frame, the Court held that "The rules contain an irrebuttable presumption of physical incompetency, and that presumption applies even when the medical evidence as to an individual woman's physical status might be wholly to the contrary." Thus the Board's mandatory leave policy was held to violate the Due Process Clauses of both the Fifth and Fourteenth Amendments.

But Justice Marshall's *Rodriguez* lament about *Reed* is surely applicable to *LaFleur* as well, since the decision far exceeds the traditional "mere rationality" review and yet does not argue for strict scrutiny for sexual classifications. It is also impossible to understand independent of a special sensitivity to sex. But what kind of sensitivity, and for what reasons?

However these questions are finally to be answered, it is clear that a rule, such as the Fourteenth Amendment—or a part of it, such as the Equal Protection Clause—is not a merely formal entity, but rather gets actively funded by subjective contributions which reflect many social concerns. And this takes place in cases such as the above in the crucial decision as to what type of scrutiny a court will bestow on a given sexual classification or claim of sex discrimination—a decision similar to that discussed by Sawer of choosing the characteristics of the precedents seen as pertinent to a case at bar. The sensitivity to the sexual classification at issue is the crucial first step towards upholding or turning down a claim of discrimination, and it very certainly does not lie outside the decision-making process itself. Thus also the essence of Justice Marshall's complaint, for this non-formalizable and subjectively variable sensitivity is at least one core ingredient in the answer to the question of whether the Supreme Court's intervention in such cases is coherent and principled—whether, in other words, the Court's treatment of such cases at this crucial first step is guided by anything but arbitrary perceptions of the social and constitutional significance of the sexual classifications concerned.

Whatever may be the answer to this question, it is still the case that the rules and principles at issue are to be interpreted actively by some value-perceptions as the judicial process instantiates its singularly important perspective on a law-as-lived. Thus, what a rule is, or what it means to have a rule, always has to be understood in terms of this living interaction. Framed in a slightly different manner, what Oliver Wendell Holmes, Jr., once said of words is also true of rules: A "word is not a crystal, transparent and unchanged, it is the skin of a living thought and may vary greatly in color and content according to the circumstances and the time in which it is used."[46] This does not mean, as we have already seen (V.3) that rules have no objective content, that they are not sedimented in an objectively instituted structure, but only to stress that the relationship of judicial speech to existing rules in a mélange of subjectivity and objectivity, law-in-act. I shall return to this at the end of this section.

We have been considering the above cases in the light of the fifth way in which judicial speech is continuous with the structure and functioning of other orders of expression, namely that it interlocks with the latter in the way they do with each other—as structures of meaning in subtle and variable relationships with each other. Such cases also illustrate the sixth and seventh similarities as well. The former consists in the fact that judicial speech, like other originary speech, is interpretative, sensitive to what is meant in addition to what is said, and finds its meanings anchored in the social world beyond the internal considerations of the law. For a simple, but not unimportant, example, consider the following book notice which might be submitted as evidence in a case on copyright infringement: "All rights reserved. No part of this publication may be reproduced, stored in a retrieval system, or transmitted, in any form or by any means, electronic, mechanical, photocopying, recording, or otherwise, without the prior permission of the Publisher." Now it is, or should be, obvious that the latter sentence cannot mean what it says. It cannot be the case that the second sentence is the literal, correct translation of the first because it leads to too many absurd consequences as well as conflicts with other legally recognized rights. In terms of the former, it forbids, *inter alia,* copying the notice itself, since it also is "part of the publication." (Logicians looking for trouble could remind the publisher of the pitfalls of self-referential statements.) It would also forbid copying a punctuation mark, or even letters marking the various signatures, from the author's text. Librarians could not write, type, or transmit by computer the International Standard Book Number to their catalogues, since it, too, is part of the publication. Nor could a purchaser copy words or phrases from the text in the margins of his or her own book. And in terms of the way the notice conflicts with other legally recognized rights, it would forbid professors from illuminating their lectures by writing some sentences from the book on their blackboards. If taken at face value, the notice would also forbid a purchaser or borrower from a library from copying out or (more commonly these days) photocopying certain pages to use non-commercially for criticism—whether in student term papers, articles in professional journals, or the preparation of papers to be read to learned societies. And the notice would even forbid photocopying or typing parts of the book in a letter to the Publisher seeking permission to reproduce them!

In short, then, instead of these (and other) "fair uses" of the text, the only connection between the purchaser or library borrower and his or her book permitted by the literal wording of the notice is reading and memory. The literal wording thus begs the question of whether a copyright is an absolute right which, in fact, it is not in many legal systems, if not in all. Consequently, the notice must be reinterpreted in terms of the social purposes of the copyright laws and conflicting claims in court must then be weighed by taking into account not only the purposes of the law plainly in view by the legislature when passing whatever law obtains in the jurisdiction concerned, but also relevant precedents, principles of justice, and the like.

The seventh similarity between judicial expression and other exercises of speech, especially clear in moral and political decision making (III.4, IV.4), consists in the fact that its creativity transcends deductive logic and that, in consequence, it can sediment new meaning within the system that it takes up and modulates. This fundamental aspect of originary judicial speech has several important legal implications and takes up a position in a certain well known debate in the philosophy of law. In the first place, it argues against a *Begriffsjurisprudenz* applied to the development of law in courts. Here also, as Jhering insisted, concepts should not be abstracted from the living conditions of social life to which they eventually refer, social purposes and the ends of law are to be kept in view to (partially) guide the judge's creativity, and legal reasoning is not to be assimilated to the deductive unfolding of the content of legal concepts derived from a "heaven of concepts" (*Begriffshimmel*).[47]

Hart points out[48] that Jhering's main target consisted of certain German academics, but much the same kinds of criticisms were directed against judges and lawyers on the other side of the Atlantic by Oliver Wendell Holmes, Jr. Deeply influenced by C.S. Peirce's pragmatism and operationalism, Holmes issued many now-famous denunciations of *Begriffsjurisprudenz* and its celestial sanctuary. For example, "The common law is not a brooding omnipresence in the sky."[49] and "the life of the law has not been logic; it has been experience."[50] He spoke of "the fallacy that the only force at work in the development of the law is logic,"[51] and of the fact that "general propositions do not decide concrete cases."[52] It was not that he thought logic unimportant in judicial decision making, but rather that he was concerned to stress that it is not primary or that by which the rest can be understood. Also, as Hart writes in "American Jurisprudence through English Eyes: The Nightmare and the Noble Dream," Holmes' replacement of experience for logic as the life of the law is perhaps "the most missued quotation from any American jurist. . . . This in its context was a protest against the rationalist supersitition (as Holmes thought it) that the historical development of the law by the courts could be explained as the unfolding of the consequences logically contained in the law in its earlier phases."[53] For the reasons given above in Part One (II.4), and also with reference to the series of cases on sex discrimination just analysed, Merleau-Ponty clearly would have endorsed Holmes' claim and viewed it merely as a special case of what is true of all history.[54]

Judicial creativity therefore transcends deductive thinking and in so doing instantiates the dynamic of all expression which infuses new life into the constituted system it takes up and makes it say more than it had said, but which it had the capacity to say. It is *making new sense.* Thus, as we have seen, judges make new law in addition to applying the existent relevant provisions of the system; their creativity is not limited to discovering merely what the law really was. The judge is not a "slot machine," an illusion for fostering which Roscoe Pound's famous essay, "Mechanical Jurisprudence," took to task the proponents of *Begriffsjurisprudenz.*[55] Nor is judicial dissent necessarily attributable to sloppy reasoning and/or being misinformed about the facts.

As a result of this likely commitment to judge-made law, Merleau-Ponty would thus join most legal philosophers today in rejecting (in English and allied systems of law) the "declaratory theory" of judicial decisions which holds that, instead of creating law, judges merely evidence what it is. This theory, although defended by Coke, Hale, Blackstone, and others, seriously misdescribes the facts. As Rupert Cross points out, "if there is no such thing as judge-made law, it is impossible to account for the evolution of much legal doctrine. For example, it is a matter of common knowledge among legal historians that the requirement of consideration in the law of contract is based on a series of decisions which can be cited by name."[56] Cross also approvingly cites Mellish, L.J. when he said that "The whole of the rules of equity and nine-tenths of the common law have in fact been made by judges."[57]

A good example of the way some judges in some legal systems can modulate the openness of the institution of law in a coming-to-be of meaning in the form of new law consists of one of the most famous tort cases in England, *Donoghue v. Stevenson,* A.C. 562 (1932). This case was a 3-2 decision in the House of Lords on an appeal from Scottish courts. The facts were these: a woman went to a café with her friend who ordered for her some ice cream and ginger beer. The former was placed in a tumbler by the café owner who also poured half the contents of the latter over the ice cream. The woman consumed part of this combination, after which the friend poured in more ginger beer. As she did so, a decomposed snail, or what was left of one, floated out as well. Since the bottle was dark, opaque glass, it had been impossible for either the café owner or the consumer to inspect the contents. Because she had drunk part of the contaminated beverage, the woman alleged that she had become seriously ill and in consequence sought damages from the manufacturer for negligence. Thus "the problem was whether the manufacturer owed a duty of care to the ultimate consumer."[58] Under existing law at the time, it was clear that the manufacturer had broken its contract with the retailer but, as most lawyers before 1932 probably would have advised, the plaintiff had no remedy from the former. Also, since she had not herself bought the drink from the café owner, she was not entitled to proceed against him for breach of contract. Hence it appeared that she had no legal remedy at all.

But the majority of the House of Lords thought otherwise: "they were not bound to follow the earlier cases, and they explained away or condemned a number of *dicta* in them. . . . the House of Lords legislated retrospectively by overruling *dicta,* if not decisions, by which the Court of Session considered itself bound."[59]

Other such examples of judge-made law abound in many legal systems, even those of code-based Roman derivation—as both Jhering in Germany and François Gény in France showed. And in the United States, for example, *Griswold v. Connecticut,* 381 U.S. 479 (1964), became a landmark case—one subset of Merleau-Ponty's "decisive sedimentations" since they set appropriately serious and enduring precedents—because it was the first time that the Justices of the U.S. Supreme Court supposedly had "found" in the Due Process Clause of the Fourteenth Amendment a guarantee of an individual right to privacy—although no such language is to be found in the Constitution. Such talk of discovery does no good by masking the truth of judge-made law, and it would be more accurate to see in the language of law which is the correlate of creative judicial speech a system of creative possibilities such that, as de Saussure pointed out for language in general, words and phrases have less a fixed definitional significance than a concrete use value.

There is also an important political implication of the rejection of the declaratory theory of law, namely, that it gives the lie to often-expressed conservative desires to appoint judges that will merely apply the law rather than make it. This is a particularly visible trend in the United States just now, because in 1984 Congress passed a bankruptcy bill creating 85 new federal district and appellate judgeships. Coupled with attrition on the bench, President Reagan has already been able to fill 114 vacancies, which is more than one-seventh of the total federal judiciary. It has also been estimated that, by the end of his second term, Mr. Reagan will have had the opportunity to appoint over half the persons serving in these lifetime positions. White House counsel Fred F. Fielding has voiced the *desideratum* of the administration as follows: "We're looking for people who view the role of the courts as interpreting the law, not enacting it. There is an imbalance in some areas of the federal courts, a tendency toward judicial activism. We want to have a balance" (*The International Herald Tribune,* March 26, 1985, p. 1). It seems clear from the context of Mr. Fielding's remarks, that is, the administration's articulated desire for "judicial restraint," that what he means by "interpretation" is what the declaratory theory of law envisages.

Even so, two conclusions follow from the remarks above about the subtle and variable relations of social structures and about the creativity of judicial expression. The first is that it will be entirely correct to predict some political, economic, and moral influence of the sort desired by the administration in the eventual judicial opinions handed down by those expressly picked for those qualities (among other things). Their decisions will be hardly indifferent to those values—represented by the fact that, for example, of all the judges appointed by Mr. Reagan thus far, one-fourth are millionaires and, with the exception of two Blacks and thirteen women, all are white men. On the other hand, for the reasons also given above, it will be wrong to believe that their opinions will be simplistic causal effects of their beliefs, values, races, and social status. Whatever attempts are made through the nomination process to engineer the design of their decisions, these attempts can at most establish subtantial political (and other) influences, not determining causes. And the second conclusion is that the creative nature of judicial expression will also underline the inadequacies of the declaratory theory of law upon which such officials rely.

Closely connected to these conclusions is another facet of judicial creativity equally illustrated by the cases analysed above, and that is what Sawer has called "the myth of decision inevitability."[60] The particular case he uses in this regard, *Ridge v. Baldwin,* A.C. 40 (1964), clearly displays different variations on the same theme in an appellate setting. The principal question in this case was whether a Chief Constable of Police had been correctly fired. There was apparently no serious issue of fact, but there were quite complex legal issues to be resolved. The plaintiff's case was dismissed in both the original trial court of the King's Bench Division and also in the Court of Appeal. But the House of Lords reversed both decisions and found for the plaintiff after all. When added up, five judges had voted against the Constable and four had found in his favor. It is not probable that one or a group of these were much more intelligent, persuasive, or better informed than another. Thus, as Sawer observes, "It is ridiculous to pretend that in such circumstances there was a 'correct' view and that it was the view that prevailed. In such cases no decision is necessarily entailed by the evidence or the law and hence while the reasoning on one side or the other provides some *justification* for the conflicting views, it does not for the *observer* satisfactorily *explain* the decision."[61] Such a decision-making situation as existed in this case also has a lot to do with a statement by Justice Jackson of the U.S. Supreme Court, namely that the Justices of that tribunal are not last because they are infallible, but rather infallible because they are last. Such a conclusion is also closely relevant to the philosophy of law advocated by Ronald Dworkin, which I shall consider briefly at the conclusion of this chapter. Just now I want to return for a moment to Hart, whose view of rules Dworkin most often takes as his target.

Up to this point, the image of judicial decision making developed here according to the model of language has contrasted sharply with one extreme view of judicial decision making, namely that governed by deductive logic as expounded by a *Begriffsjurisprudenz*. But it is also important to see how the model of judicial expression to which Merleau-Ponty would subscribe differs from an opposite extreme. This latter view, which was represented by the rule scepticism of the American Legal Realists—which, as we have seen above, Merleau-Ponty would reject— is the "Nightmare" to which Hart refers in American jurisprudence, namely that, "in spite of pretensions to the contrary, judges make the law which they apply to litigants and are not impartial, objective declarers of existing law."[62] In short, then, from the one extreme of law and judicial decision making conceived as purely objective, we are now presented with the diametrically opposite spectre that they are wholly, or at least in large part, subjective.

We have seen above (V.3) that thinking law according to the model of language entails that, like any living institution, it is a concrete unity of the subjective and the objective, a mediation of the internal and the external, and the same is true of judicial speech. Thus Merleau-Ponty's account of judicial expression would be situated between both extreme views described above and would dialectically mediate them. For judicially created speech takes up the objectively constituted system of rules and adds new sense to it, but this is always an addition controlled by the system of rules itself which both supplies and limits (in the sense of a conditioned liberty) novel judicial speech acts. Rather than unhinging the latter from the objective rule structure, judges make the rules say something new—but only, unless (in the case of lower courts) later overturned because incoherent in the system, what the rules were already capable of saying. Thus

Merleau-Ponty would argue that the best way to understand originary judicial speech—and most visibly that which sets important precedent—is as a "coherent deformation" (André Malraux) of existing rules. Such decisions decenter and recenter existing paradigms of interpretations of rules or principles (see II.3) in order to accomodate the law to social change. Were this not so, it would be enormously difficult in legal systems with written constitutions, such as that of the United States, to both maintain the coherence of the system whilst adapting it to changing social conditions. The alternative possibility, succinctly stated by Lord Wright, is that "An application of words which might be reasonable and just at some time, might be wrong and mischievous at another time."[63]

To the question, "Is there law because judges decide that such-and-such is the case, or is there law already which judges articulate and apply?" the answer is that there is some truth on both sides. Rejoining Merleau-Ponty's phenomenology of truth, we see here again from the internal point of view on rules (as-lived, in-act) that truth in judicial decision making is neither arbitrary—purely subjective—nor merely the transcription of a fixed set of rules which judges merely rediscover—wholly objective. Truth concerns, rather, "rules-for-us," a fluid system or "moving equilibrium." Like the perceptual object, law has a paradoxical objectivity of being an "in-itself—for-us." Correlatively, truth in law is also constituted in consciousness as neither wholly discovered nor completely fabricated, but as a concrete dialectic that embraces both.

But where there can be truth, there equally can be falsity, and it follows that, as noted in the previous paragraph, not all creative judicial decisions are "coherent deformations" of existing rules. There can be "incoherent" deformations as well, which would be evaluated in terms of, say, tests of constitutionality. Also, what are later decided to be unjustified decisions of a certain judge or appellate court can be corrected by a higher court, and similar decisions of a supreme court by the legislature. Nevertheless, even in applying such tests of coherence—such as in *Ridge v. Baldwin*—no tribunal (or legislative body) has at its disposal a privileged, infallible intuition of the truth—whatever that might mean here. The same basic structures of a truth-in-act such as Merleau-Ponty has outlined them (see II.4) will still obtain. Hence, this or that novelty in the law, such as the fashion of "irrebuttable presumptions," will live for a time and whether ultimately it will be judged to be true (to the system which generated it), that is, as a "coherent" deformation of the rules, will only be worked out by its subsequent history of judicial acceptance or rejection. As Merleau-Ponty put it (PM 180-81), truth lies in "anticipation, not adequation"; it is a veri-fication, in William James' phrase (see II.4), not a simple discovery. As a result, judicial decision making serves as an especially rich medium for reflecting "on the object's mode of presence to the subject, on the conception of the object and that of the subject such as they appear to phenomenological reflection, instead of substituting for them the relation of object to subject such as it conceived in an idealist philosophy of total reflection" (S 116).

§4. *La Parole Juridique and Some Main Differences from Other Speech Acts*

We have been concerned throughout the previous section with some of the main similarities between the exercise of judicial speech as it takes up a legal system of expressive possibilities and, on the other hand, the nature and functioning of speech acts in the wider social context. But this is only half the story, for there are also several key differences in the mode of judicial expression which make it unique in society, and which in two cases show plainly why, at the beginning of Chapter V, I stressed that law was analogous to language rather than being one.

One main difference between judicial speech and other social exercises thereof consists in the fact that the way courts are constituted and function results in the fact that its decisions are forced. It is true that, in some cases, dismissal of a case can take on the appearance of outright evasion, and summary judgments might be called thoughtful, delayed evasion. Even if so, however, judges at least are forced to do that much. Judges must somehow consider the cases brought into their courts and cannot defer to other decision-making entities in a legal system, unless the rules of the system indicate referral as the proper disposition of the matter.

A second major difference consists of the limitations placed on what a judge may say by the rules governing the system. For example, whilst legislative speech may and frequently does range over whatever pleases the legislators—whether relevant or irrelevant to the business at hand or even to government as such—the judge is more severely limited to the materials of the instant case and to the relevant codes, statutes, precedents, and the like, in his or her own system. As Cross puts it, "He is subject to the even greater restriction that he can only make law on such specific issues as happen to be litigated before him. Considerations of this nature led Holmes, J., one of the greatest American judges, to say: 'I recognize without hesitation that judges do and must legislate, but they can do so only interstitially; they are confined from molar to molecular motion. A common law judge could not say, I think the doctrine of consideration a bit of historical nonsense and shall not enforce it in my court.'"[64]

A third major difference between originary judicial speeh and that in other regions of the life-world, consists in the fact that the meanings sedimented in the former are done so formally, rather than informally, as in much of the rest of social life. Judges do not make law in the way that poets write verse or that customs emerge and develop. And, as alluded to in the first section of the last chapter, this is indeed one of the greatest differences between law and language.

Changes in linguistic syntax and the meanings of words not only have a different rhythm and style of development than in the law of any mature legal system, but also a different mode of birth.

Moreover, this fact is linked with the fourth major difference between judicial speech and other kinds, a difference which concerns a cluster of related considerations about the ways in which a legal system is available to judicial speech acts. This is to say that there are a number of systemic limitations imposed on judicial decision making, for a variety of reasons, that are not usually to be met with outside the law. For example, in all mature legal systems there are hierarchies of courts such that the decisions of higher courts control those of lower ones. The range of possibilities of such control is enormous, depending on the type and history of the legal system at issue, but certain generalities can easily be noted. For example, in England, because of its system of statutes and case law, there is also highly coercive precedent such that a decision by a higher court is always absolutely binding as *stare decisis* on a lower court—unless some reasonable distinction can be found in the case under consideration—and is persuasive evidence even for courts above it. In the United States, for the reasons cited above concerning problems of adjusting a written constitution to the flux of social change, *stare decisis* fits much more loosely. Even in England, however, it is not everything that the courts say that constitutes a binding precedent, but only what is taken to be the controlling reasoning in the case—the *ratio decidendi.* Other remarks are consigned in theory to a lower plane of *obiter dicta,* but it is not always easy to distinguish these two different elements.[65]

Moreover, there are different modes of taking precedent into account as the present judicial speech act takes up the past state of the legal system. Precedent can be followed, applied, consulted, ignored, contravened, and so forth, one of the more interesting features of which is that provides an involuntary dimension to judicial decisions of the sort not usually found beyond the confines of the legal world. For instance, as Cross puts it, "a precedent may be a persuasive authority although it does not persuade, especially if it has been followed."[66] Similarly, a judge may be bound by a precedent set by a higher court, or by statute or constitutional provision, without wanting to decide in the particular way indicated and even if he or she can give a good (non-legal) reason for not doing so. Thus Lon L. Fuller asks us to imagine a trial judge with a good deal of commercial experience and with a similar amount of trial experience in that area. Unfortunately, he must "live under a supreme court which he considers woefully ignorant of the ways and needs of commerce. To his mind, many of this court's decisions in the field of commercial law simply do not make sense."[67] More seriously, in the United States before the Civil War, there were judges well known for their opposition to slavery—for example, Lemuel Shaw and Joseph Story in Massachusetts—who felt constrained to enforce the (federal) Fugitive Slave Acts as well as Article IV, Section 2, of the Constitution which explicitly states that "No person held to service or labor in one State, under the laws thereof, escaping into another, shall, in consequence of any law or regulation therein, be discharged from such service or labor, but shall be delivered up on claim of the party to whom such service or labor may be due." Thus, they reluctantly issued orders to have fugitive slaves returned to their masters.[68]

There are also in code-based legal systems of Roman derivation, such as that in France, similar restrictions on the expressive possibilities open to jurists. For one thing, Article 5 of the *Code Civil* forbids a judge from positing general rules at the beginning of a decision, and if or she did so, the decision would be vulnerable to reversal on appeal. Second, French law is not at all based on an accumulated history of case law (*la jurisprudence*), but on codes which are in principle complete. No single previous decision of a higher court, or even of the *Cour de Cassation* in Paris, would bind a judge to decide a particular case in such-and-such a way. Also, district courts of appeal are not bound by their own past decisions or by those of lower courts. (Serious criminal trials are held in district assize courts. No appeal is possible from these courts except to the *Cour de Cassation* on a matter of law. The uniform consistency of French law comes, therefore, not from case law, but from the codes themselves and the opinions of the jurists who interpret them. Nevertheless, the freedom of the French judge is more limited than it may appear because, as Cross notes, "French judges and writers pay the greatest respect to the past decisions of the *Cour de Cassation*,"[69] and also because French judges, like their English counterparts,[70] tend to group a number of similar decisions together (in the French case, from the *Cour de Cassation*) to try to detect a pattern of a *ratio decidendi* which is then in actual fact very much influential in the district lower and appellate courts. A convergence (and divergence) of perspectives emergs (see II.3) in and through which the sense or pattern is constituted.

The restrictions placed by higher courts on the expressive possibilities of lower ones also underscores the second major difference between law and language to which I have alluded above (V.1), and this concerns the necessity to conform to authoritatively mandated meanings of words, phrases, constitutional provisions, and the like. To a hierarchy of courts corresponds a sliding scale of expressive possibilities such that construing the legal vocabulary to have more a concrete use value than fixed definitional significance is truer at the top of the system than at the bottom. There is a vast range of possibilities here, but this sliding scale is still consistent with legal rules, like *la langue,* being open somewhere in the system to the coming-to-be of new meaning under the impetus of an interrogatory *parole,* even though at lower levels of the system rules cannot have the indefinite use value of a "piece of change" which can be exchanged for anything on the market (CAL 257). This does not mean that judges at the lower echelons of a legal system are automatons or work out their cases solely with deductive logic and the decisions of higher courts in view, but rather to say that the work they do is carried out in the context of binding, authoritative interpretations to which they must pay heed in a way that users of a language in non-legal situations do not have to. In Hart's idiom, such judges, unlike other users of language, both have obligations and are obliged to do this.

There is one final topic which I would like to consider in the context of precedent, and that is certain claims made by Ronald Dworkin about rules and principles. I can only very briefly address this complex topic here because of the sparseness of Merleau-Ponty's texts which are relevant to Dworkin's arguments, but what relevance there is, is important. Dworkin is concerned to make at least three main, and interrelated points.[71] The first is that, as against Hart, law cannot be only a system of rules. There are, in fact, principles irreducible to rules which can and ought to guide a given judge in rendering a decision, and which form part of the law itself. For example, in the famous case of *Riggs v. Palmer,* 115 N.Y. 506, 22 N.E. 188 (1889), a New York court refused to let a man inherit from the will of his grandfather because the former murdered the latter to speed up the collection process, and the court based its decision (at least in large part) on a very old common law principle of refusing to aid and abet people who attempt to profit from their own immorality. Moreover, says Dworkin, judges have decided, and ought to decide, cases on the basis of (among other things) principles which may not be found in any given statute or any other established rule of law.[72] In one such case, the purchaser of a defective automobile was able to sue successfully the manufacturer in tort for injuries to his wife and himself caused by an accident attributable to a faulty steering mechanism. Even in the absence of written warranty protection—existing warranties limited the manufacturer's liability to "making good" defective parts—the courts agreed with the plaintiff, at one point quoting Justice Felix Frankfurter of the U.S. Supreme Court as follows: (Is) "there any principle which is more familiar or more firmly embedded in the history of Anglo-American law than the basic doctrine that the courts will not permit themselves to be used as instruments of inequity and injustice?" *United States v. Bethlehem Steel,* 315 U.S. 289 at 326 (1942).

Furthermore, although rules theoretically do not conflict, Dworkin says, principles often do. There a judge must weigh them in order to sort out which ought to be controlling. Or, taking into account a number of pertinent rules may lead a judge to formulate a principle or principles to be compared with other principles. Consequently, Dworkin's second principal claim is that judges are not seen properly as legislating or creative, but only as discoverers of what principle(s) ought to be employed in arriving at the correct legal decision. And phrasing the matter thus leads to his third main contention, namely, that there always is, at least in theory, a legally correct answer. Even in hard cases, Dworkin maintains, there is one right answer as to what the law is and the task of the judge is to find it. Thus in the chapter of *Taking Rights Seriously* entitled

"Hard Cases," he fixes on the appropriate name of "Hercules" for his imaginary jurist: "You will see now why I called our judge Hercules. He must construct a scheme of abstract and concrete principles that provides a coherent justification for all common law precedents and, so far as these are to be justified on principle, constitutional and statutory provisions as well. We may grasp the magnitude of this enterprise by distinguishing, within the vast material of legal decisions that Hercules must justify, a vertical and a horizontal ordering. The vertical ordering is provided by distinguishing layers of authority; that is, layers at which official decisions might be taken to be controlling over decisions made at lower levels. . . . The horizontal ordering simply requires that the principles taken to justify a decision at one level must also be consistent with the justification offered for other decisions at that level."[73]

It seems uncontestable that there are principles of law of the sort to which Dworkin refers. No one, indeed, denies this in legal systems such as those of England and the United States. The main difference between Hart and Dworkin on this score, however, is whether such principles are contained within a system of legal rules (or are part of the definition of law), or remain outside it. As Cross points out, all the principles which are referred to in *Henningsen* and other cases "are supported by masses of *dicta* if not by *rationes decidendi.*"[74] And I am personally inclined to see some truth on both sides of the question as to whether principles ought to be included in the definition of law. For on the one hand, excluding them entirely might lead one to think that they are insignificant, and this is patently ridiculous. Who could seriously think inconsequential hallowed common-law principles of the sort that Justice Frankfurter articulated or that "No person shall be both judge and jury"? On the other hand, making principles like these part of the definition of law yields, or tends to yield, the misleading impression that law—especially in hard cases—is more clearly certain than it really is. It seems strange at best to think of a "legally correct answer" in *Ridge v. Baldwin,* for example, and it seems to approach once again the "myth of decision inevitability" (Sawer).

Now there is not much in Merleau-Ponty's phenomenology which can clarify the triadic relationship of rules, principles, and the definition of law. On the other hand, what he does say about expression and truth, especially in the ethical and political domains suggests strongly the rejection of any one-best-wayism. As noted above, the inevitable contingency and ambiguity which surround all human choices applies as well to judicial decision making. Certainty is as much an illusion in the law as elsewhere: in *Donoghue,* for example, all the lawyers before 1932 who would have advised the manufacturer that it was not liable in tort to the ultimate consumer for allowing, or failing to guard against, a snail to get into the beverage, were not necessarily misinformed about the law or ignorant of all common law principles even conceivably relevant to the case. Quite to the contrary, the best legal advice would have been that the manufacturer was not liable. Consequently, as Merleau-Ponty knew well, certainty is more nearly the illusion of hindsight than it is the experience of being-in-the-world. In law, then, as in politics, truth is "perhaps only this art of inventing what will appear afterwards as required by the times" (AD 42). And Merleau-Ponty would not have been surprised either by Cross' statement towards the end of his rich and illuminating essay that "In several of the cases cited in this book, an analysis and synthesis of the precedents on the lines suggested by Dworkin could equally well have produced the result opposite to that reached by the court and, as a proposition of pure law, it would have commanded equal respect among the lawyers of the day."[75]

This is not to say, of course, that Merleau-Ponty, or Cross either, for that matter, has no concern for "taking rights seriously." The truth makes in exactly the opposite direction for Merleau-Ponty, as we have seen throughout Chapters III and IV, and will now examine in a legal context in the following, and final, chapter.

NOTES

1. This statement appears in a letter to Herbert Spiegelberg in response to the latter's inquiry on the subject.
2. Thus P.M.S. Hacker writes that *The Concept of Law* "has achieved the status of a classic in its field. No serious writing upon the subjects with which Professor Hart dealt can afford to neglect his work, and the key concepts with which he was concerned will, for a long time, be discussed within the parameters he laid down." "Hart's Philosophy of Law," in *Law, Morality, and Society: Essays in Honour of H.L.A. Hart,* ed. P.M.S. Hacker and J. Raz (Oxford: The Clarendon Press, 1977), p. 1.
3. On the relations of law and morality, see the references to Lon Fuller above at Chapter V, n.3. On the relation of rules to principles, see Ronald Dworkin, *Taking Rights Seriously* (Cambridge: Harvard University Press, 1977), as well as his many other writings. On the relation of duty-conferring to power-conferring rules, see J. Raz, *The Concept of a Legal System (Oxford: The Clarendon Press, 1970). And on the subject of internal versus external aspects of rules, see Neil MacCormick, Legal Reasoning and Legal Theory* (Oxford: The Clarendon Press, 1978).
4. "The Phenomenon of Law," in Hacker and Raz, pp. 85-98. For an earlier version of the discussion following, see William S. Hamrick, "A Phenomenological Critique of Hart's Concept of Rules," *Archiv für Rechts-und Sozialphilosophie—Supplementa* (Wiesbaden: Franz Steiner Verlag, 1982), Vol. I, Part I, pp. 175-84.
5. Lucas, p. 85.
6. Lucas, p. 91.
7. Geoffrey Sawer, *Law in Society* (Oxford: The Clarendon Press, 1965, reprinted 1973), p. 15.
8. Sawer, pp. 31ff.
9. *Fundamental Legal Conceptions* (New Haven: Yale University Press, 1923).
10. Sawer, p. 44.
11. Sawer, p. 44.

12. This is not to deny the possibility of, say, certain non-legal professions adopting legal modes of functioning. Such has occurred recently in the United States in medicine and education owing to the increasing prevalence of malpractice suits as well as the increasing general willingness of Americans to sue each other for almost anything.

    At the other extreme, and precisely to guard against this sort of proclivity, the emperors of the Manchu dynasty in ancient China turned the Imperial Courts into an institution of terror. For some of the chilling details of the Empire striking back, see Sawer at pp. 56-58. Two consequences of considerable relevance for modern legal systems, however, are that (1) the Imperial reasoning "reminds one of the frequent, usually groundless, worries of English judges lest permitting a new remedy would open wide the floodgates of litigation" and (2), of particular relevance to American courts, "In the case of private prosecution, an unsuccessful prosecutor incurred the penalty which the accused would have borne" (Sawer, p. 57).
13. Lucas, pp. 91-92.
14. Sawer, p. 64.
15. Sawer, pp. 52-53.
16. Sawer, p. 67. (Italics in the original text.)
17. Sawer, p. 84.
18. Sawer, p. 82.
19. Sawer, p. 25.
20. Sawer, p. 129.
21. Sawer, p. 29.
22. Sawer gives two examples, the second of which is legislative, rather than judge-made law—in addition to *Brown v. Board of Education* discussed below—namely, *Hedley Byrne and Co. Ltd. v. Heller and Partners Ltd.*, A.C. (1964) which concerns "liability in torts for failure to exercise reasonable care when giving advice or information" (p. 187) and "the Australian federal Matrimonial Causes Act 1959, which established an Australia-wide code and in doing so changed the divorce law of each of the six States and two federal territories, whose separate laws previously governed the matter" (p. 188). This law apparently did not arise out of popular sentiment for change, but was rather "an enthusiasm of the Attorney-General and of a small group of politicians and lawyers who persuaded Parliament to endorse the proposals and counted, correctly, on sufficient indifference or tepid support in the community to outweigh the vocal opposition" (p. 188).
23. One could also argue that much of the unpopularity of any Warren Court decisions throughout the late 1950's and 1960's stemmed from the fact that the Court was so consistently and, from the perspective of the history of law, a-typically, at the forefront of forging a moral vision not yet shared by the majority of American citizens. Indeed, this seems to me a good part of the meaning of the often-misused expression, "judicial activism."
24. Sawer, p. 183. One of those included in this group is Wolfgang Friedmann who provides a number of interesting examples of changes in the form of social life that yield corresponding legal changes. Citing Gustav Radbruch, for example, Friedmann points out how in Germany the civil law embodied in the civil codes had only recognized "legal subjects who conclude contracts with each other by free resolutions," whereas in the relatively new field of labor law in Germany (at the time of Radbruch's writing, in 1948) "represents the development of combinations and associations of employers and employees. This leads to a new type of legal institution, the collective agreement, which expresses this new type of social relationship. It is the *Natur der Sache,* the nature of this new type of social relationship between interest groups, that creates new legal forms, institutions, and procedures." "Phenomenology and Legal Science," in Maurice Natanson, ed. *Phenomenology and the Social Sciences* (Evanston: Northwestern University Press, 1973), II, pp. 352.

25. Several important U.S. Supreme Court cases in this regard will be discussed below in section 3. In one of them, *Frontiero v. Richardson,* 411 U.S. 677 (1973), Justice Brennan observed that "Indeed, the position of women in this country at its inception is reflected in the view expressed by Thomas Jefferson that women should be neither seen nor heard in society's decision-making councils."

    The dialectic of social and legal change set in motion by the women's movement is at least far enough advanced to make unthinkable in the United States—for reasons that have nothing to do with traditional Anglo-Saxon prudery—the type of offensive, sometimes pornographic, and even by times violent advertisements that are a commonplace of French culture and which almost justify the perception of it as misogynist.
26. From the perspective of the last quarter of the 20th-century, Merleau-Ponty certainly was gazing into a clouded crystal ball when he summarily dismissed the question "asked with enthusiasm or with anguish whether man could create life in the laboratory" as an example of "myths" appended to science "which proliferate at its fringes" (S 185-86).
27. Lucas, pp. 91-92.
28. H.L.A. Hart, *The Concept of Law* (Oxford: The Clarendon Press, 1961), p. 12.
29. It should also be pointed out that, in legal systems such as those of England and in the United States, particular trends of case law can develop, across a pattern of judicial decisions, more nearly like customs than legislation.

    With reference to Merleau-Ponty here, he writes in *Signes* that "General DeGaulle can change the laws, but he cannot change the life of France because it is not the affair of only one man, because one sole man always has too simple an idea of the system" (p. 420).
30. For instance, no one (sane) now believes, as many did once, that tampons are immoral because they bring temptations to enjoy sinful pleasures or because, in some versions, they rob a girl of her virginity. In terms of dead customs, as opposed to taboos, men no longer tip their hats to women upon meeting them in the street, largely because the custom of wearing hats itself has largely died out.
31. Sawer, pp. 130-31.
32. Sawer, pp. 137-38.
33. Sawer, p. 70.
34. Sawer, p. 10.
35. Sawer, p. 11. (Italics in the original text.)
36. Such activities have a long history; they are not limited to either contemporary dictatorships, Nazi Germany, or Franklin D. Roosevelt's famous "court packing" proposals (1937). In ancient Greece, for example, "suits and prosecutions were often brought as a means of removing a political opponent or obstructing his activities. There was even a class of vexatious litigants called 'sycophants', . . . their main purpose was to sue as a means of financial or political blackmail, on their own account or as paid agents of undisclosed principals" (Sawer, p. 74).
37. Sawer, p. 103.
38. "American Jurisprudence through English Eyes: The Nightmare and the Noble Dream," in *Essays in Jurisprudence and Philosophy* (Oxford: The Clarendon Press, 1983), p. 128.
39. For an earlier version of the discussion following, see William S. Hamrick, "A Phenomenological Critique of Hart's Concept of Rules," pp. 179ff.
40. Gerald Gunther, *Cases and Materials on Constitutional Law,* 9th edition (Mineola, N.Y.: The Foundation Press, Inc., 1975), p. 657.
41. Gunther, p. 658.
42. Gerald Gunther, "Foreward: In Search of Evolving Doctrine on a Changing Court: A Model for Newer Equal Protection," 86 *Harvard Law Review* 9 (1972).

43. In *Reed,* the Court struck down an Idaho statute that provided both a preferential ordering of classes of persons to be administrators of estates and that, in each class, men were to be preferred to women. The legislative reasoning was that men were presumed to be better candidates because of the statistical prevalence of men in the business world. The Court upheld the right to have a preferential ordering of classes of candidates, but threw out the sexual classifications within each stratum.
44. Gunther, "Newer Equal Protection," p. 34.
45. Even today, sexual classifications are not inherently suspect, and therefore entitled to "strict judicial scrutiny." What role the failure of the Equal Rights Amendment will have on this situation is far from clear. Justice Brennan is said to have regretted the absence of certain other justices on the bench, the votes of which would have enabled the *Frontiero* opinion to be written in such a way as to obviate the necessity of an Equal Rights Amendment.
46. *Towne v. Eisner,* 245 U.S. 418 (1918), at p. 425.

    As a corollary of the variations in meaning which Justice Holmes describes, one can also consider the difficulties which courts encounter in attempting to make sense out of those variations or, rather, in deciding exactly what they want words and rules to mean. Applied to the gender-based cases which we have been analysing, this means appreciating the difficulties and uncertainties involved in trying to agree on what degree of scrutiny, and for what reasons, to apply to gender-based classifications. Thus it is illuminating to read, nine years after *Reed,* Justice Rehnquist writing for the majority of the Supreme Court that "As is evident from our opinions, the Court has had some difficulty in agreeing upon the proper approach and analysis in cases involving challenges to gender-based classifications. The issues posed by such challenges range . . . to the appropriate standard of judicial review for the substantive classification. Unlike the California Supreme Court, we have not held that gender-based classifications are 'inherently suspect' and thus we do not apply so-called 'strict scrutiny' to those classifications. . . . Our cases have held, however, that the traditional minimum rationality test takes on a somewhat 'sharper focus' when gender-based classifications are challenged." *Michael M. v. Superior Court of Sonoma County (California, Real Party in Interest),* 450 U.S. 464 (1980) at p. 466.

    For the reasons stated above, it is surely obvious that the phrase, "somewhat 'sharper focus'", is hardly self-evidently clear, and is, in fact, subject to the same variations in interpretation as the other judicial gambits analysed above.
47. Cf. Neil MacCormick, "legal decisions must make sense in the world and they must also make sense in the context of the legal system" (p. 103).
48. "JHering's Heaven of Concepts and Modern Analytic Jurisprudence," in *Essays in Jurisprudence and Philosophy,* pp. 268-69.
49. *Southern Pacific Co. v. Jensen,* 244 U.S. 205 (1917), at p. 222.
50. *The Common Law* (Boston, 1881), p. 1.
51. "The Path of the Law," in *Collected Legal Papers* (London: 1920), p. 180.
52. *Lochner v. New York,* 198 U.S. 45 (1904), at p. 74.
53. *Essays in Jurisprudence and Philosophy,* pp. 129-30.
54. Merleau-Ponty also would have appreciated Holmes' attack on the excessive individualism embodied in German philosophy that dominated academic law when he (Holmes) began to write in the 1870's. As Hart puts it, "The great names were those of Kant, Hegel, and Savigny, and the theory's focal point was the respect, indeed the reverence, due to the individual and the individual will. To this, all that was problematic or in need of justification was referred. . . . To Holmes, this *Willenstheorie* seemed either unintelligible or a romantic fiction incapable of explaining even the institutions of Roman law on which it purported to be a gloss. Apart from its detailed errors this whole metaphysical approach appeared simply to

ignore the practical aims and exigencies which shape any living body of law." "Diamonds and String: Holmes on the Common Law," in *Essays in Jurisprudence and Philosophy,* p. 279. I shall come back to this theme in the following chapter.

55. Cited in Hart, "JHering's Heaven of Concepts and Modern Analytical Jurisprudence," p. 268.
56. *Precedent in English Law* (Oxford: The Clarendon Press, 1977), 3rd edition, p. 27.
57. *Allen v. Jackson* (1875), 1 Ch.D. 399 at p. 405; cited in Cross, p. 28.
58. Cross, p. 30.
59. Cross, pp. 30-31.
60. Sawer, p. 105.
61. Sawer, p. 105. (Italics in the original text.)
62. "American Jurisprudence through English Eyes: The Nightmare and the Noble Dream," p. 127.
63. "Precedents," 8 *Cambridge Law Journal* 118, at p. 125; cited in Cross, p. 18.
64. Cross, pp. 33-34, citing Holmes in *Southern Pacific Co. v. Jensen,* 244 U.S. 205 (1917), at p. 221. It is interesting that Holmes borrows his distinction of the molecular and molar from the more sinister context of a Massachusetts case over which he had presided, *Storti v. Commonwealth,* 178 Mass. 549, 60 N.E. 210, 211 (1901), "in which it was held that a statute providing for electrocution as a means of inflicting the punishment of death was not cruel or unusual punishment within the Massachusetts Declaration of Rights, MASS CONST., pt. First, art. XXVI, simply because it accomplished its object by molecular, rather than molar, motions." (!) Cited in Lon L. Fuller, "Positivism and Fidelity to Law—A Reply to Professor Hart, 71 *Harvard Law Review* 630, at p. 647 n. 15.
65. On this and other problems in appreciating the nature and functioning of precedents, see Cross, especially Chapter II, *"Ratio Decidendi* and *Obiter Dictum."*
66. Cross, p. 10.
67. Fuller, p. 646.
68. For an instructive summary of the predicament of judges such as Shaw and Story, see John Mackie, "The Third Theory of Law," *Philosophy and Public Affairs* 7, No. 1 (Fall 1977), reprinted and cited in Marshall Cohen, ed. *Ronald Dworkin and Contemporary Jurisprudence* (London: Duckworth, 1984), pp. 166-68.
69. Cross, p. 15.
70. Cross, p. 16.
71. Dworkin, *Taking Rights Seriously,* p. 23. Considering the limitations imposed by the less than adequate capacity Merleau-Ponty's phenomenology has for speaking to Dworkin's claims, what follows will be only a thumbnail sketch of what is a very important, rich, and provocative jurisprudence. For more comprehensive summaries and critiques of his position, see in general the excellent collection of essays assembled by Cohen. It is, of course, impossible to consider or even acknowledge here all the important issues they raise.
72. Dworkin, p. 23. The case at issue was *Henningsen v. Bloomfield Motors, Inc.,* 32 N.J. 358, 161 A.2nd 69 (1960).
73. Dworkin, pp. 116-17.
74. Cross, p. 216.
75. Cross, p. 221.

VII: LAW AND MORALITY

As is clear from the last four chapters, one would not find anything in Merleau-Ponty's texts resembling a fully developed discussion of law and morality. And certainly one would find nothing of the way this issue has been skewed in most discussions of it in the previous two decades of Anglo-American philosophy by being focussed almost exclusively on sexuality.[1] Instead, as with Merleau-Ponty's other references to law, those that concern morality are usually situated in the contexts of politics, economics, and history. Although productive of less exciting discussions, perhaps, these contexts do at least have the compensatory advantage of generating more interesting and thorny philosophical problems.

What we have seen so far of Merleau-Ponty's references to law and morality have established that he is committed to three separate claims, two of which are factual and the third normative. The first of the factual claims is that law is not identical to morality. As he said in his essay, "On Indochina," in relation to François Mauriac, "The war has been inconvenient enough to force him to distinguish what is legal from what is just" (S 407). The second factual claim is that, although not identical with each other, law and morality are tightly intertwined in the unitary web of social choices of which Max Weber produced such an illuminating analysis. Law and morality, as all aspects of the Gestalt structure of social orders of meaning, do not exist as atomistically distinct from each other, *partes extra partes*. On the contrary, they are interdependent rather than independent. They mutually imply each other within a given social context because they interpenetrate and signify each other.

The normative claim about law and morality is quite different. It consists of the desirability of law as a social tool to help bring about a certain kind of society—namely, that in which formal, liberal protections of freedom may be effective. Reconstructed in logical sequence, his argument would run as follows: (1) The role of politics in the new liberalism consists of holding "both ends of the chain together, the social problem and liberty" (AD 305). This is to say that politics has a double task: (i) to work towards the most humane, just society possible—which would also involve remedying past injustices—and (ii) maximizing freedom of expression and thought necessary for furthering the dialectical inquiry into truth.

(2) Effective, durable protections of liberty require formal institutions. Liberty is as fragile as it is precious (AD 313); to last, it must, therefore, be rooted in institutions rather than be left to transitory social perceptions from one historical epoch to another.

(3) In any modern, complex society (and certainly in any to which Merleau-Ponty considered the new liberalism applicable), law is one of the most crucial institutions, if not *the* most, which can provide formal protections for human freedoms and the pursuit of truth. Hence it is Parliament rather than, say, the press or the educational system, which is "the only known institution which guarantees a minimum of opposition and of truth" (AD 304). Thus, (4) law can serve as a singularly important vehicle to protect human liberties and to facilitate the pursuit of truth.

If we take into account the textual references mentioned above, others scattered throughout Merleau-Ponty's writings, as well as what can be deductively derived from other parts of the texts themselves, we can frame a coherent view of law and morality along three main lines. These are, and will be considered in this order, law and its relation to nature, interests and justice, and respect for law and fidelity to it.

§*1. Law and Nature*

Law, nature, and morality have comprised a closely related triad throughout much of the history of philosophy. In various and considerably different versions of natural law theory, law has been considered the bearer of a certain moral vision, both of which somehow having their ultimate sanction in "the nature of things." This is to say that law has often been considered to instantiate the moral point of view on life to the degree that it sought to better human existence by taking proper cognizance of the social organization and manipulation of the external order of things as well as of what best fits natural human needs and capacities. Thus law has often been thought to have built into it some kind of reference to nature in addition to culture or, in some versions of the theory, to fiat. In addition, the rational content of law, existing over and above—or, perhaps better, beneath—what is arbitrary, has been thought to enhance the dignity of law because it established the impartiality of a legal system as against the manoeuvring of private interests. In other words, there is a content of justice in a given legal system which is supposed to remain impervious to the designing interests of those who govern.[2]

One might very well conclude from the preceding chapters that, for Merleau-Ponty, law can have no foundation in nature and law and cannot really manifest any commitment to justice—to solving the social problem—which can be disentangled from the interests of the officials of the system and the majority class of a particular society. In fact, however, neither denial is quite that simple or easy, as the present discussion will show in terms of nature[3] and the following discussion will do for interests and justice.

What would lead one to the first putative denial, that is, of locating any foundation for law in nature, consists in Merleau-Ponty's claims that, as detailed above in the Introduction and Chapter II, (i) there is no pure external nature existing over against human beings, complete and locked in on itself (RC 93). (ii) Husserl's protests against the "naturalization of consciousness" are transmuted into the distinction between (human) existence and physical objects. Whereas the latter are *dans le monde,* we are *au-monde* which is intended to express the dynamics of ex-istence in which we "stand forth" as an ensemble of motor-intentional powers to be what we are not. What is most proper about us as human is, then, this power of transcendence, whereas what is "natural" about us in the mélange of culture and nature can bespeak nothing of the "not-yet": "man is the being who is not content to coincide with himself, like a thing, but who represents himself to himself, sees himself, imagines himself, gives himself his own symbols, rigorous or fantastical" (S 285). Man does not follow any in-born laws of development, like bees or trees (IV.1); therefore, as noted above in the Introduction, in Heidegger's words, "Only man exists."[4] And indeed, precisely one example of this power of transcendence, as we saw in the beginning of Chapter V, consists of the origin of basic rules and law (SNS 208).

Similarly, (iii) there is no internal human nature because, as also detailed in the Introduction, in the intertwining of culture and nature one cannot say that a particular kind of behavior is more or less natural than its contrary which is endorsed in another culture. In the interrelationships of biology and culture we are equally natural and cultural, for culture is not a veneer layered on an immutable substratum of (human) nature (PhP 220-21). Nor (iv), for the same reason, can culture rightly be thought to be a "second nature." Marxist criticisms of such a notion are entirely correct, for culture and humanity itself are, within the limits of a conditioned liberty, "an interworld which we call history, symbolism, truth to be made" (AD 269). History (v) teaches negatively, as we saw above (II.5), such that the main lessons we learn from the intertwinings of nature and culture from one historical epoch to another consists in discovering what will not work. Rather than grant the rationalist premise that the universe is through-and-through intelligible, history reveals sense emerging from a background of non-sense, order amidst disorder, reason situated in un-reason, and necessity menaced by contingency. Thus, the utility of nature as a guide for living would correspondingly be diminished. As a result, then, (vi) nature, whether thought of as internal or external, cannot for Merleau-Ponty function as a norm for deductive reasoning about a supposedly proper legal and moral development of either an entire society or for its individual members.[5]

Such a view implies straight away a repudiation of one version of natural law theory in which law consists of a set of conclusions supported ultimately by a metaphysical or ontological doctrine. Basic principles of law are held to follow from such a doctrine and are asserted to have their moral sanction in the same ontology. Further, this particular version of natural law theory may or may not be framed in a religious context. When it is—as, say, for St. Thomas Aquinas—natural law is considered to be a reflection of the eternal, divine law. But both the religious and non-religious variants of this version of natural law theory are untenable if there is no immutable substratum of human nature, if nature and culture are inseparably mixed up with each other and if, as Merleau-Ponty believed, what is claimed to be "natural" and "unnatural" is supported only by culturally conditioned intuitions that such is the case. Or, in a different idiom which emerged above in Part One (II.4), phenomenology functions as ideology critique in the measure in which it shows us that what is interpreted as natural is in fact ideological because what is ideological is perceived by us as natural.

This is precisely the position taken by the Scandinavian legal realist, Alf Ross. "The history of natural law," he observes, "reveals two striking points: the arbitrariness of the fundamental postulates concerning the nature of existence and of man; and the arbitrariness of the moral-legal ideas that are evolved on this basis."[6] Ross considers, for example, that the "chapter on family law" within natural law systems "always makes amusing reading" "because it so clearly reflects the moral prejudices of the age. . . . The ludicrous dryness of rationalism is reflected in Kant's definition of marriage as a contract between two persons of different sexes for the lifelong mutual possession of their sexual capacities; sexual intercourse is only permitted in wedlock; if any one of the marriage partners gives himself or herself into another's possession, the other marriage partner is invariably entitled to 'recover' the runaway, like a material object, into his possession."[7]

The result is that, "Like a harlot, natural law is at the disposal of everyone"; as Merleau-Ponty perfectly appreciated in the domain of politics, "The ideology does not exist that cannot be defended by an appeal to nature."[8] And as Merleau-Ponty also would have observed, the putative epistemological warrant for such claims lies not in a rigorous dialectic of reflective, critical thought securely anchored to concrete empirical evidence, but rather in a supposedly incorrigible and private intuition. Every ideology can be defended as "natural" "since the ultimate basis for every natural right lies in a private direct insight, an evident contemplation, an intuition. Cannot my intuition be just as good as yours?"[9]

In American law, there was an important series of Supreme Court cases which perfectly well illustrates not only Ross' point, but also much of what was discussed in the previous chapter in terms of judicial decision making and Sawer's criticisms of Hohfeld's table of legal relations. These cases are also completely in concert with the political position adopted by Alain (see IV.1) and had similar disastrous results because they all frustrated legal remedies for pressing economic problems. This was so because, in the course of developing a doctrine known as "substantive due process," the Court held that all the legislation or other state regulation concerned violated a natural right for employees to make contracts for themselves which was "found" to be guaranteed by the Fifth and Fourteenth Amendments. H.L.A. Hart provides a handy summary of some of these cases as follows: "For the development of this doctrine see . . . *Lochner v. New York,* 198 U.S. 45 (1905) (Fourteenth Amendment 'liberty of contract' prohibits state from regulating the maximum hours per day or week a bakery employee may work); *Adair v. United States,* 208 U.S. 161 (1908) (Fifth Amendment 'liberty of contract' bars federal prohibition of 'yellow dog' employment contracts for employees of interstate railroads); *Coppage v. Kansas,* 236 U.S. 1 (1915) (Fourteenth Amendment 'liberty of contract bars state prohibition of 'yellow dog' employment contracts); *Adkins v. Children's Hosp.,* 261 U.S. 525 (1923) (Fifth Amendment 'liberty of contract' prohibits District of Columbia from prescribing minimum wages for women)."[10] (Ross discusses the last of the cases briefly.)

There are also two other cases, one before *Adkins* and the other after it, which Ross could well have utilized in his critique. Both afford handsome examples of paternalistic opinions which purportedly are grounded in the very warp and woof of "the nature of things."

In the former, *Bradwell v. Illinois,* 16 Wall. 130 (1873)—which is also cited exactly 100 years later by Justice Brennan in *Frontiero*—the United States Supreme Court upheld a state law barring women from the practice of law. Justice Bradley's concurring opinion contains the following illuminating passage: "Man is, or should be, woman's protector and defender. The natural and proper timidity and delicacy which belongs [*sic*] to the female sex evidently unfits it for many of the occupations of civil life . . . . The paramount destiny and mission of woman are to fulfill the noble and benign office of wife and mother." Justice Bradley also confidently ascribes this "noble and benign office" to the "Will of the Creator" and, in an ancillary argument, considers that any contrary view taken by the Court would be violative of the divinely ordered "nature of things." One role of the courts, on this view, would then be to make society as legally a "second nature" mirroring the primary Nature as possible.

The second case, as Wolfgang Friedmann describes it, consists of a "1953 decision of the West German Supreme Court, interpreting the legal status of the married woman in the light of the Bonn Constitution of 1949. The Court declared it to be in the *Natur der Sache* that the husband, as head of the family, represents it toward the 'outer world' (*nach aussen*), while the wife devotes herself to the 'inner order' (*innere Ordnung*). This interpretation . . . is, of course, simply an infusion of the Court's own very conservative view of the respective social functions of husband and wife into the Constitution, a by no means uncommon phenomenon. . . . Like the related, though not identical, natural law philosophy, the *Natur der Sache* thus can easily serve to give to specific political and social ideologies the halo of 'immanence' or 'a natural order of things.'"[11]

The interest of the reasoning in these cases is not exhausted simply by their being period-pieces of benighted paternalism. Rather, what is much more important about them is that they were not very extraordinary in terms of the prevailing attitudes of positive morality. Indeed, the decisions very likely seemed self-evident to Justice Bradley and to the West German justices (and to all similarly inclined persons) precisely to the degree that they appeared "natural." But the attitude formally endorsed, in terms of the "proper" relationship of men and women which is supposedly inscribed into the stonework of the universe and, at least in American eyes if not also on the other side of the Atlantic, underwritten by the divine Will, has not been limited to the confident moralizings of a few invincibly ignorant jurists. Instead, the staggering complacency of the judicial mind at work in these cases is probably due at bottom to the fact that their results may fairly be said to express the majority view not only before 1873, but right down to our very days. It is only with the advent of contemporary feminism, as I argued in the previous chapter, that this view has definitely begun to change—although hardly universally. Also, "advent" is an especially appropriate description in the sense that Merleau-Ponty borrows it from Paul Ricoeur—culture as advent conceived as a coming-to-be of new meaning (S 85).

Phenomenology functions here as ideology critique to show us that what is taken to be natural is really ideological because it (phenomenology) makes us aware that there are two significantly different senses of seeing through ideologies. The first way is roughly equivalent to seeing through glasses, that is, as naively conditioned by the framework of interpretation without perceiving it as a framework. But the naive, uncritical view of passive acceptance is transcended by the sceptical criticism embodied in the second sense of "seeing through," namely the way that a detective sees through a ruse or a plot. Here the framework of interpretation is recognized for what it is—an ideology—and debate then becomes not merely concerned with details within the framework, but rather primarily with challenges to the framework itself.[12] When feminists and others talk about raising people's consciousnesses, effectively the object is to lead them from the first sense of "seeing through" to the second. It might also be said that this shift of perspective summarizes as well the path Merleau-Ponty's thinking followed from *Humanisme et terreur* to *Les Aventures de la dialectique* as illustrated above (at IV.3).

Moreover, such sceptical interrogation makes us realize that there is not just one framework of interpretation, but rather many competing perspectives, not all of which are compatible with each other. There is no one all-inclusive perspective—as noted above in Part One (II.4), such would in fact be a self-contradiction. Rather, there is only a multiplicity of perspectives and rationality, far from being threatened by this fact, appears only at the intersection of various perspectives which engage each other like gears (II.4).

Something of the same reasoning also appears in Merleau-Ponty's consideration of language (see I.4) when he rejects the notion of an ideal language somehow inscribed in the nature of reality and against which all existing empirical languages could be measured as imperfect realizations (as Husserl advocated in the fourth of his *Logical Investigations,* that is, "the idea of an eidetics of language and of a universal grammar which would set the necessary forms of signification for any language" [S 105].) Along the same lines, thinking law according to the model of language would lead one to reject the notion of an ideal law, a universal law (of nature) written into the foundations of "reality," and in general, as we saw at the end of the last chapter, any "one-best-wayism" in legal decision making which ultimately rests on an appeal to "the nature of things."

Another important application of the same reasoning leads to a different, but related consequence of seeing phenomenology as ideology critique. Namely, human experience is through and through interpretative, even in its most basic modes of constituting the perceptual field, rather than being founded on the passive reception of sense-data from the perceptual and/or cultural worlds. No "absolute, presuppositionless evidence" is possible (PhP 453) because experience is essentially mediated by culture and history. One crucial effect of this omnipresence of interpretation and mediation is to cast considerable doubt on the concept of self-evidence—of some doctrine, for example, being self-evidently true, as the relationship of men and women was for Justice Bradley and the West German justices. Phenomenology considered as ideology critique leads us to perceive the need to be sensitive investigators of the constituting activities of consciousness in and through which something appears (better: is made to appear) as self-evident. Although Merleau-Ponty does not say it just this way, his view is essentially that self-evidence is always a self-fulfilling prophecy.[13]

This statement of his view, if I have construed it correctly, is not without problems of its own, as I shall show momentarily in terms of rights. But to see that this is so, we need to widen our consideration of nature and other versions of natural law theory to realize that there are senses in which "the nature of things" may be appealed to, and other ways that nature might be normative, that are considerably different than serving as a source of deductive reasoning to arrive at "the right answer." And here, as we shall see, despite all the contrary indications noted above, Merleau-Ponty's phenomenology consistently can endorse a relevance of law to nature which will also turn out to be important to the goal of respect for law.

This is to say that although nature may not be immutable or a normatively controlling datum, it is, nevertheless, an important ingredient in our lives. It serves as a reference point and source of evidence for countless individual decisions, social policies, and laws. It presents itself to us as objective and as constraining us to recognize it if we wish to make successful decisions. For example, successful laws which adequately settle or obviate disputes and give form to social institutions must refer to nature in a multiplicity of different ways. To take only three widely different instances, humankind cannot long live with unrestrained industrial pollution, so laws regulating commerce eventually have to take into account the effects of poisoning the ecosystem or melting the polar ice-caps. Or again, successful laws dealing with torts must take into account the relevant facts of free will, human passions, the possibility of causally explaining human behavior, and so forth. And third, fruitful, intelligent laws governing the flow of commerce, property rights, and the like, must be anchored successfully in "the facts"—that is, in what will work best in the particular situations affected, so that human beings are benefitted rather than harmed. Otherwise, law would be consigned to the position of abstract theories criticized by Merleau-Ponty—in the case of law, abstractions from the social organization of nature which it is supposed to formalize and protect.

Such a view of the relation of law to nature has had many adherents at different times and places throughout the history of Western philosophy (as well as that of the East), and it is hence neither possible nor necessary to consider all its prominent variations. For brevity as well as for the sake of what is most relevant to Merleau-Ponty, I shall consider only two such versions here, one of the earliest and then one of the most recent. The former consisted of the view adopted by Roman lawyers—not sweeping generalizations proposed by writers such as Seneca and Cicero, but rather how law was perceived by practicing lawyers themselves. For example, at the very beginning of Justinian's *Digest,* law is defined as *ars boni et aequi,* "the art of the good and the equitable." These lawyers did not consider law, as A.P. D'Entrèves points out, "a complete and ready-made system of rules, but essentially a means of interpretation, almost, as it were, the 'trick of the trade' which they resorted to and used in a masterly fashion. In shaping a body of laws which would apply to the whole civilized world they had no abstract theories in mind, but aimed at the workable and the practical. . . . Clearly, this is not a philosophical position. It looks much rather like the 'science of an art.'"[14]

D'Entrèves refers to this particular version of natural law theory which, as it turns out, he rejects (along with the ontological version detailed above), as the "technological" view of natural law. He further indicates that one of the most recent variants of the theory consists of Lon L. Fuller's arguments that law is ineluctably an antinomy of reason and fiat, law discovered and law created. Exactly why D'Entrèves rejects the "technological" view will be discussed below in the context of the ideal of respect for law. (We shall see that, among other things, he advances criticisms of Fuller which are most central to the place of law within Merleau-Ponty's new liberalism.) But first, let us briefly consider the relevant parts of what Fuller himself says. He terms his view of law "eunomics" in order to avoid misleading associations brought about by the over-worked label of "natural law theory." In particular, he wishes to avoid confusion with the ontological view of natural law described above whilst also rejecting various forms of legal positivism from Bentham and Austin to Hart which cannot, on his view, adequately plan or account for the ideal of fidelity to law.

For Fuller, law in general—and, perhaps most visibly, case law in the courts in particular—always manifests a Janus-like face of reason and fiat. Neither is reducible to the other, but it is also true that an analysis of one side of the figure sooner or later reveals its insufficiency and leads to the other side. Fiat refers to the power relationships that the will of law-making authorities brings into existence—which constitute for Hart the primary attribute of secondary rules—such as the ability to sue because one is the owner of a piece of land on which trespass has been committed. Fiat also refers more generally to that aspect of law created through the will of law-making authorities that happens to be arbitrary—that is, that for which "no good reason" can be found. For example, while it is certainly not arbitrary that wills should have witnesses, it cannot be decided on the basis of reason alone whether there ought to be, say, two or three. One just has to choose.

The reason side of law is, however, significantly different. It represents the way law refers to the nature of things, as in the examples cited above about industrial pollution, tort law, and contracts in commerce), in order to express the deeper social purpose of law to secure goods for humankind which cannot be attained without law. As with the Roman lawyers, the emphasis is on "the workable and the practical," to use D'Entrèves' phrase, social organization of nature in order to increase human well-being. Hence, Fuller advises, our approach to nature should not be that of deducing legal implications from basic metaphysical principles. Nor should it "be that of one doing obeisance before an altar"; rather, it should be "more like that of a cook trying to find the secret of a flaky pie crust or an engineer trying to devise a means of bridging a ravine."[15]

There is much in Merleau-Ponty's phenomenology of the social world to show that he could accept Fuller's view of the relationship of law and nature, or at least a view much like it. For the "technological" view conflicts with none of the claims about nature summarized in the beginning of this section, and it also accords well with much else to which Merleau-Ponty is committed. First, the "technological" view is not bound to any "one-best-wayism" or "decision inevitability." Just as political decision making, legal reasoning is inventive and practical, but it does not follow from the fact that a practically reasonable solution has been found to a certain problem that there were not other possible, and even better, solutions. There usually exists in any given problem-solving situation, within or external to law, a variety of means to the same end—just as there is more than one way to bridge successfully a ravine or produce a flaky pie crust. Thus once again, legal (and other) rules have an instrumental value (see III.4, V.3), which allows them to be used as adaptable tools in various contexts of expression.

Second, Merleau-Ponty's insistence on a mélange of nature and culture coheres well with Fuller's insistence that law is a bi-polar reality composed of reason and fiat. It is true that Fuller considers them as an antinomy, but it is also the case that, because an analysis of either side of law leads one to see that it is not self-sufficient, each side presupposes the other and eventually leads the investigator to it. Hence, as with Merleau-Ponty's analysis of culture and nature, what is claimed to exist is a concrete reality with dual aspects rather than adualism of independent, *partes extra partes* components. In Merleau-Ponty's idiom, a full understanding of the cultural world must include a reference to its basis in nature, and conversely, our view of nature is always culturally filtered. This, I believe, is an important part of what he meant when he wrote that "There is something to say in favor of the 'natural light.' Men secrete culture in some way without knowing it. The human world, so different as it might be from the natural or animal world, is in some way *natural for man*" (SNS 208-09).[16] Consequently, the fact that cultural significations of our incarnate existence transcend biological givens does not imply that the latter are unimportant or negligible in the making of law. As Marx certainly knew well, and Merleau-Ponty after him, there are certain constant and fundamental demands for food, clothing, shelter, work, and so forth, the satisfaction of which imposes on a particular society legal problems and on its law-making authorities basic moral and legal obligations. Such obligations may be said fairly to lie at the very heart of the social problem which the new liberalism is supposed to address. I shall come back to this in both the following similarity and in a discussion of rights below.

The third similarity concerns what Merleau-Ponty says of the tight connection between nature and history and the fact that history teaches us negatively. Of two possibilities, let us recall (from II.5), history cannot teach us that "one might be *more true* than the other, although we can say that one is more false, more artificial, and less an opening on a less rich future" (RC 65). Thus we do not learn from history that capitalism will not triumph or that the proletariat will. Neither result is sketched out in advance in a heaven of ideas or inscribed in the foundations of nature. But for all that, it is certainly the case that historical understanding can encompass an awareness of how, for example, a given economic system sought to culturally modulate nature and, given the intentionality of consciousness, how this attempt defined the members of the society whose system it is—both those who actively participate in and benefit from the system as well as those who do not (those with more and less rich futures). As in

Lochner or *Adkins,* these are crucial lessons for legislators and judges seeking to become artists of "the workable and the practical." The science of this art can then address data of considerable temporal thickness, rather than being limited to one isolable decision after another, because, as Merleau-Ponty put it in *Humanism and Terror,* "History only has a sense if there is something like a logic of human existence which does not make any adventure impossible, but which at least, by a *natural selection,* eliminates in the long run those who diverge from *permanent necessities* of men" (pp. 163-64; italics in the original). Law-making authorities can ignore these "permanent necessities," what was referred to above as constant and fundamental demands of human existence, only at their peril and—as we shall see below—at the risk of losing all respect for law.

The fourth point of similarity is that there is a close parallel between the idea of law having a touchstone in nature by looking for what will be most "workable and practical" in a particular case and, on the other hand, two claims of Merleau-Ponty detailed above (at II.4): that (i) truth is an active process of verification (à la William James) instead of the secure possession of a private, infallible intuition (as Ross denied, and as the previous chapter has given us reasons to reject for judicial decision making) and (ii) rationality emerges from a convergence of social (and perceptual) perspectives in the constitution of objectivity. In judicial decision making, like that which is political, creative speech aims at bringing about what will later be seen as necessary for its particular times. And for this to occur, all possibly relevant perspectives must be utilized; none must be arbitrarily omitted. Legal speech in general, whether legislative or judicial, must therefore be based on all the materials at hand—nature very much included—if it hopes to be efficient and successful in solving problems.

The fifth and final similarity between Merleau-Ponty's phenomenology and what Fuller says of law concerns the nature and origin of rights. For both thinkers it seems to me that the best way to describe their notion of rights in terms of valid claims or another similar expression which suffices to indicate that their source is clearly not that of cultural manufacture (fiat), either in positive morality or in law. With regard to law, construing moral rights as legal fiat—as certain 19th-century theorists did—makes them legal powers. One main result of such a view is that it leaves no room for legally unrecognized moral rights such that, for example, there is no way to say consistently of slaves in slave-owning cultures that they have moral rights to be free. By parity of reasoning, if Merleau-Ponty accepted this view of moral rights, he would have no way to complain of the (legal) treatment of workers in capitalist societies or that the Communist Party ought to be legal in regimes in which it was not already so. (It was also on the basis of rejecting such a view of rights that Sawer [VI.1] claimed that considerable legal development in recent times had stemmed from an ambiguous usage of the word "right.")

Rather than being of cultural manufacture, it appears that, for both Fuller and Merleau-Ponty, rights are given in our very humanness (see above at III.2). That is to say, rights are grounded, in a broad sense, in "the nature of things." But for Merleau-Ponty in particular, this does not mean nature as what was distinguished from human existence conceived as a power of transcendence of what (naturally) is, but rather the involuntary base of that existence in the pre-reflective, lived-body which always has—despite anyone's fiat—"permanent necessities." Furthermore, as detailed above in Chapter IV, what very likely sustained Merleau-Ponty's commitment to Marxism for so long, and why he clung to the doctrine of the triumph of the proletariat against what were to become increasingly clear and persuasive counter-examples, was his belief that, despite the considerably hostile moral and legal fiat of capitalist societies, workers had valid claims to the provision of basic goods of survival, to be treated with respect as ends in themselves. Indeed, as also underlined above in the context of politics, it was partly a defense of this claim, coupled with what he perceived to be insurmountable epistemological problems with Marxist theories of historical explanation, that finally decided his break with Marxism and directed his programme for a non-Communist left.

It is precisely this commitment which exposes Merleau-Ponty's views of self-evidence and "natural" rights—understanding by "natural" whatever is not of cultural derivation or "fiat"—to criticisms of inconsistency. That is, just as he was himself ideological during the period of *Humanism and Terror* in clinging to the notion of the triumph of the proletariat, why was he not equally so with regard to its most important premise, workers' non-culturally-generated rights to be respected as ends in themselves? It is the case that the premise can be defended, and has been several notable times in the history of philosophy, without being put in the service of a proletariat. But it is nonetheless true, and singularly striking, that there is never any interrogation of the premise in Merleau-Ponty's writings, before or after *Humanism and Terror.* It is always mentioned as though it were self-evident, and its role in Merleau-Ponty's thought is to be the silent, hidden, but indispensable fulcrum on which his social views are balanced.

But of course, it need not remain so, for this hidden premise can be pried out and challenged. For one thing, there have not been lacking a variety of historical alternatives—not least those of multiple variants of capitalism—each defended with its own (what we call) ideology. For another thing, Merleau-Ponty's view is not the only logically possible way of regarding what is just for human beings, whether these alternative schemes have actually existed or not. To take merely one of a number of long-familiar examples, while there are good reasons[17] for rejecting the sort of utopia which Aldous Huxley long ago worried about in *Brave New World,* there is nothing self-contradictory about the proposed modes of existence therein. Indeed, Huxley was quite right to observe, and would have had even more evidence today for so claiming,[18] that the difference between the lifestyles of citizens in his future society and those of our own is one of degree rather than of kind.

Merleau-Ponty could respond that the right to be treated as an end in oneself is either self-evident after all or that this claim can be defended in some other way. I am not certain what his considered response would be, since it is not unambiguously clear in the texts themselves. (It is, in fact, a "bad" ambiguity therein.) But on the basis of what we have already seen of his ethics, it seems likely that the following reconstructed line of reasoning best expresses his view of the matter. Also, this reconstructed view is directly relevant to the ideal of respect for law that governs the lives of the persons whose rights are under discussion.

The argument would run roughly this way: (i) Human existence is a power of transcendence, expression, and self-determination. It incarnates a liberty of self-fulfillment through which the self is seen as a center of well-being. It constitutes and institutes meanings through being situated in and conditioned by what is whilst aiming at what is not yet. (ii) What comprises the difference between more and less rich futures—for individuals as well as sub-cultural groups and whole societies—is, in an important part, the degree to which the conditions of one's situation are capable of soliciting and nourishing one's creativity. (iii) "Human flourishing"[19] thus is helped materially by (a) the provision of basic goods in life which positively encourage it as well as by (b) the absence of conditions which would harm it. At a very rudimentary level, food, clothing, and shelter are examples of (a), whilst starvation, crippling disease, and authoritarian repression are different sorts of instances of (b). But over and above this rudimentary level, there exists a multiplicity of goods to flesh out the list begun in (a) by the basic necessities of life. One needs knowledge, aesthetic experience, freedom of expression, and so forth, to answer all the complex and varying ways we can flourish. Since (iv) being treated as an end in oneself means being respected as an autonomous source of flourishing, respecting people as ends in themselves is tantamount to respecting existence itself or, what is the same, a commitment to helping people become as fully human as possible. This is the regulative ideal of the new liberalism in the domain of politics and law, that is, in a world in the grips of class struggle, to work toward future conditions in which the struggle is replaced by universal respect—with, however, a full realization of the contingency with which the sedimentation of meaning is always menaced.

By contrast, (v) treating someone as *merely* a means to an end—the contradictory of the desideratum of (iv)—is to use the other exclusively as a tool, something to manipulate in such a way that the individual concerned no longer counts. In treating someone considered as a source of flouishing only as a means to an end, (vi) one abuses him or her, which effectively can poison the center of flourishing at its very core. Moreover, (vii) when such adverse attitudes take on the serious weight of social institutions, limits are imposed on the freedom of expression, dignity, and self-determination of whole classes of people. Sexism and racism are obviously prominent examples, and so, in Merleau-Ponty's view, is capitalism—to which, say, films such as *The Bostonians, A Passage to India,* and *The Tree of Wooden Clogs* provide eloquent visual testimony. And (viii) when written into law, as in *Bradwell* or *Adkins,* such dehumanizing obstacles to human flourishing become formal, coercive restraints. Thus Fuller complained of certain constitutions which had "come into existence since World War II" that they not uncommonly had built into them "a host of economic and political measures of the type one would ordinarily associate with statutory law. It is hardly likely that these measures have been written into the constitution because they represents aims that are generally shared. One suspects that the reason for their inclusion is precisely the opposite, namely, a fear that they would not be able to survive the vicissitudes of an ordinary exercise of parliamentary power. Thus, the divisions of opinion that are a normal accompaniment of lawmaking are written into the document that makes law itself possible. This is obviously a procedure that contains serious dangers for a future realization of the ideal of fidelity to law."[20]

The ideal of fidelity to law will be considered in detail below, in the final section of this chapter. In the present context, however, Merleau-Ponty's reconstructed argument has at least three other features of interest. The first one is that it does not actually succeed in establishing what it set out to, namely, a right to be treated as an end in oneself. This is so because the argument is purely descriptive and rights are prescriptive, and it has been known at least since Hume that what ought to be the case cannot be deduced logically from what is the case. At most, the argument establishes a Kantian-like hypothetical imperative, namely, "if one wanted to encourage (develop, solicit, nourish, maximize . . .) human flourishing, then one ought to treat each person as an end in him-or herself. As we shall see below, this hypothetical limitation is in fact why D'Entrèves rejects the "technological" view of natural law—that is, that it can never establish categorically the desirability of the antecedent clause.

Second, the (bad) ambiguity in Merleau-Ponty's writings as to whether the right to be treated as an end in oneself is self-evident or arrived at in some other way has a parallel ambiguity in terms of the way he wants to use the right in question to judge institutions such as capitalism and bourgeois legal systems. Namely, as noted above (III.4), it is not certain whether, on his view, values come from history or whether we use them to interpret history (or both). The right here in question was certainly not self-evident for Nietzsche, for whom in consequence Kant's *Critique of Practical Reason* ranked prominently on his list of philosophical frauds. But for Merleau-Ponty, if the contemporary hero is not Prometheus (see III.3), he or she can hardly be Zarathustra (or, more accurately, the Overman whose self-proclaimed herald Zarathustra is). Merleau-Ponty might respond at this point that, as in the parallel reconstructed argument in Chapter III about values and the interpretation of history, history has taught us negatively that all other views of rights are insufficient. That is, history broadly consists of a case-book of examples of the unhappy consequences for human beings when they are not respected as ends in themselves, and this provides the new liberalism with enough evidence to make such a view of rights a regulative ideal for a world in struggle. And such a view of history is not only considerably more likely than that of Zarathustra, but it is also the case that, in a nuclear age, demonstrations of competing views might well be the last such case studies. They would gain for the planet as a whole the sagacity of W.C. Fields whose last words before being hanged at the end of *My Little Chickadee* were, "It'll sure be a lesson to me."

But whatever be the source of the right to be treated as fully human, Merleau-Ponty accords it to everyone as a regulative idea to pursue. It is not a privilege or a right to be earned; it exists already, not as an objective value to be copied, but as an objective demand to be satisfied—a "permanent necessity," the actualization of which requires only the elimination of dehumanizing social and legal conditions. It is not thus something merited by virtue of race, sex, mental accomplishments, or economic standing. As regards the latter, for example, it would impeach the views that rights to adequate health care or heat in winter are functions of one's ability to pay. The results of such contrary social policies have obvious and unhappy consequences for the ideal of respect for law, for if one does not respect as ends in themselves the members of society whose law it is, there hardly seems any point in respecting the law itself. Respect for law must be earned and planned for, as Fuller says, but the same cannot be said rightly of respect for persons.

A final feature of interest of the argument reconstructed above concerns the list of goods begun at (iii) (a) which, if completed, would correspond to all the essential and important ways in which human flourishing can occur. In essence, what John Finnis attempts in Part II of his interesting and intriguing essay, *Natural Law and Natural Rights* is to complete this list. He seeks to illustrate and defend the claim that there are self-evident basic goods in life which augment human flourishing—and the absence of which contributes to human diminishment—and that, in consequence, it is always "practically reasonable" to pursue such goods.

Merleau-Ponty's reactions to Finnis' claims clearly would be shaped by his perception of phenomenology as, among other things, an ideology critique. And it is certain that he would have endorsed Alf Ross' own ideology critique, as detailed above. Moreover, there are three arguments articulated in Part One which, on the surface at least, appear inimical to *any* kind of defense of natural law or natural rights. These three arguments consist of the denial of the normativity of nature for human existence, the rejection of "exterior rules" and "objective values," and the critique of rationalism as a historical adventure rather than being capable of demonstrating any rational order in "the nature of things." There is, instead, only reason set amidst unreason, logic set in the unavoidable context of contingency. The critique of rationalism is also, as we have seen (I.3), tightly related to the dogmatic universality which Merleau-Ponty found in Husserl's analyses of language and finally in structuralism itself.

On the other hand, Merleau-Ponty's phenomenology strongly converges on Finnis' theory in what concerns the latter's list of "basic goods" and also the former's view of decision making—in ethics, politics, and law—of creating the best "pictures," or concretizing the richest set of humane values possible in a given context. Thus, although it is obvious that nothing Finnis says is binding on Merleau-Ponty, it is worth pausing to consider a brief overview of his theory in order to underscore the most important similarities and differences. What substantial agreement does exist in their views will also have the merit of demonstrating the wide variations in meaning possible for the label "natural law."

The basic goods which Finnis is concerned to elaborate are knowledge, life, play, aesthetic experience, sociability (friendship), practical reasonableness, and "religion."[21] All except the last two require little explanation, but by "practical reasonableness" is meant the capacity to use one's intelligence effectively in actions which shape one's character and one's relationship with others[22] in bringing the basic goods into being. As in political, ethical, and legal decision making for Merleau-Ponty, the emphasis is on thinking in contact with the facts of one's situations in order to make values real. At the same time, for reasons given in the reconstructed argument above in (i)-(iv), a concern for making values real also makes human beings more fully human. This is so because "the basic forms of good are opportunities of *being;* the more fully a man participates in them the more he is what he can be."[23] "Religion," on the other hand, is not self-explanatory because the word is used as an admittedly awkward label for the good concerned. Hence, Finnis himself encloses it in quotation marks.[24] For rather than referring to dogma or creed, which Merleau-Ponty would not accept, it underlines the reasonableness of the belief that it is particularly important to have thought carefully (and, if possible) correctly about a divine order of things—no matter whether the best answer appears to be adoption of the religious hypothesis, agnosticism, or atheism. And this was a subject about which Merleau-Ponty himself was long and painfully exercised.[25]

Further, practical reasonableness has nine basic requirements which are interrelated and interdependent. The first is that one ought to have a "rational plan of life," in the sense that there is some "harmonious set of purposes and orientations, not as 'plans' or 'blueprints' of a pipe-dream, but as effective commitments."[26] This concept, which is taken over from John Rawls' *A Theory of Justice,*[27] simply expresses the requirement that, if reason is to be practical rather than a diffuse waste of effort and time, priorities must be coherently ordered so as to establish goals and plans for achieving them. And indeed, it is just as difficult to imagine successful moral, political, or legal decision making as Merleau-Ponty has described them in the absence of this requirement as it is to conceive that Merleau-Ponty would accept what Finnis also rejects here.

The second requirement is that, in our actions, there be no arbitrary preference or neglect among the basic goods—that is, all count equally.[28] Similarly, the third requirement states that there can be no arbitrary preferences between persons.[29] As argued above, for Merleau-Ponty, each person deserves to be treated as an end in him-or herself; such a right is not earned, but rather given in our very humanness. In a world in struggle, however, this is a regulative ideal. The fourth requirement is one of detachment, by which Finnis means to distinguish between particular projects and the rational plan of life they embody.[30] The idea here is that, even if the former fail to achieve what goods we wish them to, this does not justify abandoning the rational plan of life which they embody. Failure of certain projects does not empty our lives of all meaning. Rather, it calls for renewed thought to find more creative means to actualize the values concerned. Or, as we saw in Chapter III, rules are instrumental means, but only that. Their value comes from their ability to help us concretize what Finnis calls "basic values." And this is the fifth requirement of practical reasonableness, fidelity or commitment to basic values.

Together the fourth and fifth requirements constitute a considerable overlap with what Merleau-Ponty says about values—both moral, political, and legal. For, (i) despite apparently contradictory language, Finnis' view coheres well with what Merleau-Ponty defended in terms of a contextualist theory of ethical values in place of "objective values" and "exterior rules." This is so because what Finnis describes, unlike what Merleau-Ponty rejects, is not inconsistent with a creative human freedom working practically to discover concrete solutions for bringing values into being. What Merleau-Ponty rejects in ethics (Kant), politics (Alain), and in law (the school of *Begriffsjurisprudenz*) is the view that would make decisions simple deductions from general principles applied to facts. A second close similarity (ii), therefore, between the fourth and fifth requirements and Merleau-Ponty's view of decision making consists in the fact that detachment and commitment jointly establish an effective strategy for reasonably achieving social goals across a complex network of conflicting individual interests. But at the same time, (iii) they serve to distinguish acting on principle—commitment to the basic good(s) at issue in particular actions, social policies, or laws—from mere opportunism or "sub-rational complacency of habit, mere urge to conformity, etc."[31] As we have seen above (IV n.50), this distinction was also very much on Merleau-Ponty's mind in the context of his discussion of Machiavelli. I shall come back to this in the "Epilogue" below.

The sixth requirement, which overlaps that of a rational plan of life, is that, in attempting to bring values into being, one should be as efficient as possible instead of wasting time in non-utilitarian actions, or with those which are unfit for the purposes desired.[32] Again Merleau-Ponty would not disagree, for it is inherent to an instrumental view of rules that there be some rational relationship between means and end and that the tool should be as closely appropriate to the task as possible. On the other hand, he would have a considerable qualification to offer for the seventh requirement, that one should respect every basic value in every action.[33] Perhaps it would be better to express this requirement negatively, that is, not to disrespect any value in any act, because not all (or perhaps any) acts have all values in view. And perhaps some have none in view. But if one takes seriously the Marxist perspective of a world in struggle—as Merleau-Ponty certainly does and as Finnis apparently does not[34]—then, for the reasons given above, the seventh requirement becomes more a regulative ideal than what is actually possible. One might also therefore conclude that Merleau-Ponty would have the same opinion of the eighth requirement as well, namely that we should respect the common good of society at the expense of private interests conflicting with it—even, or especially, our own.[35]

That is, although one might be tempted to say that, on Merleau-Ponty's view, class struggle should always have pride of place over the common good—or better, that the common good is ultimately best served by allowing class struggle to continue, albeit, in the programme of the new liberalism, within formal liberal structures—there was at least one time in his life, in supporting Pierre Mendès-France, that he held the opposite view. As Sonia Kruks points out, Mendès-France came to power with the Keynsian "idea—so stale today, but still novel in France in 1954—that the state, as a neutral force, should actively intervene to moderate and contain class struggle for the national good."[36] And as Kruks goes on to note, "Mendès-France appealed to all Frenchmen to act as citizens, beyond their own narrow class interests and to participate in the democratic process from which the decisions of the state must derive. As Merleau-Ponty put it in one of his articles in *L'Express* (23.9.54), the 'ideology of state intervention without state production . . . addresses itself to political consciousness, to the citizen as such.'"[37]

In the context of Finnis' eighth requirement of practical reasonableness, we have thus been brought face to face with the problem of justice and interests which comprises the subject of the following section. Before leaving it here, however, let us at least be clear that Merleau-Ponty endorses the general desirability of acting for the common good. The problems that this poses for the rest of his view of law and society will be left for the next section.

Finnis' final requirement of practical reasonableness, the ninth, is that one acts according to what one's conscience tells one to do or avoid doing.[38] This requirement is obviously tightly related to the fourth and fifth, detachment and commitment, participation in which indicates that one is acting out of principle. For the reasons given above in discussing these requirements, I do not think Merleau-Ponty would be troubled by this one either. For what Finnis means by "conscience" has nothing to do with the style of ethics and politics which Merleau-Ponty rejected under that label, that of pure intentions detached from the consequences of one's actions (Kant and Alain). Rather, in Finnis' sense, the meaning is very close to what Merleau-Ponty meant in stressing the tight connections between morality, law, and politics as interwoven orders of social meaning, a conclusion equally relevant to the relationship of justice to individual and class interests.

§2. *Interests and Justice*

The second major strand of Merleau-Ponty's thinking about law and morality consists of the relationship of interests and justice.[39] (The ideal of respect for law also emerged several times in the preceding section and will be implicated here as well. But since it requires discussion which is not reducible to either section, it will be reserved for special consideration below.) Now in some systems of law, such as those of England or the United States, rights are conceived as legitimate interests. I have an interest in protecting my reputation, for instance, and so I have a right against others that they do not slander or libel me. But Merleau-Ponty's consideration of interests and justice is wholly different. Namely, it is restricted to economic interests and basic human needs as well as the injustice of capitalist and communist societies which do not satisfy those needs.

The relationship of interests—both moral and legal—and justice, again both moral and legal, played a role in previous analyses of morality (III.2, 3), politics (IV.2), and law (V.2), as well as in the preceding section of this chapter (with reference to Finnis' eighth requirement of practical reasonableness, namely, that one should act to seek the common good.) From these analyses we have learned that, in Merleau-Ponty's view: (i) the situation of law within the Gestalt-structure of other social phenomena brings it about that the actual functioning of a legal system as well as meanings assigned to constitutions, positive laws, codes, evolving bodies of case law, and the like, are strongly colored by—even if not simplistic copies of—whatever political, economic, moral, and religious interests dominate in a given society from one synchronic state to another. (ii) Both the solidarity of the juridicial with other orders of social meaning, as well as the way that law usually develops to solve problems and formally ratify moral and other social values (instead of initiating new forms of life), underline the significance of the ways in which law both reflects and reinforces other social values. And (iii), we saw that, what is the relevant case in point for Merleau-Ponty's critique of liberal democracies in his earlier writings, a democracy of formal rules facilitates and abets the establishment and maintenance of bourgeois capitalism.

Moreover, (iv) in Merleau-Ponty's view as it stood at the conclusion of *Humanisme et terreur,* interests and justice in Western societies were simply opposed to one another, both morally and legally. As noted above, justice, though never carefully defined, amounted roughly to treating all members of society as ends in themselves; hence "justice" and "universality" are used interchangeably (see III.2). But in a world in struggle, justice in this sense is a regulative ideal which could be accomplished only through the abolition of classes and the formal institutions, such as law, which protect them. Western democratic (bourgeois) justice is empty and even hypocritical because, whilst on the one hand protecting existing class disparities (through the control of the means of production, private ownership of natural resources, and the like), such justice on the other hand ignores the violence of such arrangements by taking refuge in a scheme of merely formal rules—that is, those that insulate the content of social arrangements legally protected from critical examination and change. It is in this sense of "formal rules," as we have seen in Chapters III and IV, that he indicts the doctrines of "formal democracies" as being "in ruins" (S 31). Such doctrines, like those of Alain, comprise a "juridicial dream" (HT 66) because they ignore the consequences of living in a heaven of principles, namely, polarization of interests and violence such as one finds in the "substantive due process" cases sketched above.

Thus, as we have seen in Part One (IV.2), what Merleau-Ponty effectively does in *Humanisme et terreur* is to expand and generalize Fuller's critique of constitutions noted above by applying the latter's criticisms to all Western societies which falsely contrast communism, lies, and propaganda, on the one hand, with respect for truth, law, and individual freedoms, on the other. This is only a "liberal mystification" (HT 9); the Marxist knows, on the contrary, that "each human initiative polarizes interests all of which are not acknowledged" (HT 87). Therefore, in Western, bourgeois democracies, since interests and justice are so thoroughly opposed to each other, and given the emptiness and hypocrisy of Western "justice"—no matter how even-handed things appear on the surface—a proper critique of Western law ought to lead to the dismantling of their legal systems and allied formal institutions. There is surely much more than a small Nietzschean influence running through such a perception—not of Zarathustra, to be sure, but rather of *The Twilight of the Idols,* the sub-title of which is "How One Philosophizes With a Hammer." The aim in both cases is to use the tuning fork of a more sensitive and enlightened consciousness to expose the hollowness of the old idols—even though, or especially when, superficially the truth looks to be quite otherwise.

When one goes beyond Merleau-Ponty's earlier writings to the framework of the new liberalism of *Les Aventures de la dialectique,* one finds a vastly different consideration of legal and moral interests and justice. For as detailed in Part One (III.3, IV.3), the task of the new liberalism is not a polemic aimed at overthrowing all formal institutions on the grounds of a diametrical opposition of interests and justice. It is, rather, a question of how to utilize institutions such as parliament in order to recognize and give effect to individual freedoms whilst on the other hand enabling justice (universality) to emerge. However, before outlining the important problems for the philosophy of law posed by this later view, it is worth pausing a moment to consider one way of objecting to the earlier one and how Merleau-Ponty would respond to it. For both the objection and the response will prove relevant to the later view and to the ideal of fidelity to law.

The objection is framed by H.L.A. Hart in the context of his criticisms of Sir Patrick Devlin's views on the enforcement of morals. Hart wishes to distinguish between the "formal values" and "material values" that are both necessary features of "the practice of any social morality."[40] The latter refers to the content of the morality dominant in a given society for which we may fairly expect substantial overlap in law in the ways explained in the previous chapter. The former, however, is radically different. It consists of what is necessary to preserve the moral point of view itself: "In moral relationships with others the individual sees questions of conduct from an impersonal point of view and applies general rules impartially to himself and to others; he is made aware of and takes account of the wants, expectations, and reactions of others; he exerts self-discipline and control in adapting his conduct to a system of reciprocal claimis. These are universal virtues and indeed constitute the specifically moral attitude to conduct."[41]

The distinction is important in morality, to be sure, but also in politics and law, for it allows us to disentangle two different senses of preserving morality. One is a moral conservatism that tries to "freeze into immobility the morality dominant at a particular time in a society's existence,"[42] and hence is concerned with the "material values of a social morality. As Hart points out, the greatest danger in such a view, as Mill in *On Liberty* and de Tocqueville in *Democracy in America* were concerned to underscore, "was not that in fact the majority might use their power to oppress a minority, but that, with the spread of democratic ideas, it might come to be thought unobjectionable that they do so."[43] The "central mistake" of such a view is "a failure to distinguish the acceptable principle that political power is best entrusted to the majority from the unacceptable claim that what the majority do with that power is beyond criticism and must never be resisted."[44] And it is precisely from the point of view of "preserving morality" in respect to "formal values" that effective criticism is often possible and necessary. For preserving the moral point of view can and should be unhinged conceptually and existentially from the crystallization of particular interests in law.

How might Merleau-Ponty respond to Hart's distinction? Certainly he would agree—even within the framework of *Humanisme et terreur*—about the dangers of legally freezing into immobility dominant moral (and related political and economic) interests. And he equally clearly would endorse the view that the majority class of a society ought not to be insulated from criticism. But beyond these concessions, there is little to suggest that he would accept such a form/matter distinction as capable of reviving a sense of justice in Western democracies such that their legal systems would merit respect. Since capitalist systems are already unjust, even-handedness in their administration along the lines that Hart has sketched out as formally constituting the moral point of view—for instance, in the impartial application of general rules—could not salvage the respectability of the system itself, morally or legally. The hollowness of the idol remains when law is but the trappings of an inner core of violence. The only way, then, that Merleau-Ponty ultimately could see Hart's distinction as an effective defense of the ideal of respect for law in formal democracies in which law implements and consolidates a capitalist system is if under taking "account of the wants, expectations, and reactions of others" in a "system of reciprocal claims" Hart could come to include Marxist criticisms of capitalism. And there is no evidence that he would do so.[45] It is not that Hart's distinction is wrong, so much as it is abstract. It must be radicalized to encompass the presuppositions of social values rather than focussing exclusively on their legal administration.

Such a conclusion parallels and extends critiques by J.R. Lucas, as we saw in the last chapter, and by Lon Fuller, of the ways in which Hart's treatment of law abstracts the legal skeleton too much from the social and political body which it supports. Fuller, in focussing more closely on the social function of law, rejects the concept of law as purely managerial control. Rulers do not exercise a purely managerial control over their subjects. On the contrary, as we have seen above (V.2), both are bound by the same general rules that reflect and sediment the same societal values. As a result, as John Finnis summarizes Fuller's position, "There is thus an essential component of collaboration and reciprocity in the enterprise of subjecting human conduct to the governance of legal as distinct from merely managerial norms."[46] And in a way quite similar to that in which both Lucas and Fuller anchor their views of law in its social functions, we have seen in Chapter IV that the programme of Merleau-Ponty's new liberalism is predicated upon a honest recognition of conflicting interests and, more generally, of class struggle. As opposed to the "empyrean politics" of thinkers such as Alain, class struggle exists and, indeed, must exist because there are classes, which is to say those who are systemically disfavored (AD 303). The task of the new liberalism is thus not unlike that which faced the founders of *Les Temps Modernes,* namely, to go beyond existing parties by "rethinking the whole" and "recreating principles in contact with the facts" (AD 255). This is why that, as explained in Chapter IV, the Communist Party ought to be legal, namely, that it is a "useful danger" in that it helps to pose "the social problem in terms of struggle" (AD 303-04).

The upshot of the changed perspective of the new liberalism is, then, first, the goal of justice remained the same: to bring into being a future society in which each member could be treated humanely, as an end in him-or herself. "The misery and exploitation of the most disfavored are the last arguments," Merleau-Ponty tells us, "and, as Péguy said, the city in which a single man suffers injustice is an unjust city" (AD 207). Second, if we persist in "recreating principles in contact with the facts" and ask what conditions are necessary for these regulative ideals to be actualized in the manner suggested in *Les Aventures de la dialectique* and afterwards, it immediately becomes clear that one such condition is that law must be something more than the crystallization and reinforcement of dominant moral, political, and economic interests. In other words, law must be able to rise higher than the state of being a tool of moral or political conservatism—although, for reasons given above and in the last chapter vis-à-vis judicial decision making, law can be fairly expected to reflect whatever other social values predominate. Law must allow class struggle to exist and work toward a state in which those systemically disfavored can be fully respected, but it cannot do this if it becomes a pawn of a given (majority) class. This is why Merleau-Ponty wrote of the necessity of resisting capitalism and "its imperious laws of functioning" (AD 305).

But this sort of view leads to two different sorts of critical questions, the first of which is whether "the facts" of the current world political situation make it likely or even plausible to suppose that the programme of a non-Communist left could meet with any more success in our own day than it did in Merleau-Ponty's own. This is an empirical question to which I shall return at the end of this section and in the Epilogue below. The second question, however, is of a very different nature. It is whether the theoretical distinction between the solidarity of law in the social Gestalt and the subtle and variable relations between the "parts" of the Gestalt is really sufficient to sustain the political and legal hopes of the new liberalism. It was this distinction that was employed in the last chapter to differentiate political, moral (and other) influences on judges from a causally deterministic account of those influences. But in the much wider and different context of parliamentary democracy, one might well think such a distinction too fragile to bear the weight Merleau-Ponty would place upon it for the sake of law working effectively to solve "the social problem." And if not, then the new liberalism would run the risk of becoming, like its obsolete predecessors, a superficial, optimistic reduction of history "to speculative conflicts of opinion, political struggle to exchanges of viewpoint on a clearly posed problem, and human existence to the relations of cocitizens in an empyrean politics" (AD 303). This was, after all, precisely the Marxist objection Merleau-Ponty posed to his own view, as well as how Sonia Kruks criticized it (IV.3).

It is not clear to me that Merleau-Ponty was even fully aware of this problem, let alone provided a detailed answer to it. For, it is striking how there is no attempt in the Epilogue of *The Adventures of the Dialectic* to consider the efficacy of parliamentary democracy in the light of either Weber's analysis of historical explanation which appears earlier in the text or the more general sorts of remarks cited above several times about the solidarity of the juridicial with other orders of meaning in society. And indeed, the description of the subtle and variable relations of social structures is to be found in *Signs* rather than in his last major work on politics. As a result, the best answer which his phenomenology can give to such an objection must be constructed from separate textual references.

One such argument he could give would run as follows: (i) As noted above in relation to Finnis' eighth requirement of practical reasonableness, narrow class interests should be transcended for the sake of the common good. This is so because, among other reasons, (ii) the welfare of the whole society turns on benefitting the most disfavored. As he indicated in his article, "Où va l'anti-communisme?" in *L'Express* (25 June 1955), bringing prosperity to France's "poorest sons" may indeed cause short-term conflicts of interests, but these will converge in a national unity in the long run.[47] But (iii), what grounds (i) and (ii) is the necessity of formal institutions—chiefly that of parliament—to protect everyone's liberty. (As Finnis pointed out, it is not "practically reasonable" to arbitrarily disregard the welfare of any given member or class of society.) One key function of institutions is, thus, as Kruks fails to appreciate (see IV.3), to provide a temporally thick, enduring structure for human liberties. It is as naive to think that genuine freedom emerges with the overthrow of an entire legal system as it is to consider, as Kruks also does (IV.3), that a legal institution such as parliament necessarily reduces class struggle "to healthy intellectual opposition always to be maintained within the status quo."

Further, (iv) taking into account the openness to change in living human institutions such as law, we incur the double responsibility of maintaining institutions, such as parliament, but also keeping them accessible to the advent of new meaning and available to all. Doubtless political conservatives would attempt to forestall fundamental, presuppositional challenges to the system itself in the form of certain actions, social policies, or even the constitutional unfairnesses of which Fuller complained, but presumably Merleau-Ponty would class these under the "parliamentary manoeuvrings" that could be denounced in parliament itself. And certainly one argument new liberals could make would be that attempts to drive alienating wedges between the members of society and their institutions are arbitrary and unjust because they contravene the basic goods (in Finnis' language) of knowledge and truth which sustain the dialectic. Such attempts would also clash with the third requirement of practical reasonableness, to avoid arbitrary preferences amongst persons, and with the eighth requirement, to seek the common good.

But it is not only law-making authorities in stable constitutional democracies that are tempted to close off parliaments from fundamental changes or to allow them to serve as a vehicle for making basic changes in society, or even to suppress them entirely. History, both past and present around the globe, has no want of such leaders who resort to parliament only when convenient and expedient—which is to say, maintaining only a hypocritical, deceitful openness of the democratic process—and usually transparently so at that. As noted above in Part I (IV.3), a *parlement de convenance* is no more thought to attract serious commitments that a *marriage* of the same genre. In extreme cases of attempting to close off institutions such as parliament, when no effective legal speech is possible in such situations, the institutions themselves may decay and die. But absent these *in extremis* cases, the difference between an institution such as parliament being open or closed usually will be one of degree rather than of kind. Hence Merleau-Ponty would also argue normatively for complete openness in order to maximize the chances of success of the dialectic in arriving at a solution to the social problem. As a result, the openness of institutions functions in his view both descriptively—as a factual account of the very nature of a living social structure—and prescriptively, as a norm for human flourishing.

Saying just this much, although true to Merleau-Ponty's thinking on such matters, nonetheless still misses the full sweep of his concern for the openness of parliament. The full significance of his claim only becomes clear when we consider that he intends an openness of legal institutions in terms of both content and form. The latter means unrestricted access to all members, parties, and classes of society; thus, as noted before, he took particular pains to insist that the Communist Party must enjoy the right to legal representation. But openness to new meaning in terms of content is very different. For what this would entail—for any society "in struggle," and thus in Western capitalistic ones—would be a legal system which, throughout the whole range of the law of social administration and lawyer's law, permits law to democratically work against whatever codes, statutory law, and/or constitutional provisions there may be which prevent the emergence of justice. And we have already seen that, considering the solidarity of law within the social Gestalt, it would be reasonable to expect much overlap here. As a result, the new liberalism poses the social problem as a struggle for power, but it is the power to change the content and sometimes the form of institutions—economic, political, and legal—rather than scrapping them entirely. Indeed, the feminist movement shows us clearly that, despite all external appearances and predictions based on them from the external point of view, in Hart's sense, from the internal point of view institutions are still human, that effective struggle to change their content and even basic value presuppositions can in principle go on within them, and that, finally, these possibilities are two faces of the same reality. Or, as Lucas put it, "The long-held belief that law not only is not opposed to freedom, but positively constitutes it, makes sense only if law is regarded primarily from the internal point of view."[48]

Such a conclusion leads us directly to the ideal of respect for law, but it also points toward a balancing note of caution. The previous paragraphs have argued that, in Western capitalistic democracies, the hope which the new liberalism would invest in parliament would not be misplaced, although there would be enormous, countervailing pressures against the basic legal and political reform desired by a non-communist left. It would thus be a chance, albeit a slim one, to concretize humane values. Hence the note of caution consists in the realization that political and legal institutions are not easily amenable to the forces of change. This is partly why, as we saw above (IV.3,4) the new liberalism is not a solution to the social problem in the sense of a solution to a cross-word puzzle, and that what is indicated is the much more modest and realistic view of *virtu* without resignation, of reason set ineluctably in the context of non-reason, and of necessity situated in contingency. Since institutions embody the weight of history, effective and substantial changes usually also require a countervailing history. Feminism, after all, did not spring into being, whole and complete, like Athena from the head of Zeus—a usual, stock-in-trade, but hardly appropriate analogy! Rather, it was *en route* for a long time, across centuries of injustice. So the new liberal must remain alive to the differences between political and legal synchrony, on the one hand, in which desired institutional changes may well not crystallize as desired, and the perspective of diachrony in which changes may be better noticed and measured. And from all that appears, Merleau-Ponty's oscillation between hope and despair in the "Préface" of *Signes* (pp. 31-32) reflects this sensitivity to synchronous and diachronous interpretations and a hesitancy about drawing premature conclusions.

But however this may be, it seems clear that, on Merleau-Ponty's view, legal institutions provide the conditions which are necessary, rather than sufficient, for the new liberalism's struggle for legal and political power and for the emergence of justice from a welter of conflicting interests. Perhaps it would be best to say, then, that the new liberalism is committed to the struggle of a concrete dialectic through law, no more and no less. No more because there is no satisfactory moral alternative, and no less because of the indispensability of legal institutions for the pursuit of truth and human dignity. If reliance on legal institutions, such as parliament or the courts, sometimes leads to mischief and injustice, eliminating them would practically guarantee it.

§3. *The Ideal of Respect for Law*

A number of different perspectives over the last two chapters converge on the subject of respect for law in Merleau-Ponty's phenomenology of law as here interpreted. To begin with, for the reasons given in the previous section, respect for law is a regulative ideal, rather than a datum or a *fait accompli.*[49] In a world in struggle, a world unacceptable (E 49) both morally and legally, respect for law would accrue only insofar as, within a given legal system, law-making authorities shared a commitment to make law an instrument of justice. This commitment, as in Finnis' stress on basic goods as modes of being in which we participate, must not lapse back into a morality of pure intentions, but rather work to concretize values. Liberalism, like reason or the Absolute, must not be denied, but rather brought down to earth. Correlatively, law-making authorities must be resolved to interpret abstract legal words such as "rights," "equality," "citizenship," "democracy," and "justice" in terms of the tissue of living human relationships to which these words, as well as grandiose constitutional slogans, refer in a particular society, and then more realistically work to humanize the social world.

Second, as discussed above, there must be an openness of legal institutions in terms of both form and content. Correlatively, as described in Chapter IV, freedom of expression and tolerance of political and other differences must be defended. Such openness is a necessary condition of modulating such institutions for the sake of concretizing values such as those "basic goods" which Finnis elaborates. On the other hand, although it is certain from the texts that Merleau-Ponty would defend freedom of expression and of inquiry, as well as toleration of political and philosophical differences in recreating liberal principles "in contact with the facts," there is not enough textual evidence to indicate where he would draw the limits of free expression. Almost all, if not all, societies governed by parliamentary democracies have thought it necessary to limit freedom of expression to protect other basic social goods as well as free speech itself.[50] But virtually the only conclusions which one can draw from the textual description of the new liberalism are that (i) freedom of expression is a good through which can operate the dialectical search for truth and the solution of the problem of social justice. (ii) Freedom of expression must not be restricted merely on the grounds that it threatens public order, where the latter refers to moral conservatism in what concerns the "material values" of society. In a society in struggle, sanctioning restrictions on free expression merely because it threatens public order—effectively honoring "the heckler's veto"—would condemn not only a Communist Party, but also the new liberalism or any other minority group or party to a programme of pure intentions and mere words shorn of their consequences. Also, it would be a plainly hypocritial notion of toleration—as well as logically inconsistent with the concept of parliamentary democracy—to tolerate political and legal opposition only until it begins to show results.

But "threatening public order" can mean something much more serious than the likely impact of the heckler because it can entail activities, plans, and social forces set in motion that are plainly inconsistent with parliamentary democracy itself. At the antipodes of moral conservatives who wish to restrict freedom of expression which disrupts, or tends to disrupt, public order, there are groups preaching intolerance that wish to take advantage of free speech in order eventually—once in power—to eliminate it. Thus Merleau-Ponty would also hold that (iii) given the necessity of formal institutions of law—and chiefly parliament—for the pursuit of the dialectic, freedom of expression must not be allowed to be inconsistent with the maintenance of those institutions themselves. With particular reference to the Communist Party, as explained above in Chapter IV, where it is a question of actions taken outside the democratic process, these would be tolerated only so long as they are not inconsistent with the maintenance of the democratic process itself. In the case of activities within the democratic process, these must be tolerated provided that its politics are governed by the rules of the institution of parliament itself. And as also pointed out in Chapter IV, this latter sort of toleration creates puzzles about how liberal the new liberalism can be if the Communist Party's danger would no longer be "useful" because it had triumphed democratically. This is just another way of saying that parliamentary democracy is essentially risky, and taking the risks impartially binds all players in the game, no matter in what direction the electoral wheel of fortune happens to turn. In any case, the new liberalism cannot consistently disenfranchise the Communist Party (or any other) group for that reason alone, but only if its danger is no longer "useful" because of its activities outside the democratic process. In that sort of situation, Merleau-Ponty might have recourse to something resembling Oliver Wendell Holmes' "clear and present danger"test from *United States v. Schenk:* "The most stringent protection of free speech would not protect a man in falsely shouting fire in a theatre, and causing a panic. . . . The question in every case is whether the words used are used in such circumstances and are of such a nature as to create a clear and present danger that they will bring about the substantive evils that Congress has a right to prevent. It is a question of proximity and degree" (249 U.S. 47 [1919], at 51, 52).

If this is a correct rendering of Merleau-Ponty's views, it would follow that he would also endorse certain types of laws meant to protect the integrity of legal institutions. On the grounds of a public harm principle—that is, that freedom of expression and other behavior rightly can be restricted to prevent harm to public institutions—he could argue for laws against, say, contempt of courts and legislatures. (He could also defend a private harm principle—namely, that liberty correctly can be infringed by the State for the purpose of preventing harm to particular individuals—for all the various reasons known explicitly since Mill's *On Liberty,* and which in consequence make such a principle virtually uncontroversial.) For, neither society at large nor its institutions of law can survive for long in the absence of restraints on the free use of violence.

In terms of problems associated with tolerating groups such as the Communist Party, it would also follow that Merleau-Ponty could endorse sedition laws, at least in principle. The latter qualification is important because the principle at issue amounts to distinguishing between actively fomenting revolution—which, because of (iii), he would almost surely wish to proscribe—and merely advocating it—which, because of (ii)—he presumably would not wish to to restrict. Correlatively, therefore, the new liberalism would be committed to working out legislation to provide conceptually clear and legally enforceable distinctions between the two. Urging or counselling others to bomb public institutions, riot, or assasinate leaders—after the manner of *Action Directe*—would be examples of the former, whilst claiming as a part of a political theory that social circumstances morally justify such actions would fall under the latter category. Of course, these examples are over-convenient legally because of their clarity and simplicity. In most legal proceedings in the United States concerned with sedition, it has proved notoriously more difficult to disentangle incitement to revolution from mere advocacy.[51]

Another important strand in Merleau-Ponty's thinking about respect for law is the way that it transcends mere fiat by relating to "the nature of things" in human existence. As described above, in taking account of the *exigences permanentes* of human life, law merits respect to the degree that it applies a vision of justice to what is real and practical. Legal praxis and moral principles are not fundamentally unhinged from each other, as in the "juridicial politics" of Alain (S 299), but rather are harnessed together in the task of actualizing values. Only by situating the latter project in the context of "the workable and the practical" (D'Entrèves) can legal subjects be actually—rather than merely theoretically—respected. If legal officials want to work toward the goal of respect for law, then, as Fuller expresses it, they cannot afford to ignore, any more than in terms of politics, the complex and multiform ways in which law mediates our relationships with nature. Otherwise, as underscored above, the social functions of law in settling disputes and moulding behavior would remain abstract and empty. Law and society would fail to engage each other like gears, to use one of Merleau-Ponty's favorite similes, at the very foundation which supports them both.

But can the "technological" view of natural law, as elaborated earlier on, suffice to provide respect for law? D'Entrèves considers that it will not because, "In plain, everyday language, the objection is that the 'best working' law is not necessarily the 'best' law. But that objection can also be put in a more philosophical idiom by recalling the capital distinction between 'technical' and 'categorical' imperatives. . . . If anything, both the *jus naturale* of the Roman lawyers and Professor Fuller's 'natural law of the social order' are hypothetical or technical imperatives in the Kantian sense."[52] And J. Raz voices much the same criticism by comparing the best working law to a "sharp knife" which can be required for morally good aims, but is equally serviceable for evil ones."[53]

But these are mistaken criticisms of Fuller, who seeks to distinguish law from mere violence in terms of "the internal morality of law itself."[54] The case in point for Fuller in his debates with Hart consists of the legal status of wicked German laws during the Nazi regime. There, unlike the unjust social system illuminated by *Huckleberry Finn* (see V.2), there was not the slightest pretence of a concern for the common good (Finnis' eighth basic good) in what concerns the criminal law. (By and large, the Nazis did not tamper with the civil law inherited from the Weimar Republic.) There existed a hypocritical and empty show of reciprocity and cooperation as a thinly disguised and purely managerial control dictated only by expediency.[55] *Thoroughly* iniquitous regimes cannot qualify as law because, as Finnis correctly observes, "A tyranny devoted to pernicious ends has no self-sufficient *reason* to submit itself to the discipline of operating consistently through the demanding processes of law, granted that the rational point of such self-discipline is the very value of reciprocity, fairness, and respect for persons which the tyrant, *ex hypothesi*, holds in contempt. . . . such regimes are in business for determinate results, not to help persons constitute them*selves* in community."[56] Thus, "coherence and goodness have more affinity than coherence and evil"[57], not because of any tactical considerations such as Hobbes advanced in *Leviathan*—namely, that it is always in the prudent ruler's interest to behave humanely toward his subjects in order to keep his throne—but rather because law is shorn of its social purpose and loses its structure of reciprocity and cooperation when it slides into purely managerial control. And managerial control, like a "sharp knife," can be employed for evil as well as good aims—as the Nazis were far from the least significant example of showing us.

As regards Merleau-Ponty, as we have seen across the last two chapters, the legal systems of capitalist societies, although the latter are inherently unjust, are still apparently valid law. On the other hand, he does want to distinguish law from mere violence in terms of both its social purposes and resulting structure of cooperation and reciprocity—structures it shares with language and politics and which, in Finnis' words, "help persons constitute them*selves* in community." Hence it would follow that, on Merleau-Ponty's view, although law and morality are not identical, the former cannot be entirely neutral to the scheme of values in the latter that particular society would embrace, and still deserve the name of law. There must be at least a minimal floor of cooperation and reciprocity aimed at the common good to keep law from degenerating into violence.

It also follows from the same argument that Hart places too much weight on secondary rules in defining the nature of a mature legal system (see V.3). As Lucas shows, by denying the conceptual links between law and morality and social custom, Hart is led wrongly to the view that, with a valid rule of recognition still in place, a wicked regime might still fairly claim to be guided by the rule of law. But the truth is that, even if a regime maintains some minimum content of morality as Hart argues in *The Concept of Law,* great moral evils in the system effectively change the nature of the game being played. As Lucas puts it, "The rule of recognition cannot override great substantive wrong. It is only a meta-rule, subsidiary to the system of substantive rules, often unformulated and depending on the substantive rules for its real significance.[58] In terms of the criminal law, at least, the German in Hitler's regime was situated similarly to a cricketeer "when the umpire starts giving all black men out and awarding sixes to all Australians over six feet tall."[59] The cricketeer may then ignore the umpire or, if that is imprudent—if the official is armed—he may then give lip service to the umpire whilst acknowledging that what he is doing is no longer cricket. As in games, so in law: a German citizen might not be able to resist the Nazis, but—again with regard to the criminal law (a qualification absent in Lucas' account)—"could not claim that the rulings of the Hitler regime had any legal validity, even though Hitler's original appointment to office, like the umpire's, had been legally valid."[60]

As noted above in Part One (IV.4), the structure of reciprocity and cooperation emerges first in Merleau-Ponty's writings in terms of language and is then applied to politics. Accordingly, let us return to language itself in order to illustrate the final strand of his thinking which is relevant to the ideal of respect for law, namely, the distinction between validity and efficacy. Now as we saw in Chapter V, most developed societies—if not all—are marked by a certain tension both linguistically and legally between those who accept the rules of the system as reasons for doing or abstaining from doing certain things, and those who do not. The former—who constitute the majority of a stable society—see rules from "the internal point of view," in Hart's idiom, whilst the latter approximate the "external point of view" of the observer who does not him- or herself participate in the system. In language, the creative activities of the latter group can lead to the emergence of new genres of poetic expression, theatre, or of literature, to be sure, but also to that of new dialects. Furthermore, the latter are sometimes linked to statements of cultural identity on the part of a certain sub-cultural group. In the view of such groups, the use value of the received language has atrophied, such that they wish to work out a new linguistic synchrony within the contours of the accepted framework. And if the break is decisive enough, a completely new diachrony eventually may result as well.

People who are concerned with such linguistic phenomena sometimes make two claims about the internal and external aspects of rules which are of some considerable interest from the point of view of respect for law. One of these claims, which we have already seen is correct, is that existing rules are not the only possible ones and not necessarily the best. There is no ideal language and no one-best-wayism of expression. These doctrines are untenable in the light of the fact that rules change across a certain temporal duration according to the sufficiency of their internal uses and what proportion of a given society desires what changes and when. Thus, from the point of view of diachronous aspects of language (and law), the distinction between validity and efficacy tends to get blurred, even if it does not vanish entirely (see V.3).

But as also noted in Chapter V, this conclusion about diachrony does not imply that, in a synchronic perspective, we ought to be fuzzy about the distinction between validity and efficacy. The denial of this fact constitutes the second claim that proponents of new dialects sometimes make about rules, but in this they are mistaken. That is to say, from the perspective of a given minority group which no longer accepts the language system of the majority, the latter will manifest itself as something to be accepted just because the majority do. In other words, its validity will be interpreted solely in terms of its efficacy, an efficacy which is a coercive threat expressed in, say, grading school examinations, applications for jobs, and the like. The internal aspect of a certain rule, its being a reason for speaking in particular ways, will be lost in the external point of view which sees only linguistic coercion. Correlatively, of course, respect for the rules will dissipate as the internal aspects of rules become less and less visible. In practice, legally as well as linguistically, the line between validity and efficacy in a given synchronic perspective on rules may be thin indeed, but it may also be thinner than it ought to be. For in a particular legal or linguistic framework, a certain rule is not presented synchronically to consciousness in the internal point of view as a reason for conforming to it *because* the majority happen to do so. As Hart pointed out, validity does not reduce to habits of obedience merely. Rather, the converse is the case: the majority conform to it because it is constituted in consciousness as a reason for doing so. And this is the case regardless of the fact that one can recognize simultaneously that the historical origins of the valid rule at issue are diachronically sedimented in empirically contingent patterns of usage, or efficacy. But, as pointed out in Chapter V, this does not imply that, synchronically, validity is equivalent to efficacy since, in the short run at least, both legally and linguistically, a rule can both exist and be disobeyed at the same time.

What are the consequences for the ideal of respect for law of maintaining the distinction between validity and efficacy within a society in struggle and also committed to structuring that struggle through the legal processes of parliamentary democracy? First, respect for law is correlated synchronically with validity rather than efficacy, since as we have seen (V.1), law is not reducible to pure force or violence. A crucial lesson for the majority party in parliament will thus be that the ideal of respect for law cannot be defended solely on the grounds of fiat, that a particular rule is the law, and effectively by the threat of sanctions for non-compliance. This was, as detailed in Chapter V, Austin's mistaken account of validity which Hart was correct to attack on the grounds of a more sophisticated account of (what is unavailable in Austin's theory) rules. It also follows here, therefore, that the Austinian defense of respect for law must undergo a similar adjustment.

Another crucial lesson for the majority is, secondly, that, since appeals to force (efficacy) do not comprise the last, or even the first, arguments in favor of respect for law, the latter is presented as open to critical examination. This is to say that, using Fuller's language, law manifests itself as more than mere fiat. Its reason side, which expresses the social function of law as it is grounded in "the nature of things," underlies the rationales which can be given by the majority for seeing a given rule as a reason for obeying it. And it is this reason side which is always and unavoidably open to interrogation and challenge by minorities.

Such reasoning also points to a necessary precision about the internal point of view itself by means of which Finnis criticizes Hart, and with which, for reasons given below, Merleau-Ponty would agree. That is, Finnis points out that Hart's description of the internal point of view is in reality a mixture of different kinds of viewpoints. Hart says, for instance, that "allegiance to the system may be based on many different considerations: calculations of long-term interest; disinterested interest in others; an unreflecting inherited or traditional attitude; or the mere wish to do as other do."[61] But, as Finnis observes, this is an "unsatisfactory and unstable" mixture because it glosses over differences of attitudes which are, in practical terms, real and important, and so we should distinguish further between "the central from the peripheral cases *of the internal or legal point of view itself.*"[62]

A legislator motivated by the latter two attitudes, for example, would hardly be likely to give a very compelling account of why law should be respected and indeed would be most prone to identify validity with efficacy and respect for law with fear of sanctions. But such an equation of respect for law with a prudential action or policy of staying out of harm's way can hardly express the focal point of meaning in the internal point of view on law. At best, it is only peripheral to what is more central. And that is, as Finnis phrases it in such a way as also to give voice to the regulative ideals of the new liberalism, "a viewpoint in which the establishment and maintenance of legal as distinct from discretionary or statically customary order is regarded as a moral ideal if not a compelling demand of justice."[63] Such reasoning merely states in another way earlier arguments to the effect that the dignity of law is enhanced insofar as legal institutions are kept open to critical examination and justification.

There is, finally, a third lesson in the distinction between validity and efficacy for the ideal of respect for law. This is an important consideration for minorities, those who do not have the controlling political and legal power (efficacy) at which they aim. The fact that validity does not equal efficacy also entails that not (yet) having power does not for that reason alone invalidate existing law and make it unworthy of respect. There may be, of course, other reasons for holding such views—for instance, like the Nazis, the system may come to be so thoroughly morally odious that it can hardly merit the name of law. Such, in fact, might be the best description of South Africa today. And within an incontestably valid legal system, it would still be possible for minority groups to find no reason to respect particular laws. But in terms of the legal order as such, respect for it does not turn on the empirically contingent and variable state of one's political (and legal) fortunes. No serious appreciation of, nor respect for, the formal aspects of parliamentary democracy could rest on such purely self-interested considerations.

This is to say, once more, that it is in the interest of all members of society—even, or especially, minority groups and parties—to protect the dignity, and maintain the openness, of legal institutions of parliament, the courts, and the like. This is also why, in democratic, freedom-loving societies—including any, therefore, of which the new liberalism might be the controlling power—toleration of the intolerant is such a thorny problem and a sensitive issue. From this point of view, it is irrelevant whether it is a question of, say, fascists on the extreme right or the dictatorship of the proletariat on the extreme left.[64] And especially at the interior of the parliamentary process itself, the challenge and *angoisse* of the new liberalism would be to hold together both ends of another chain: at the one end, the preservation of formal democratic institutions, because they are necessary conditions of instituting freedom and solving the social problem; and at the other end, keeping those institutions unlimitedly open to all parties which could even come to the point of voting democratically to abolish parliament itself. But in any society in which the new liberalism allowed the latter to occur, Merleau-Ponty's parting shot at Marxism—"Revolutions are true as movements and false as regimes" (AD 279)—would redouble on the new liberalism itself.[65]

NOTES

1. For a good discussion of the way that the relationship of law and morality has been distorted through an exclusive focus on sexuality, see the "Preface" of Richard Wasserstrom, ed. *Morality and the Law* (Belmont, CA: Wadsworth Publishing Co., 1971.) For further details, see also the instructive articles in that volume in addition to H.L.A. Hart, *Law, Liberty, and Morality* (Oxford: Oxford University Press, 1963), and Sir Patrick Devlin, *The Enforcement of Morals* (Oxford: Oxford University Press, 1965).
2. Hence, for example, the moral principle derived from natural law traditions which, among many others, made its way into the Anglo-Saxon common law, namely, that "No man is above the law." Of course, this principle has been disputed vigorously from time to time, as for instance, Lord Coke found to his peril in James I's Star Chamber. And in the minds of some, even after almost 200 years of Constitutional history, the principle was lost on Richard Nixon in his response to Watergate.
3. For an earlier version of the discussion following, see William S. Hamrick, "Humanity, Nature, and Respect for Law," in A.-T. Tymienieka, ed. *Analecta Husserliana* (Dordrecht: Reidel, 1983), Vol. XIV, pp. 245-56.

   It is true that one could simply put an end to the difficulty by making a virtue of the differences between the earlier and later texts in what concerns our relation to nature, and then adopting the perspective of the later texts. For, as we saw above in the Introduction, *L'oeil et l'esprit* tells us that, "Visible and mobile, my body is as and amongst things, it is one of them, it is taken up in the tissue of the world and its cohesion is that of a thing. But because it sees and moves itself, it holds things in a circle around it; they are an annex or extension of the body, they form part of its definition and the world is made of the same stuff as the body" (p. 19). Nonetheless, I want to carry on the present discussion in relation to Merleau-Ponty's earlier, rather than later, texts because, as also explained in the Introduction, it is in the former, rather than in the latter, that he is clearly committed to both phenomenology as a method for doing philosophy and to understanding the social world. Still, it is undeniable that the present discussion could only be helped by the even closer *entrecroisement* of the body and nature as described in the later works. And a similar conclusion follows for the discussion of the ideal of fidelity to law.
4. *Was Ist Metaphysik?* (Frankfurt a.M.: Vittorio Klostermann, 1965), p. 16.
5. For a similar view in a different context, see D.W. Robertson, *A Preface to Chaucer* (Princeton: Princeton University Press, 1962), p. viii: "This importance of social change as a determining factor in man's psychic constitution has recently been stressed in a brilliant book by J.H. van den Berg, *The Changing Nature of Man,* which sets out to show that 'earlier generations lived a different sort of life, and that they were *essentially* different.' . . . Their 'human passions,' although not very different from ours biologically, may have been stimulated and elaborated in ways that seem strange to us, and their art, in consequence, may have been appealing in ways that we do not readily understand" (italics in the original text).
6. *On Law and Justice* (Berkeley: University of California Press, 1959), p. 258.
7. Ross, pp. 259, 260.
8. Ross, p. 261.
9. Ross, p. 261. It is interesting to compare in Merleau-Ponty's own legal context the first sentence of the Committee draft of the *Code Napoléon:* "Il existe un droit universel et immuable, source de toutes les lois positives; il n'est que la raison naturelle, en tant qu'elle gouverne tous les hommes." In the same vein, the *Constitution Française du 3 septembre 1791* begins with its "Déclaration des droits de l'homme et du citoyen" and lists seventeen "droits naturels,

inaliénables et sacrés." L. Dugit, H. Monnier, and R. Bounard, *Les Constitutions et les principales lois politiques de la France depuis 1789,* rev. ed. by Georges Berlia (Paris: Librairie Générale du Droit et de Jurisprudence, 1952), p. 1.

10. "American Jurisprudence through English Eyes: The Nightmare and the Noble Dream," *Essays in Jurisprudence and Philosophy* (Oxford: The Clarendon Press, 1983), p. 125, n.8.
11. Wolfgang Friedmann, "Phenomenology and Legal Science," in Maurice Natanson, ed. *Phenomenology and the Social Sciences* (Evanston: Northwestern University Press, 1973), II, p. 363.
12. Naive, passive acceptance and critical reflection are diametrically opposed extremes. In actual practice, one might well find many different variations in attitude along the spectrum from one extreme to the other. Suspicion, for example, can occur before hardening into the certainty of sceptical rejection.

    In a parallel way, schizophrenic children are sometimes embroiled in this contrast between two different senses of "seeing through." See William S. Hamrick, "Language and Abnormal Behavior: Merleau-Ponty, Hart, and Laing," *The Review of Existential Psychology and Psychiatry,* Volume XVIII, Nos. 1, 2, & 3, 1982-83 (but actually published in 1985), pp. 181-203.
13. As noted above in the Introduction, one of the most significant differences between Merleau-Ponty's earlier and later works is that in the latter, there is apparently a great desire for unmediated immediacy and to obviate the standing requirement (now perceived as an obstacle) of interpretation in consciousness. It is hardly any accident that this changed attitude goes hand in hand with the remarkably different consideration of nature (see n. 2 above).
14. "The Case for Natural Law Re-examined," *Natural Law Forum* I (1956), pp. 27-46. Reprinted and cited in *Natural Law,* 2nd. edition (London: Hutchinson University Library, 1970). The passage cited is at p. 148.
15. "Reason and Fiat in Case Law," 59 *Harvard Law Review* (1946), 371.
16. As also noted above, one must be careful not to read into Merleau-Ponty's usage of "lumière naturelle" any moral content. This is quite clear in his return to this theme in *Signes* more than a decade after *Sens et non-sens:* the "lumière naturelle" is an "opening to being" which manifests itself "equally well in the most cruel forms of sadism as in Italian painting" (p. 304).
17. This is so because human beings are capable of a much richer and more fulfilling happiness than that with which *Brave New World* inhabitants are besotted—of immediate sensuous gratification, or an *infantile* happiness.
18. This is true not only of a plethora of forms of effective social conditioning, but also of its most successful accomplishment which is the conception of happiness framed by a suffusion of sex, drugs (whether legally recognized as such or not), the fetish of wealth, together with its ancillary dreary cycle of buying and having; and the acceptance of the deceitful promises of electronic media (chiefly television) for instantaneous solutions to life's problems.

    For an interesting argument in favor of censorship based on the observations of the previous paragraph and in note 17, see Irving Kristol, "Pornography, Obscenity, and the Case for Censorship," *The New York Times Magazine,* 28 March 1971. Kristol's views have been legally influential at least once when they were cited with approval by the United States Supreme Court in upholding a State's right to control the exposition of pornographic materials even when viewed only by consenting adults in private. See *Paris Adult Theatres v. Slaton,* 413 U.S. 49 (1973), at p. 64.
19. The expression is that of John Finnis in *Natural Law and Natural Rights* (Oxford: The Clarendon Press, 1980), *passim.* I shall return to Finnis' essay at the conclusion of the present section.

20. "Positivism and Fidelity to Law—A Reply to Professor Hart," 71 *Harvard Law Review* 643 (1958).
21. Finnis, pp. 59-99.
22. Finnis, pp. 88-89.
23. Finnis, p. 103. (Italics in the original text.)
24. Finnis, p. 89.
25. Jean-Paul Sartre, "Merleau-Ponty [I]," translated with introduction by William S. Hamrick, *Journal of the British Society for Phenomenology,* Volume XV, Number Two, May 1984, pp. 134-35.
26. Finnis, pp. 103-04.
27. (Cambridge, Mass.: Harvard University Press, 1977), pp. 408-23.
28. Finnis, pp. 105-06.
29. Finnis, pp. 106-09.
30. Finnis, pp. 109-10.
31. Finnis, p. 110.
32. Finnis, p. 111.
33. Finnis, pp. 118-25.
34. Marx gets scant and insignificant attention in Finnis's essay, Lenin even less, and Engels none at all.
35. Finnis, p. 125.
36. Sonia Kruks, *The Political Philosophy of Merleau-Ponty* (Sussex: The Harvester Press, 1981); published simultaneously by The Humanities Press (Atlantic Highlands, N.J.), p. 125.
37. Cited at Kruks, p. 126; translation Kruks'.
38. Finnis, p. 125.
39. A previous version of this section appeared in "Interests, Justice, and Respect for Law in Merleau-Ponty's Phenomenology," in William L. McBride and Calvin O. Schrag, eds. *Phenomenology in a Pluralistic Context* (Albany: State University of New York Press, 1984), pp. 39-48.
40. *Law, Liberty, and Morals,* p. 71.
41. Hart, p. 71.
42. Hart, p. 72.
43. Hart, pp. 77-78.
44. Hart, p. 79.
45. On matters of a closely related nature, see William L. McBride, *Fundamental Change in Law and Society* (The Hague and Paris: Mouton, 1970), pp. 50-63 and 216-25.
46. Finnis, p. 9. See Lon L. Fuller, *The Morality of Law* (New Haven: Yale University Press, 1964), pp. 210ff.
47. Something of the same reasoning has been present in the body of American case law which is most concerned with "affirmative action" plans, and what some have interpreted as "reverse discrimination," in attempts to deal justly with members of minority groups traditionally discriminated against. Effectively, the U.S. Supreme Court, as well as lower federal courts, have seen that treating such systematically disfavored members of society as Kantian-like selves, as pure ends in themselves, would be to inhabit a heaven of principles out of contact with the facts of violence that would thus be further entrenched. For appeals to (only) equal consideration in any given job-hiring or school admission decision—with no reference to race or sex—would do nothing to eliminate the lingering effects of past discrimination which, because of inequalities in the historical situations of the applicants, substantially disadvantage the preparation of minority-group members in competing for social goods.

It also follows from Merleau-Ponty's similar reasoning that the new liberalism would further have to wrestle with the tensions inherent between goals of freedom and equality.

48. "The Phenomenon of Law" in P.M.S. Hacker and J. Raz, eds. *Law, Morality, and Society: Essays in Honour of H.L.A. Hart* (Oxford: The Clarendon Press, 1977), p. 94.
49. In this particular, Merleau-Ponty would find himself in agreement with Fuller in the latter's critique of positivism in "Positivism and Fidelity to Law—A Reply to Professor Hart," pp. 642ff., and especially at p. 646.
50. "In the United States, as in every other system of system of constitutional government, the protection of free speech and discussion has had to be balanced against other community interests, such as the security of the State, the maintenance of public order and decency, the protection of reputation, and the need for fair trial proceedings." Geoffrey Marshall, *Constitutional Theory* (Oxford: The Clarendon Press, 1971), pp. 167-68.

    Cf. Finnis (p. 220): "In short, just as the right of free speech certainly requires 'limitation', i.e. specification, in the interests of free speech itself and of many other human goods, so too the procedure for settling the 'limits' of this and other human rights will certainly be enhanced in reasonableness by a wide freedom of cultural and political debate, in any society in which there is a sufficiently diffused respect for discussion and compromise as ways of being reasonable in community."
51. See Marshall, pp. 179-83, and Joel Feinberg, "Limits to the Free Expression of Opinion" in Joel Feinberg and Hyman Gross, eds. *Philosophy of Law* (Encino, CA: Dickenson, 1975), p. 149, where the author points out that after the Russian Revolution flamboyant spokesmen for working-class parties in America "were commonly charged with violations of the Federal Espionage Act during and after World War I, of state sedition laws in the 1920s, and, after World War II, of the Smith Act," but their trials "for advocacy of revolution tended to be extremely difficult and problematic partly because it was never clear whether revolution in any usual sense was something taught and approved by them, and partly because it was unclear whether the form of reference to revolution in the Marxist ideology amounted to 'advocacy' of it."
52. D'Entrèves, p. 149.
53. J. Raz, "The Role of Law and its Virtue," 93 *Law Quarterly Review* 195, at 208 (1977).
54. Fuller, pp. 644ff. See also *The Morality of Law,* pp. 210ff.
55. The fact that the Nazis did not do much mischief with the civil law prevents one from drawing any simple conclusions about whether there was a valid legal system under Hitler or not. For a charming (and classic) discussion of this problem, see "The Problem of the Grudge Informer," appended to Fuller's *The Morality of Law.*
56. Finnis, pp. 273-74. (Italics in the original text.)
57. Fuller, "Positivism and Fidelity to Law—A Reply to Professor Hart," p. 636.
58. Lucas, p. 95.
59. Lucas, p. 95.
60. Lucas, p. 95.
61. *The Concept of Law* (Oxford: The Clarendon Press, 1961), p. 198.
62. Finnis, p. 13. (Italics in the original text.)
63. Finnis, p. 14.
64. It is striking how many pretended versions of the latter style themselves as "popular democracies" when in fact they are anything but democratic and are profoundly unpopular in terms of both representation in legal processes (if any) as well as public sentiment.
65. Albert Rabil, Jr., observes that Merleau-Ponty "might have added that it is the difficulty of every human institution." *Merleau-Ponty: Existentialist of the Social World* (New York: Columbia University Press, 1967), p. 111. Jefferson counselled a new revolution in every gener-

ation, but one does not get from Merleau-Ponty a sense that the integrity of legal and political *institutions* is normally of such a short duration.

Still, Rabil is surely correct to stress the applicability of Merleau-Ponty's remark well beyond the domains of politics and law, and not least in philosophy itself—as anyone can attest who wishes to escape the stultifying, choking atmosphere of the *salon des beaux arts* approach of academic (institutional) philosophy, in order to recover the freshness of experience out of which enduring philosophical questions emerge. One of Nietzsche's sub-titles was "A Philosophy for Good Teeth." A similar ascription for academic thought might be "A Philosophy for Good Stomachs"—as when a cow endlessly chews its cud, before swallowing it, the taste is also quickly gone.

EPILOGUE

It has now been a quarter-century since the appearance of *Signes,* with its "Préface" which (in part) alternates between political despair and hope. And this time next year will see the same anniversary for the death of the author himself. Since that unexpected and tragic event, his has become one of "the voices of silence" in contemporary French culture, though not yet, as noted in the Introduction, on the other side of the Atlantic. This silence is certainly regrettable because, among other things, it is intriguing to speculate how, had he lived, he might have reacted to the current non-communist left government of François Mitterand. But it is even more interesting to consider how he might have judged the current world political (and legal) situation. Another way of saying this is to ask what lessons can be drawn from his phenomenology of the social world—as interpreted here to include the phenomenology of law—for understanding and judging the contemporary political landscape. Much might be said on this topic—indeed, far more than could reasonably be attempted here. Thus I shall restrict myself to only some brief remarks about the Soviet Union, France, and the United States.

With regard to the first of these three countries, there is little in Soviet history since 1961 that would have surprised him—except perhaps for the fact that so little has changed. (Plus ça change. . . .) The silencing, imprisonment, and exile of political dissidents, the invasion of Prague and the crushing of the Dubcek regime—tellingly known at the time as "communism with a human face"—the invasion of Afghanistan, and the connivance with Polish authorities to destroy the Solidarity labor union—all provide converging perspectives on Merleau-Ponty's indictment of the U.S.S.R. for institutionalizing violence instead of being the genuine bearer of proletarian humanism. Moreover, there is some evidence that the Gulag has even been reactivated. According to a recent issue of *Le Figaro Magazine* (24 May 1985), satellite photographs have revealed the existence of 2000 functioning concentration camps in the Soviet Union, of which 119 are for women and children, and counted in this total are 273 prisons and 85 psychiatric hospitals. Over 4 million people are said to live in such camps, condemned to various terms of forced labor in the most bestial of living conditions. Also, in terms of the abuse of "law" as an instrument of terror, there are three reported in the above article worth mentioning as continuous with Merleau-Ponty's critiques in "L'U.R.S.S. et les camps" (S 330-43). The first of these is that anyone without work for a few weeks is prosecuted for "parasitism," and then sent to forced-labor camps. Thus the Gulag permits the Kremlin to claim that unemployment does not exist (Q.E.D.). The second and third laws are apparently new: any prisoner in the Gulag can have his or her sentence prolonged without legal proceedings or anything remotely suggesting "due process," which entails that some prisoners will live out their lives in the camps. The third law, however, applies outside the Gulag: any Soviet citizen making unauthorized contact with a foreigner can be imprisoned for three years. In sum, even if the claims made in this story are only a tenth true, the Soviet Union remains as far removed from Marx as it was during Merleau-Ponty's lifetime.

On the other hand, as Merleau-Ponty would also point out, in all living institutions it is still the case that there can emerge a coming-to-be of new meaning. No institution is impervious to change or time or human creativity. And with recent changes in the "Old Guard" of the Kremlin leadership—in favor of younger, differently formed men—one may yet see in this century less terror and more humaneness in Russia. I shall return to this possibility below, in connection with the United States.

With regard to France, Merleau-Ponty would clearly have welcomed the election of a non-communist left, although he might have been surprised it could come to pass. Also, it is equally certain that he would have applauded its attempts to socialize rights—concretizing values within the formal liberal protections of a legal system, rather than leaving them as empty abstractions—and hence making law more worthy of respect. The "Declaration of the Socialist Rights of Man," recently signed by all the eminent members of the Socialist Party, affirms that "Capitalism is only legalized theft," and that all citizens have a right to housing, leisure, work, information, and an adequate standard of living—among others.

The conservative reaction, on the other hand, has been that these *desiderata* are all "admirable aspirations for security," but only "pretended rights of man" which, if adopted as "real rights," would lead to communism. This is the way, for example, Alain Madelin, a conservative member of the French Parliament, argued in "The Rights of Man are Not Socialist," in *Le Figaro Magazine* of 9 February 1985. Further, Madelin offers an intriguingly simple linguistic solution for determining real from pretended, or alleged, rights. That is, the former are expressed as "droit de," and the latter as "droit à." There are admittedly some exceptions to this rule, since language is not quite the Protean bed he would like it to be, but it is still the case that all the socialists' "pretended rights"—for instance, "le droit à un niveau de vie suffisant" (the right to an adequate standard of living) or "le droit au logement" (the right to housing)—are examples of "droit à," whilst all the "real rights" in the French *Déclaration des droits de l'homme* of 1789 are examples of "droit de."

Well, if anything is true, as Merleau-Ponty would have responded, it is certainly doubtful that the unemployed and homeless are as fond of grammar as they are of work, human dignity, and self-respect. And in any case, as we have seen at various junctures of this essay, linguistic rules are not cemented in reality the way that the "natural" rights referred to above are asserted to be. In a different synchrony, far removed from the present, perhaps the prepositions ("de" and "à") will even come to be reversed—as Merleau-Ponty's sceptical humanist rejection of an ideal language could point out.

It would also be intriguing to have Merleau-Ponty's assessment of the Mitterand government from the point of view of the distinction between acting on principle and out of a sense of political expediency. One of the more interesting of recent political events in France, which serves as an adequate measure of the desperation felt by the administration, has been to change the electoral process from a scheme of direct to one of proportional representation in the National Assembly. It appears that the controlling motive was to give more power to right-wing extremists than they otherwise would have had, precisely in order to force the electorate to vote for socialist candidates as the lesser of the two evils. Certainly this sort of political accomodation wears the appearance of expediency more than principle—on which conservative and other critics were quick to capitalize in the ensuing uproar. In addition, for reasons that Lon Fuller gives about the manoeuvrings of constitutions for the sake of private interests, as we saw in the last chapter, such actions do little to enhance the goal of fidelity to law and respect for it.

On the other hand, if the non-communist left fails to instantiate effectively the values it has in view, and also fails to gain re-election either as the majority in the National Assembly (in 1986) or at the Presidential level (in 1988), will the theory of Merleau-Ponty's new liberalism be falsified as a theory? Merleau-Ponty himself, be it recalled, was always concerned to recreate values "in contact with the facts," but what can uncongenial facts, if such they turn out to be, show us? And if it is not the falsity of the new liberalism, can this denial be consistent with his rejection of the doctrine of proletarian humanism? Would not the new liberalism become a new ideology?

I am not convinced that Merleau-Ponty does in fact have a satisfactory answer to the problem of consistency unless he would be willing, as is the present writer, to unhinge the defense of a moral position from the likelihood of its historical realization. But Merleau-Ponty might argue his case in the following manner. (i) History has not shown us any palatable moral alternative. (ii) The non-communist left ought still to work out a politics of hope, a "*virtu* without resignation" (S 47), with the full consciousness of the contingency of success.

And (ii) will be the case because (iii), as noted above in Chapter I, it is impossible to specify *a priori* how much falsifying evidence—diverging perspectives—is necessary to defeat a theory and (iv) we shuld remember the long-range perspective on the diachronous aspects of culture and history in addition to those which manifest themselves in the contemporaneousness of synchrony. Further, (iv) is required to support (iii) both to differentiate the content of the values at issue and because (iii) by itself cannot provide a distinction between the new liberalism which Merleau-Ponty would accept under the conditions imagined and the doctrine of proletarian humanism which he rejected under actual historical conditions. This distinction would call attention to the fact that, in France, the concretization of values is *en route* and one has to take a long-range view of things rather than judge by immediate consequences. As we have seen above, to prevail against the weight of historically sedimented values, a countervailing history is usually required. But in the Soviet Union, by contrast, proletarian humanism is not *en route;* it has led, rather, to a dictatorship against the proletariat, the destructive consequences of which are *already* clear and the values of which are sharply in contrast with the best interests of humanity. Thus a succession of synchronies of that kind of commitment could teach us nothing new about the desirability of the value-scheme implicated therein. There could be no hopeful awaiting the outcome of history, as in the case of France.

Merleau-Ponty might well also be drawn to point out a dimension of the new liberalism largely missing from his own speculative sketch of it in *Les Aventures de la dialectique* and elsewhere, and that is the international forces at work which can encourage or frustrate the concretization of humane values. For, the greater part of the socialists' problems in France today are economic, and the latter in turn are due to the robust capitalism of the Reagan administration across the Atlantic. As Merleau-Ponty pointed out, although all orders of meaning in society are tightly related, one of them may become dominant—stand out as a focal point—in a particular era. In our own, the prevailing foci of meaning are the threat of nuclear holocaust and, in some ways closely connected with it through a defense build-up, the economic side of life typified by Reaganomics.

Indeed, the influence of the latter is world-wide. Even the Chinese have now joined in and, in fact, since it introduced market incentives into agriculture six years ago, its harvest of grain has been augmented by one-third. Moreover, for the first time ever, it is reported in the press, China can feed itself in staple foods. The Chinese scheme is also quite similar to the famous New Economic Policy (NEP) instituted by Lenin in 1925 and which was eliminated by Stalin in 1929 for the sake of the state monopoly that persists to this day. (It is apparently still true, for example, that peasant farmers cannot even own their own horses.) However, in April 1984, the journal *Problems of History* issued a call to reform in both an editorial praising Nikita Kruschchev's similarly inspired reforms of

1953-64—which remain the *bête noire* of Kremlin conservatives—and in an article urging the immediate reintroduction of a plan like the NEP. The party organ, *Kommunist,* responded in a predictably hostile manner, but this war of words may mean that economic reform is again on the agenda at the highest levels of the Kremlin.

But although capitalism is in high gear on a world-wide scale, in the United States at least it is impossible not to be cognizant of its more sordid consequences. Some of these are (i) the obsolescence of the family farm, which must spend enormous, unaffordable sums to buy the equipment required to compete in the market created by capitalist-driven technology—a market on too vast a scale for most small farmers. There are also (ii) the devastated steel towns riddled with unemployment for the same reasons. And (iii) individual savers, such as those affected by the recent debacle of 71 Ohio savings-and-loan institutions that went bankrupt, are threatened with ruin. In a deregulated market, it is much easier and more predictable for foolish bankers to make bad deals—lured by the greed endemic in the system, which not only solicits, but actually encourages such behavior. These are not the failures of capitalism, in the style of the current American practice, but rather signs that the system is working. And it is, of course, the exact reverse of Mendès-France's programme of state intervention in the economy as a neutral force for the common good.

It seems plain that Merleau-Ponty would indict such a scheme for its principles and its effects, both of which bear striking resemblances to the *illusions perdues* of Alain. And yet with the same blindness, for hidden beneath this spurious respect for the individual from whom the burdens of governmental intervention are supposedly being lifted, is a violence visited on those who, for one reason or another, cannot compete within the system, who are done in by the very machine which they have helped to fuel. But these are only the most visible examples of the pervasive social need, as Merleau-Ponty pointed out quite clearly, not to have the protections of formal liberal institutions withdrawn, but to have them strengthened. Nor is such withdrawal conducive to a respect for law or for encouraging a fidelity to it. The Roman lawyers knew better who insisted on *res, non verba.* However, the *res* of overriding importance in America today is success in the market, and this being so, Merleau-Ponty would apply to the United States the same argument sketched above for distinguishing the situation in France from that of the Soviet Union. Just as in the case of the latter, a succession of synchronies is not necessary to teach us the destructive quality of the value-scheme now in play.

In sum, then, had Merleau-Ponty lived another twenty-five years, he equally could not have been a communist or an anti-communist, in the sense of siding with the Soviet Union or the United States and its allies. He would have found a promising overture to the concretization of humane values in the present French government, but like most French (non-communist) leftists today, he would be anxiously awaiting the next historically decisive events—whether they originate from within or outside France itself. To repair to an old French proverb, *Le vin est tiré, il faut le boire:* a sequence of events has been set in motion and we can only await the outcome.

* * *

The unplanned lengthy interval since the completion of this book has provided an unexpected opportunity to extend this Epilogue briefly. From all that appears, nothing has happened over the last nineteen months to disturb the conclusion of the preceding paragraph. First, about the Soviet Union, Merleau-Ponty would not find, I think, any compelling evidence of institutional humaneness tempering violence, especially in what concerns political dissidents and human rights violations. On the other hand, he probably would be surprised at the degree to which capitalism has caught on in some Eastern-bloc countries. Hungary, it was reported quite recently in the *New York Times,* is now even closing unprofitable factories and laying off workers.

About France, he would have been perhaps somewhat less morose, but probably not surprised either. With the advent of "cohabitation" between a socialist President and a conservative Prime Minister, a number of socialist gambits have already been undone. There is, for instance, no more election by proportional representation, and so the government's strategy of making itself more attractive than extreme right-wing zealots has backfired. It is also the case that many prices have been decontrolled, many nationalized businesses privatized, and it has become easier to fire workers.

Even more seriously, however, rather than a fundamental cooperation to cure the ills of the Fifth Republic, Mitterand and Chirac seem to be playing cat-and-mouse games with the electorate by pointing accusing fingers at each other. From all that appears, the aim is to survive with the least tarnished image. Mitterand can keep a low profile and blame domestic woes on Chirac's policies, and the latter can always lament the constraints of his boss—whether it is a question of allegedly buying off terrorists in Syria or of confronting student protests at home in the Latin Quarter. It remains to be seen, however, whether cohabitation will be a unique event or whether it itself will develop into an institution. Its historical significance, then, remains to be constituted much farther down the road. Among the many questions to be answered is whether socialism can survive whole and intact, or only as a graft on another political organism.

With reference to the United States, there are at least four different, but related, kinds of events and historical processes at work mentioned above which Merleau-Ponty would continue to find interesting and pertinent to his phenomenology of the social world. The first is the persistent success of Reaganomics and its consistent and continual diminishment of social welfare programs designed to help the least advantaged members of society. The second is the use of new biological technologies in the service of free-market enterprise that severely threatens the existence of some parts of the work force. This is particularly true of farmers who are going out of business in droves. As mentioned above, technology fueled by capitalism has already brought it about that the average farmer must spend hundreds of thousands of dollars on equipment to compete with super or 'mega'farms owned by large corporations. But to add to these usual woes, genetic engineering is being used more and more these days in the dairy industry in order to increase the supply of milk. It is hardly surprising that only the super, corporate farms can afford the loss of revenue occasioned by glutting the market with milk and that small farmers cannot afford the technology necessary to compete in the market. Were Merleau-Ponty alive today, he probably would not miss the opportunity to comment on these phenomena in the light of the *Manifesto of the Communist Party* (Preface to the Russian Edition of 1882) that, in America, "Step by step the small and middle landownership of the farmers, the basis of the whole political constitution, is succumbing to the competition of giant farms".

It is also worth pointing out, in the context of genetic engineering, that concern for some of the issues discussed in Chapter VI has intensified over the last several months, especially in regard to bio-hazards from agricultural testing and in respect to legal and moral conflicts over surrogate mothers. The pending court case in New Jersey about Ms. Mary Beth Whitehead, a surrogate mother who changed her mind and wishes to reclaim her ("her"?) child, will doubtless be a landmark decision.

The third phenomenon of American life today which is pertinent to the preceding pages, especially Chapter VI, concerns the continued reshaping of the Federal courts through conservative Presidential appointments. Nothing has occurred essentially in this regard to change the arguments advanced above. But it is appalling—considering Merleau-Ponty's contention that formal institutions are necessary to protect liberty—that one of the (unsuccessful) nominees has said in a recent article in a national periodical that he considered the Constitution to be on balance a bad idea. Also, the Attorney-General has made some rather stupefying claims about Supreme Court decisions not being binding except on the parties to the cases decided by that tribunal. And during the past year, a variety of public figures—newspaper columnists, legislators, and Supreme Court justices, including the new Chief Justice—have all given speeches or written articles which converged on the conclusions of Chapter VI about the differences between influence and deterministic causality.

Chief Justice Rehnquist particularly has made some illuminating comments on the fate of a Justice's political loyalties to the President who nominated him or her once that Justice takes his or her place on the Supreme Court. In his view, within the dynamics of the institution of the Court, the Justice quickly learns that independence and individual thinking are valued much more highly than political loyalties, and the latter are damped to the fringes of the Justice's consciousness. They are, perhaps, "always on the agenda," as Freud said in another context, but they are only that. And, as with any aspect of experience on the fringes of consciousness, what role they play in a given judicial experience will depend on the context. One wonders, for example, what will happen when judges who have been appointed to the bench for, among other things, their beliefs in minimal governmental intervention in free-market enterprise, will have to rule on protectivist tarifs and trade-sanctions which are being increasingly advocated by various conservative members of Congress and by labor and industry lobbying groups.

Last, but very definitely not least in terms of the previous chapter's concern for fidelity to law and respect for it, the scandal of the Iranian payoffs and subsequent diverting of funds secretly to the Nicaraguan Contras merely continues a schizophrenic attitude of the present administration toward the virtues of law and order. It has been some time now since the World Court ruled against the United States in funding the Contras in the first place, but the administration seems blissfully unaware of the contradictions in thumbing its nose at the World Court on the one hand and preaching the virtues of law, freedom, and human dignity on the other. Perhaps Merleau-Ponty would read the latest developments as just an unusually explicit disclosure of the underlying layers of violence of a capitalist system, much as the American socialist, Corliss Lamont, once said that fascism is only "capitalism in the nude." But the ridicule to which these contemporary events have left open the administration's own conception of respect for law makes one uncertain as to whether it is Lamont, H.L. Mencken, or perhaps P.T. Barnum, who is most needed in Washington.

—St. Louis, December 1986

WORKS CONSULTED

Primary Sources of Merleau-Ponty Most Relevant to this Study

1942

La Structure du comportement. Paris: Presses Universitaires de France. English translation: *The Structure of Behavior.* Translated by Alden L. Fisher. Boston: The Beacon Press, 1963.

1945

Phénoménologie de la perception. Paris: Gallimard. English translation by Colin Smith. New York: The Humanities Press, 1962; London: Routledge and Kegan Paul, 1962.

"Le Roman et la Métaphysique," *Cahiers du Sud,* 22: 270 (March-April), pp. 194-207; also in *Sens et non-sens* (1948).

"La Guerre a eu lieu," *Les Temps Modernes,* 1: 1 (October), pp. 48-66; also in *Sens et non-sens.*

"La Querelle de l'existentialisme," *Les Temps Modernes,* 1: 2 (November), pp. 344-56; also in *Sens et non-sens.*

"Le Doute de Cézanne," *Fontaine,* 8: 47 (December), 80ff.; also in *Sens et non-sens.*

1946

"Pour la vérité," *Les Temps Modernes,* 1: 4 (January), pp. 577-600; also in *Sens et non-sens.*

"Le Cult du héros," *Action,* No. 74 (1 February), pp. 12-13; also in *Sens et non-sens* under the title "Le Héros, l'homme."

"Autour du marxisme," *Fontaine,* 9: 48-49 (February), pp. 309-31; also in *Sens et non-sens.*

"Foi et bonne foi," *Les Temps Modernes,* 1: 5 (February), pp. 769-82; also in *Sens et non-sens.*

"L'Existentialisme chez Hegel," *Les Temps Modernes,* 1: 7 (April), pp. 1311-19; also in *Sens et non-sens.*

"Marxisme et philosophie," *Revue Internationale,* 1: 6 (June-July), pp. 518-26; also in *Sens et non-sens.*

"Le Yogi et le prolétaire," *Les Temps Modernes,* 2: 13 (October), pp. 1-29. Some of this article in also in *Humanisme et terreur,* I, 2.

"Le Yogi et le prolétaire," *Les Temps Modernes,* 2: 14 (November), pp. 253-87. Some of this article is also in *Humanisme et terreur,* I, 2 and II, 1.

"Le Primat de la perception et ses conséquences philosophiques," *Bulletin de la Société Française de Philosophie,* XLI, reporting on the meeting of 23 November 1946), pp. 119-53. English translation by James M. Edie in *The Primacy of Perception and Other Essays,* edited by James M. Edie. Evanston: Northwestern University Press, 1964, pp. 12-42.

1947

"Le Yogi et le prolétaire," *Les Temps Modernes,* 2: 16 (January), pp. 676-711. Some of this article is also in *Humanisme et terreur,* II, pp. 1-2.

"Indochine S.O.S.," *Les Temps Modernes,* 2: 18 (March), pp. 1039-52. (This was an unsigned editorial. This article also appeared in *Signes* as "Sur l'Indochine."

Humanisme et terreur. Paris: Gallimard. Citations are from the 1972 edition. English translation by John O'Neill. Boston: The Beacon Press, 1969.

"Le Métaphysique dans l'homme," *Revue de Métaphysique et de Morale,* 52: 3-4 (July-October), pp. 290-307. This article also appeared in *Sens et non-sens.*

"Le Cinéma et la nouvelle psychologie," *Les Temps Modernes,* 3: 26 (November), pp. 930-43. This article also appeared in *Sens et non- sens.*

"Lecture de Montaigne," *Les Temps Modernes,* 3: 27 (December), pp. 1044-60. This article also appeared in *Signes.*

1948

Sens et non-sens. Paris, Nagel. Citations are from the 5th edition, 1966. English translation by Hubert L. and Patricia A. Dreyfus. Evanston: Northwestern University Press, 1964.

"Un Auteur scandaleux," *Le Figaro Littéraire* (3 January). This article also appeared in *Sens et non-sens.*

"Communisme et anticommunisme," *Les Temps Modernes* 4: 34 (July), pp. 175-88. This article also appeared in *Signes* as "La Politique paranoïaque."

1949

La Conscience et l'acquisition du langage, Cours de Sorbonne. Paris: Centre de Documentation Universitaire. Cited in *Bulletin de Psychologie,* n° 236 tome XVIII 3-6, November 1964, pp. 26-259. English translation by Hugh J. Silverman. Evanston: Northwestern University Press, 1973.

"Note sur Machiavel," *Les Temps Modernes,* 5: 48 (October), pp. 577-93. This article also appeared in *Signes.*

1950

"Les Jours de notre vie," *Les Temps Modernes,* 5: 51 (January), pp. 1153-68. This editorial, also signed by Sartre, appears additionally in *Signes* as "L'U.R.S.S. et les camps."

1951

"Le Philosophe et la sociologie," *Cahiers Internationaux de Sociologie,* 10, pp. 55-69. This article also appeared in *Signes.*

Les Sciences de l'homme et la phénoménologie : Introduction et première partie, Cours de Sorbonne. Paris: Centre de Documentation Universitaire. English translation by John Wild in *The Primacy of Perception and Other Essays,* pp. 43-95.

1952

"Sur la phénoménologie du langage," in *Problèmes actuels de la phénoménologie,* edited by H.L. Van Breda. Paris: Desclée de Brouwer. This essay also appeared in *Signes.*

"Le Langage indirect et les voix du silence," *Les Temps Modernes,* 7: 80 (June), pp. 2113-44; 8: 81 (July), pp. 70-94. This essay also appeared in *Signes.*

1953

"Un Inédit de Maurice Merleau-Ponty," *Revue de Métaphysique et de Morale,* 67: 4 (October-December 1962), pp. 401-09. English translation by Arleen B. Dallery in *The Primacy of Perception and Other Essays,* pp. 3-11.

Eloge de la philosophie. Paris: Gallimard. English translation: *In Praise of Philosophy.* Translated by James M. Edie and John Wild. Evanston: Northwestern University Press, 1963.

1954

"La France va-t-elle se renouveler?", *L'Express,* 23 October, pp. 3-4."Sur les faits divers," *L'Express,* 18 December, pp. 3-4. This essay also appeared in *Signes.*

1955

Les Aventures de la dialectique. Paris: Gallimard. English translation by Joseph Bien. Evanston: Northwestern University Press, 1973. Also London: Heinemann, 1974.

"A quoi sert l'objectivité?", *L'Express,* 29 January, p.4.

"Einstein et la crise de la raison," *L'Express,* 14 May, p. 13. This essay also appeared in *Signes.*

"Où va l'anticommunisme?", *L'Express,* 25 June, p. 12.

1956

"Le Grand rationalisme," in *Les Philosophes célèbres* (editor), Paris: Lucien Mazenod.

"Sur la destalinisation," *L'Express,* 23 November, pp. 13-17. This essay also appeared in *Signes.*

1958

"La Démocratie peut-elle renaître en France?" (interview) *L'Express,* 3July, pp. 15-17. This essay also appeared in *Signes* as "Demain . . ."

"Sur Madagascar" (interview), *L'Express,* 21 August. This essay also appeared in *Signes.*

1959

"Le Philosophe et son ombre," in *Edmund Husserl 1859-1959.* Edited by H.L. Van Breda and J. Taminiaux. The Hague: Martinus Nijhoff. This essay also appeared in *Signes.*

"Bergson se faisant," *Bulletin de la Société Française,* LIV (January-March), 1960 (reporting on the Bergson Congress, 17-20 May 1959). This essay also appeared in *Signes.*

"De Mauss à Claude Lévi-Strauss," *La Nouvelle Revue Française,* 7: 82 (October), pp. 615-31. This essay also appeared in *Signes.*

1960

Signes. Paris: Gallimard. English translation by Richard C.McCleary. Evanston: Northwestern University Press, 1964.

"Préface" to Dr. A. Hesnard, *L'oeuvre de Freud et son importance pour le monde moderne,* pp. 5-10. Paris: Payot.

1961

"L'oeil et l'esprit," *Art de France,* 1: 1 (January). Reprinted in *Les Temps Modernes* (November), and as a separate book, *L'oeil et l'esprit,* Paris: Gallimard, 1964. The originally published article and the book contain illustrations chosen by the author himself, but which most unhappily are left out of the English translation by Carleton Dallery in *The Primacy of Perception and Other Essays,* pp. 159-90.

1964

Le Visible et l'invisible, suivi de notes de travail. Texte établi par Claude Lefort. Paris: Gallimard. English translation by Alphonso Lingis. Evanston: Northwestern University Press, 1968.

1968

Résumés de Cours, Collège de France, 1952-60. Paris: Gallimard. English translation *Themes from the Lectures at the Collège de France (1952-60),* translated by John O'Neill, Evanston: Northwestern University Press, 1970.

1969

La Prose du monde. Texte établi par Claude Lefort. Paris: Gallimard. English translation by John O'Neill, Evanston: Northwestern University Press, 1973.

1974

"Philosophie et non-philosophie depuis Hegel," I-II, notes de cours, texte établi et présenté par Claude Lefort. *Textures,* nos. 8-9 (1974), pp. 83-129, and nos. 10-11 (1975), pp. 145-73. English translation of these notes of Merleau-Ponty's lectures at the Collège de France in 1961 by Hugh J. Silverman. "Philosophy and Non-Philosophy since Hegel," *Telos,* no. 29, Fall 1976, pp. 39-105.

WORKS CONSULTED

Secondary Sources

Amselek, Paul. "The Phenomenological Description of Law," translated by Raoul Mortley in Maurice Natanson, ed. *Phenomenology and the Social Sciences*. Evanston: Northwestern University Press, 1973, II, pp. 367-449.

Austin, John. *The Province of Jurisprudence Determined.* New York: The Noonday Press, 1954.

Bourdieu, Pierre. "Le champ littéraire: Préalables critiques et principes de méthode," *Lendemains* 36, 1984, p. 5.

Bingham, Joseph. "What is the Law?", 11 *Michigan Law Review* 2-23 (1912).

Cooper, Barry. *Merleau-Ponty and Marxism: From Terror to Reform.* Toronto: University of Toronto Press, 1979.

Cross, Rupert. *Precedent in English Law.* Oxford: The Clarendon Press, 1977, 3rd edition.

Dauenhauer, Bernard P. "Merleau-Ponty's Political Thought: Its Nature and Its Challenge," in William L. McBride and Calvin O. Schrag, eds. *Phenomenology in a Pluralistic Context.* Albany: State University of New York Press, 1984, pp. 14-25.

______"Hope and its Ramifications for Politics," *Man and World* 17: 453-76 (1984). Reprinted in J.N. Mohanty, ed. *Phenomenology and the Human Sciences.* Dordrecht: Martinus Nijhoff Publishers, 1985.

DeBeauvoir, Simone. "Merleau-Ponty et le pseudo-sartrisme," *Les Temps Modernes,* 10: 114-15 (April-May 1955), pp. 2072-2122.

D'Entrèves, A.P. "The Case for Natural Law Re-examined," *Natural Law Forum* I (1956), 27-46. Reprinted in *Natural Law.* London: Hutchinson University Library, 1970 (2nd edition).

DeSaussure, Ferdinand. *Cours de linguistique générale,* édition critique, préparée par Tullio de Mauro. Paris: Payot, 1960.

Devlin, Sir Patrick. *The Enforcement of Morals.* Oxford: Oxford University Press, 1965.

DeWaelhens, Alphonse. "Une Philosophie de l'ambiguïté," the Préface of Merleau-Ponty's *La Structure du comportement.* Paris: Presses Universitaires de France, 1942.

Dewey, John. *The Quest for Certainty.* New York: Capricorn Books, 1960.

Dugit, L., Monnier H., and Bounard, R. *Les Constitutions et les principales lois politiques de la France depuis 1789.* Ed. Georges Berlia. Paris: Librairie Générale du Droit et de Jurisprudence, 1952.

Dworkin, Ronald. *Taking Rights Seriously.* Cambridge, Mass: Harvard University Press, 1977.

Edie, James M. Foreward to Merleau-Ponty's *Consciousness and the Acquisition of Language,* trans. Hugh J. Silverman. Evanston: Northwestern University Press, 1973.

______"Merleau-Ponty: The Triumph of Dialectics over Structuralism," *Man and World* 17: 299-312 (1984). Reprinted in J.N. Mohanty, ed. *Phenomenology and the Human Sciences.* Dordrecht: Martinus Nijhoff, 1985.

Feinberg, Joel. *Social Philosophy.* Englewood Cliffs: Prentice-Hall, Inc., 1973.

______"Limits to the Free Expression of Opinion," in Joel Feinberg and Hyman Gross, eds. *Philosophy of Law.* Encino, CA: Dickenson, 1975.

Finnis, John. *Natural Law and Natural Rights.* Oxford: The Clarendon Press, 1980.

Frankena, William. *Ethics.* Englewood Cliffs: Prentice-Hall, Inc., 1973, 2nd edition.

Friedmann, Wolfgang. "Phenomenology and Legal Science," in Maurice Natanson, ed. *Phenomenology and the Social Sciences.* Evanston: Northwestern University Press, 1973, II: 343-65.

Fuller, Lon L. "Positivism and Fidelity to Law—A Reply to Professor Hart," 71 *Harvard Law Review* 630-73 (1958).

______*The Morality of Law.* New Haven: Yale University Press, 1963.

Gunther, Gerald. "Foreward: In Search of Evolving Doctrine on a Changing Court: A Model for Newer Equal Protection," 86 *Harvard Law Review* 9 (1972).

______*Cases and Materials on Constitutional Law.* Mineola, N.Y.: The Foundation Press, Inc., 1975, 3rd edition.

Hacker, P.M.S. "Hart's Philosophy of Law," in P.M.S. Hacker and J. Raz, eds. *Law, Morality, and Society: Essays in Honour of H.L.A. Hart.* Oxford: The Clarendon Press, 1977, pp. 1-25.

Hamrick, William S. "Towards a Phenomenology of Legal Rules," *Journal of the British Society for Phenomenology,* Vol. X, No. 1 (January 1979), pp. 9-22.

______"A Phenomenological Critique of Hart's Concept of Rules," *Archiv für Rechts-und Sozialphilosophie—Supplementa.* Wiesbaden: Franz Steiner Verlag, 1982, Vol. I, Part 1, pp. 175-84.

______"Humanity, Nature, and Respect for Law," in A.-T. Tymieniecka, ed. *Analecta Husserliana.* Dordrecht: D. Reidel Publishing Company, 1983, pp. 245-56.

______"Interests, Justice, and Respect for Law in Merleau-Ponty's Phenomenology," in William L. McBride and Calvin O. Schrag, eds. *Phenomenology in a Pluralistic Context.* Albany: State University of New York Press, 1984, pp. 39-48.

______"Redeeming the Earth: Tragic Wisdom and the Plains Indians," *Journal of the British Society for Phenomenology,* Vol. XVI, No. 1 (January 1985), pp. 36-54.

______"Language and Abnormal Behavior: Merleau-Ponty, Hart, and Laing," *Review of Existential Psychology and Psychiatry,* Vol. 18 (1985), pp. 181-203.

Hart, H.L.A. "Positivism and the Separation of Law and Morals," 71 *Harvard Law Review* 593-629 (1958).

______*The Concept of Law.* Oxford: The Clarendon Press, 1961.

______*Law, Liberty, and Morality.* Oxford: Oxford University Press, 1963.

______*Essays in Jurisprudence and Philosophy.* Oxford: Oxford University Press, 1983. This volume is a collection of Hart's essays ranging from "Definition and Theory in Jurisprudence" (1953) to "The House of Lords on Attempting the Impossible" (1981).

Heidegger, Martin. *Was Ist Metaphysik?* Frankfurt a.M.: Vittorio Klostermann, Neunte Auflage, 1965.

James, William. *Pragmatism: A New Name for Some Old Ways of Thinking.* New York: Longmans, Green, and Co., 1910.

______*Essays in Pragmatism.* New York: Haffner Publishing Company, 1948.

Kelsen, Hans. *General Theory of Law and State.* New York: Russell and Russell, 1961.

______*The Pure Theory of Law.* Berkeley and Los Angeles: The University of California Press, 1967.

Kristol, Irving. "Pornography, Obscenity, and the Case for Censorship," *The New York Times Magazine,* 28 March 1971.

Kruks, Sonia. *The Political Philosophy of Merleau-Ponty.* Sussex: The Harvester Press, 1981. Published simultaneously by The Humanities Press, Atlantic Highlands, N.J.

Kuhn, Thomas. *The Structure of Scientific Revolutions.* Chicago: The University of Chicago Press, 1962.

Laing, R.D. and Esterton, A. *Sanity, Madness, and the Family.* London: Penguin Books, 1970.

Lucas, J.R. "The Phenomenon of Law," in P.M.S. Hacker and J. Raz, eds. *Law, Morality, and Society: Essays in Honour of H.L.A. Hart.* Oxford: The Clarendon Press, 1977, pp. 85-98.

MacCormick, Neil. "Law as Institutional Fact," 90 *Law Quarterly Review* 102 (1974).

______*Legal Reasoning and Legal Theory.* Oxford: The Clarendon Press, 1978.

Mackie, John. "The Third Theory of Law," *Philosophy and Public Affairs* Vol. 7, No. 1 (Fall 1977), reprinted in Marshall Cohen, ed. *Ronald Dworkin and Contemporary Jurisprudence.* London: Duckworth, 1984.

Madison, Gary Brent. *The Phenomenology of Merleau-Ponty.* Athens, Ohio: Ohio University Press, 1980. Translated from the original French edition by the author himself. *La Phénoménologie de Merleau-Ponty, une recherche de la conscience.* Paris: Editions Klincksieck, 1973.

Marsh, James L. "Phenomenology as Ideology Critique," *Philosophy Today,* Fall 1980, pp. 272-84.

Marshall, Geoffrey. *Constitutional Theory.* Oxford: The Clarendon Press, 1971.

McBride, William L. *Fundamental Change in Law and Society.* The Hague and Paris: Mouton, 1970.

Nardone, Henry F. "Creativity in Art and Aesthetics," *The Journal of Aesthetics and Art Criticism,* Vol. XXXIV, No. 2, Winter 1975, pp. 183-90.

Popper, Karl. *The Logic of Scientific Discovery.* London: Hutchinson, 1959.

Pound, Roscoe. *Outlines of Lectures on Jurisprudence.* Cambridge, Mass.: Harvard University Press, 1943.

Rabil, Albert, Jr. *Merleau-Ponty: Existentialist of the Social World.* New York: Columbia University Press, 1967.

Raz, Joseph. *The Concept of a Legal System.* Oxford: Oxford University Press, 1970.

______"The Role of Law and Its Virtue," 93 *Law Quarterly Review* 195 (1977).

Richir, Marc. "Le Sens de la Phénoménologie dans *Le visible et l'invisible,*" in *Maurice Merleau-Ponty, Esprit,* No. 66, June 1982, pp. 124-45.

Robertson, D.W. *A Preface to Chaucer.* Princeton: Princeton University Press, 1962.

Ross, Alf. *On Law and Justice.* Berkeley and Los Angeles: The University of California Press, 1959.

Sartre, Jean-Paul. "Merleau-Ponty [I]," trans. William S. Hamrick, *Journal of the British Society for Phenomenology,* Vol. XV, No. 2 (May 1984), pp. 123-54.

Sawer, Geoffrey. *Law in Society.* Oxford: The Clarendon Press, 1965; reprinted 1973.

Schiff, David. "Phenomenology and Jurisprudence," *Liverpool Law Review,* Vol. 4, No. 1 (1982), pp. 5-18.

Schutz, Alfred. *Collected Papers*. Edited by Maurice Natanson. The Hague: Martinus Nijhoff, 1962.

Simons, Margaret A. and Benjamin, Jessica. "Simone de Beauvoir: An Interview," *Feminist Studies* 5, No. 2 (Summer 1979), p. 339.

Spiegelberg, Herbert. *The Phenomenological Movement: A Historical Introduction*. Dordrecht: Martinus Nijhoff, 1982, 3rd edition.

Spurling, Laurie. *Phenomenology and the Social World: The Philosophy of Merleau-Ponty and its Relation to the Social Sciences*. London: Routledge and Kegan Paul, 1977.

Wasserstrom, Richard. Editor, *Morality and the Law*. Belmont, CA: Wadsworth Publishing Co., 1971.

Whitney, Peter. "Jean-Paul Sartre's Notebooks," *Journal of the British Society for Phenomenology,* Vol. XV, No. 2 (May 1984), pp. 109-22.

INDEX